"The world is always trying to replace Christianity with a spiritual counterfeit that is another religion entirely, as J. Gresham Machen pointed out a century ago. Rosaria Butterfield exposes today's ideologies that seek to force the church into the mold of sexual perversion and self-deification. And she reminds us in this well-written and easy-to-read book that the answer to these soul-destroying lies remains the same as it always was: knowing and abiding in God's word so that the truth will set us free. Highly recommended!"

Joel R. Beeke, President, Puritan Reformed Theological Seminary, Grand Rapids, Michigan

"In a culture marked by sexual confusion and moral chaos, Rosaria Butterfield bursts through the fog of confusion with unflinching clarity. Defining words like *male* and *female*, and the biblical roles assigned to them, this book speaks plainly and unapologetically about the beauty of God's design and purpose for gender, sex, marriage, and family. If the five lies of our anti-Christian age she confronts are like idols in Daniel's Babylon, be inspired to join Butterfield as she, like Daniel's three friends, stand amongst the thousands of bended knees and boldly assert, 'We will not serve your gods.'"

Alisa Childers, Host, *The Alisa Childers Podcast*; author, *Another Gospel?* and *Live Your Truth and Other Lies*

"Falsehood abounds not only in the world but also, sadly, in the church. The truth must attack the lies of the age for the sake of God's honor and glory, the good of people, and the health of the church. In this deeply courageous book, Rosaria Butterfield addresses topics that many are afraid to confront and expose. On the one hand, this is grievous, but I am especially grateful for the gifts God has given to Butterfield, who is in many respects uniquely able to expose these five lies of our anti-Christian age. You may weep reading this book, but I am convinced you will also rejoice."

Mark Jones, Senior Pastor, Faith Presbyterian Church, Vancouver, British Columbia

"As I read this cogent, trenchant, and timely declaration of gospel sanity, I was constantly reminded of the words of Christ: 'You will know the truth, and the truth will set you free' (John 8:32). Rosaria Butterfield has afforded us a much-needed caveat to the prevailing untruths of our day while simultaneously redirecting us to the pathway of freedom."

George Grant, Pastor, Parish Presbyterian Church, Franklin, Tennessee; author, *The Micah Mandate*

"Rosaria Butterfield has written a landmark book on the lies our culture is rapidly adopting regarding sexuality, what she calls 'the idol of our time,' namely LGBTQ+ ideology. In all the subjects she raises—in particular feminism, homosexuality, and transgenderism—her treatments are broad, deep, and fair. She offers profound, and deeply convincing, reflections on Christian spiritual issues of temptation, sin, envy, and modesty, as well as the doctrines of the Scriptures and ecclesiology. As a converted lesbian, now a committed pastor's wife and mother, no one is better placed to cover this material than Butterfield. Her book will surely go down as a classic."

Peter Jones, Executive Director, truthXchange

"A timely and vital exhortation to the church, this book is a much-needed resource for Christians facing ever-increasing confusion in the world. With clear, biblical truth, Rosaria Butterfield cuts through key lies of our current culture, which have crept into the church like the serpent in the garden. This is a must-read!"

Becket Cook, author, *A Change of Affection*; Host, *The Becket Cook Show*

"Rosaria Butterfield speaks the truth in love, exposing and refuting five big lies widely accepted in our culture. She draws on her profound understanding of the Bible as well as her wide reading and personal experiences. May this important book strengthen Christians and be used to call many, not only to the truth but also to repentance and faith in Christ."

W. Robert Godfrey, President Emeritus and Professor Emeritus, Westminster Seminary California; Teaching Fellow, Ligonier Ministries

"Rosaria Butterfield is one of those rare individuals who lives out her convictions with utter consistency—earlier as a lesbian professor of feminist and queer studies and now as a Christian and a pastor's wife. In this book, she confronts some of the most pervasive falsehoods of our age."

Nancy Pearcey, Professor and Scholar in Residence,
Houston Christian University; author, *Love Thy Body* and
The Toxic War on Masculinity

"Few authors consistently write books with such clarity and power, rightly dividing the primary issues of the day, like Rosaria Butterfield. Drawing from her unlikely conversion, literary eloquence, philosophical fluency, and theological mastery, she has again composed another tour de force in *Five Lies of Our Anti-Christian Age*. Addressing identity, sexuality, feminism, and transgenderism, this masterpiece uncovers the deceptive lies infiltrating the church and points to the lifegiving and timeless truth of God's word. Like a watchman on a wall, Butterfield grounds her courage and passion in her love for neighbor. Will we take the wide road of compromise leading to death or the narrow path of suffering leading to life in Christ? Read this book. You will not be pampered but challenged. Most of all, expect that the gospel of Christ will be exalted without any wavering to the left or the right."

Christopher Yuan, speaker; author, *Holy Sexuality and the Gospel*;
creator, *The Holy Sexuality Project* video series

"With surgical precision, Rosaria Butterfield names, assesses, and dismantles the secular religion of our time. She makes the agenda of the enemy before us come into razor-sharp focus. But she doesn't stop there. Like any good surgeon, after dismantling the cancer, she sews the patient back up—in this case, demonstrating how to battle lies with the truth. *Five Lies of Our Anti-Christian Age* is a handbook for how to use God's word to fight joyfully against an often baffling world around us."

Summer Jaeger, Cohost, *Sheologians*

"In *Five Lies of Our Anti-Christian Age*, Rosaria Butterfield is doing the good work of 'destroying arguments and every lofty opinion raised against the knowledge of God' and of 'taking every thought captive to obey Christ' (2 Cor. 10:5). As a result, this book is a punch in the mouth to the reigning worldly ideologies of our day, and Butterfield is like Jael with warm milk and a tent peg. Butterfield pulls no punches but boldly confronts five lies that are bedeviling God's people, and she faithfully refutes those lies with biblical truth. While this book will be edifying for all believers, Butterfield sets her sights on warning women in particular. Butterfield has a gift for saying hard things in profound and incisive ways. This is a powerful book that confronts the conceits of our age, and I cannot recommend it highly enough."

Denny Burk, Professor of Biblical Studies, The Southern Baptist Theological Seminary; President, Council on Biblical Manhood and Womanhood; Teaching Pastor, Kenwood Baptist Church, Louisville, Kentucky

"In *Five Lies of Our Anti-Christian Age*, Rosaria Butterfield takes a wrecking ball not only to the obvious lies of modern culture but even more to the comfortable Christianese shibboleths we thoughtlessly mouth because we've heard so many others in church repeating them. They are the most dangerous deceptions of all. And the challenge running through every chapter of this book is this: choose this day whom you will believe—the word of God or the accommodationist counterfeits. Keep your highlighter handy—you will be reaching for it constantly."

Megan Basham, Culture Reporter, *The Daily Wire*; author, *Beside Every Successful Man*

Five Lies of Our Anti-Christian Age

Five Lies of Our Anti-Christian Age

Rosaria Butterfield

Foreword by Kevin DeYoung

CROSSWAY®

WHEATON, ILLINOIS

Library of Congress Cataloging-in-Publication Data

Names: Butterfield, Rosaria Champagne, 1962– author.
Title: Five lies of our anti-Christian age / Rosaria Butterfield.
Description: Wheaton, Illinois : Crossway, 2023. | Includes bibliographical references and index.
Identifiers: LCCN 2022005727 (print) | LCCN 2022005728 (ebook) | ISBN 9781433573538 (hardcover) | ISBN 9781433584060 (pdf) | ISBN 9781433584084 (epub)
Subjects: LCSH: Truthfulness and falsehood—Religious aspects—Christianity. | Christianity and culture. | Church controversies. | Women—Religious aspects—Christianity. | Families—Religious aspects—Christianity.
Classification: LCC BV4647.T7 B88 2023 (print) | LCC BV4647.T7 (ebook) | DDC 261—dc23/eng/20220603
LC record available at https://lccn.loc.gov/2022005727
LC ebook record available at https://lccn.loc.gov/2022005728

For Will and Hope Roberts,
faithful Christian friends who have raised their daughters,
Grace Bennett and Faith Roberts, to fear God, not man.
This book could not have been written without your witness, courage,
kindness, friendship, prayers, advice, and countless meals.
We live as the church militant until we join with the church
triumphant upon the return of our Lord and Savior, Jesus Christ.
I am grateful that our Lord gave us marching orders together.
Revelation 19:11–13

*Now I saw heaven opened, and behold, a white horse. And
He who sat on him was called Faithful and True, and in
righteousness He judges and makes war. His eyes were like a
flame of fire, and on His head were many crowns. He had a
name written that no one knew except himself. He was clothed
with a robe dipped in blood, and His name is called The Word
of God. And the armies in heaven, clothed in fine linen, white
and clean, followed Him on white horses. Now out of His mouth
goes a sharp sword, that with it He should strike the nations.
And He Himself will rule them with a rod of iron. He Himself
treads the winepress of the fierceness and wrath of Almighty God.
And He has on His robe and on His thigh a name written:*

*KING OF KINGS AND
LORD OF LORDS.*

REVELATION 19:11–16 (NKJV)

Contents

Foreword

THE DEVIL IS A LIAR.

And not just any old liar, a very good one. He normally avoids direct assaults. He prefers deceit, and misdirection. Think of the snake in the garden of Eden, merely *suggesting* that God's word might not be fully trustworthy. The devil specializes in traps and snares (2 Tim. 2:26). He masquerades as an angel of light (2 Cor. 11:14). He blinds the minds of unbelievers (4:4). Our enemy, that ancient serpent, who is called the devil and Satan, is wicked, tricksy, and false (Rev. 12:9). He is a father of lies (John 8:44).

The devil lies to us in many ways. He may not speak through a snake, but he knows how to make his voice heard. Sometimes he may bring something directly to mind. Or perhaps he keeps us from seeing and hearing what we should. More often, I imagine, he speaks through the half-truths and quarter-truths we find in a thousand movies, television shows, and "news" reports. His voice can be heard in our universities and from the halls of power. If we listen carefully, we may detect his slithering speech in Christian books and in spiritual blogs, even from pastors and churches.

That is why the book you are holding is so important. Make no mistake, this courageous book is bracing. You won't agree with every sentence. But it is hard to imagine anyone who shouldn't listen to what Rosaria has to say. Strike that—not what Rosaria has to say, but what God has said that Rosaria knows we need to hear. Rosaria Butterfield is a friend of mine, and she is eager to speak to you as a friend too—if you will let her. She is smart, caring, self-deprecating, and—here's one thing I hope you'll learn to love—in a world awash in soft heads and brittle hearts, Rosaria isn't afraid to tell you what she really thinks. May her tribe increase.

There is a war raging between good and evil in our world, and though we might prefer the conflict to be fought somewhere else, we don't get to pick the times in which we live. The front lines today are battles over sex, gender, and identity. We must be ready for a fight in precisely these places. Don't underestimate the power of your opponent. The devil wants us to join him in his rebellion against God. He wants to make us cowards and traitors. He wants us to believe the myth of our own autonomy. He wants us to raise the white flag and side with the enemy—the enemy without or the enemy within, it doesn't matter to him. The devil hates every spiritual blessing in Christ. He hates Christ's power. He hates Christ's forgiving grace. He hates Christ's transforming grace. He hates the gospel and the church. He hates happy marriages and well-ordered families. He hates personal holiness and obedience. The devil hates Christians who stand their ground.

Have you ever noticed the central command for the Christian as he conducts spiritual warfare? Read over the passage in Ephesians 6 on the armor of God. The exhortation is not to cast out demons or bind territorial spirits. The command, repeated several times, is simply "stand" (vv. 11, 13, 14). Don't give up. Don't give in. Don't back down. It's as if Christ our captain is yelling out instructions to his troops: "Hold your lines, men! Don't break ranks. Stand your ground!"

And how do we stand? It's quite simple really. We live by truth, not by lies. There are five implements in the armor of God that are defensive: a belt, a breastplate, shoes, a shield, and a helmet. There is one offensive weapon, a sword. All six pieces of armor are meant to reinforce the same two things: the truth about God and the truth about ourselves. That's how wise Christians have always done battle with the devil. That's how the fight must be fought in our day.

The devil says to us, "If God is a God of love, how can he judge? You have nothing to fear if you sin." But with the belt of truth, hear God's voice saying, "Do not be deceived: God is not mocked, for whatever one sows, that will he also reap" (Gal. 6:7).

And when the devil accuses us of falling short of the glory of God, we stand ready with the breastplate of righteousness, knowing that God "made him to be sin who knew no sin, so that in him we might become the righteousness of God" (2 Cor. 5:21).

And when the evil one bids us to walk in resentment and bitterness with our brothers and sisters, we will not follow, because our feet are fitted with the gospel of peace, knowing that Christ himself is our peace, who has made the two one and has destroyed the barrier, the dividing wall of hostility (Eph. 2:14).

And when the devil comes with his enticements to sin, we will take up the shield of faith and will choose, like Moses, to be mistreated along with the people of God rather than to enjoy the pleasures of sin for a short time (Heb. 11:25).

And when Satan tries to convince us that God is unwilling to save us or unable to change us, we will trust that the name of the Lord is a strong tower; the righteous run into it and they are safe (Prov. 18:10).

And when Satan tells us that we are hopeless, that sanctification is hopeless, and that endurance is hopeless, we will strike back with the sword of the Spirit. "No, Satan, there is no condemnation for those who are in Christ Jesus (Rom. 8:1). I am dead to sin and alive in Christ by the Spirit (8:10). I do not consider the sufferings of this present time worth comparing with the glory that is to be revealed (8:18). We have hope for what we do not see, and we will wait for it with patience (8:25). The Spirit will help us in our weakness and intercede for us with groanings too deep for words (8:26). We know that for those who love God all things work together for good (8:28). We believe that if God is for us, no one can stand against us (8:31). We believe that we are more than conquerors through him who loved us (8:37) and that neither death nor life, nor angels nor rulers, nor height nor depth, nor anything else in all creation, will be able to separate us from the love of God that is in Christ Jesus our Lord (8:38–39)."

Five Lies of Our Anti-Christian Age has everything to do with the armor of God, because this book is a book about truth—truth you may have never heard, truth you may have forgotten, or truth you already know but haven't dared to embrace. Don't follow the great dragon; that's what this book is about. He has already been defeated. Follow the one who *is* truth (John 14:6). Listen to him. Love him. Learn from him. Do not fall for the lies of our age. Stand your ground.

KEVIN DEYOUNG
Senior Pastor, Christ Covenant Church,
Matthews, North Carolina

Preface

THIS BOOK IS FOR CHRISTIANS, especially Christian women, who aren't ashamed of the Bible and its teachings—or who are and want to change. For young married women, my hope is that this book will encourage you to press on in holy faith and living. For young single women, I hope that you will aspire to be faithful and fruitful Christian wives, that is, to be helpers, wise counselors, and devoted homemakers to a godly man raising children to the glory of God. For older single and married women, my hope is that you will take up your role of honor as spiritual mothers to young women in the church.

Making the honor of the Christian family your priority and serving the Christian family with your life and your time is not some domestic cop-out. Indeed, it is part of how the great promise of Revelation 11:15 comes into focus: "The kingdom of the world has become the kingdom of our Lord and of his Christ, and he shall reign forever and ever."

This book is for those who know that marriage between a man and a woman is sacred and cannot be modified to appeal to cultural whims. We didn't make this sacred covenant, and we can't remake it. This book is for Christians with loved ones trapped in lesbian relationships and transgender confusion who know that helping them requires staying connected without joining them in their indoctrination. Only because we serve a God who can be truly known can we stay connected to lost loved ones and be of any godly use. We are of no good to God or our loved ones if we believe the lies the culture feeds us about what it means to be a man or a woman.

This book is for Christians not embarrassed by the Bible and its teaching on women's roles and callings. An unbreakable biblical logic connects God's design for men and women, God's standards for sexual behavior, and the Bible's teaching on sex roles in the family, church, and world. God created men and women in marriage to do different and complementary things: husbands lead, protect, and provide, and wives submit, nurture, and keep the home.

Because Satan would like you to think that my previous sentence is conspiratorial hate speech, strong Christian women need to know what the Bible says on this matter rather than what some famous almost-Christian feminist blogger says on Twitter. In fact, being wise in Scripture and ignorant of Twitter may be the first step. Of course, being a helpmate, wise counselor, and homemaker are not our only responsibilities—many others fill each day. When our obligations give us public positions in the world, we seek to conduct ourselves as godly women in these public spheres (as did the famed Proverbs 31 woman). But some of us believe, as I do, that God's design for women determines our roles and our priorities. The Christian family matters, and its neglect is deadly.

The covenant blessing that God gives to married women with children extends to unmarried or childless women in the church who support this high calling. We are the body of Christ, under the covenant of grace, and if our priorities are in order, God will bless us, all of us, with no second-class citizens or people left out or passed over. This does not mean that all Christian women will be married; it does mean that all Christian women who value biblical marriage and childbearing and rearing will be blessed.

Finally, for those women who have loved ones lost for now and held in the grips of our nation's reigning idol, a formidable monolith represented by the letters LGBTQ and the symbol +, this book intends to arm you with God's words of courage, comfort, and boldness so that you may pray without ceasing. My prayer is that you will stay indestructibly connected to your loved one without falling victim to the indoctrination that has bewitched her. If *bewitched* seems like a strong word, listen to how the apostle Paul puts it: "Some will depart from the faith by devoting themselves to deceitful spirits and teachings of demons, through the insincerity of liars whose consciences are seared" (1 Tim. 4:1–2). Innovations to the gospel are more accurately understood as false teaching. Nothing good comes from this.

My prayer is that our generation would be known for faithful prayer, fervent worship, diligent church membership, and sacrificial hospitality, blessed by and magnified by the Holy Spirit. May your faith fail not, and may you see your loved one restored to truth and to Christ.

Introduction

The grass withers, the flower fades,
but the word of our God will stand forever.

ISAIAH 40:8

YOU TREK DOWN THE STEPS and onto the street, heading toward
the big warehouse grocery store, favorite coffee mug in hand, two
youngest children in tow. "Bigot!" "Hater!" These are the words that
greet you as soon as your feet hit the sidewalk. You look around,
wondering who was just shouting these accusations and to whom.
In utter disbelief, you realize that the shouter was a brother in the
Lord. And he was angrily yelling at you. Brothers and sisters are
clashing with each other in hurt, confusion, and rage—right here
on Main Street. Fingers are pointing, and accusations are flying
high and hard. And these people aren't outsiders—they are members of your tribe. All around you, people are bustling around in
self-righteousness and scornful disdain.

Seemingly overnight, a civil war within Christianity has
broken out.

You arrive at the grocery warehouse emotionally exhausted.

You hoist your little ones into the grocery cart seat, hand each one a snack cup with Cheerios, pull out your membership card, and flash it to the check-in girl. "Thank you, Miss," you say while entering the colossal warehouse through the electronics section. Mountainous TV screens cover the walls, and you try to adjust your eyes to the glare. On one screen, you witness a news reporter shoving a microphone under a beleaguered mom's chin and posing a cheeky question in a language you faintly recognize. The reporter appears to speak English but uses words and phrases like *intersectionality* and *gay Christianity*. The reporter keeps using the third-person plural (*they*) to refer to a singular subject (*he* or *she*), which only serves to proliferate your confusion and disorientation.

Suddenly, you realize that the check-in girl is trying to get your attention. You check your pocketbook for your membership card, thinking maybe you dropped it, and she is kindly trying to return it. It turns out that's not why she is running toward you. She is shaking her fists in rage. "I go by the pronouns *he* and *him*!" the girl shouts over the din of the TVs.

"Your heteronormativity abuses me!" Her face is contorted with anger and rage.

What is *heteronormativity*, you wonder?[1]

As if she read your mind, the reporter speaks directly to the camera: "We are on a full-scale war against heteronormativity, the horrific belief that heterosexuality is normal."

You smile at your daughters, trying to draw their attention away from the blaring TV. You ponder the word *heteronormativity* as you esteem your daughters' dark brown eyes, something they inherited

---

1 Heteronormativity is the belief that heterosexuality is an abusive form of social control and manipulation, not the natural order of the created world.

from your husband. Ruminating on whether a second cup of coffee would help, you try to understand what is not normal about a husband and a wife and the children God graciously gives them.

What kind of culture goes to war against this?

You hurry past the newscast because your three-year-old notices *Blue's Clues* on the next big screen and wants to get out of the cart and dance and sing along. Something seems off as you draw near, and that's when you notice it. The show's title is "Blue's Clues Pride Parade Sing-Along Featuring Nina West."[2] You had no idea that the fluffy blue dog, beloved by preschoolers everywhere, hung out with drag queens. Your toddler is spellbound. Rushing past Ru Paul's protégé at full tilt, you find yourself at the foot of another gay performance, the San Francisco Gay Men's Chorus performing "A Message from the Gay Community." It contains the haunting refrains "We're coming for your children" and "We'll convert your children."[3] This one really takes you aback. The lead tenor, with his foppish eyebrows and sinister smirk, signals that, well, yes, he really is coming for your children. As the other members of this large choir combine voices for the crescendo, you realize that now you are the one spellbound.[4] You didn't know that gay men joke so openly these days about pedophilia.[5] Back in ancient history, like, five years ago, that would have hit a little too close to home.

---

2   "The Blue's Clues Pride Parade Sing-Along Ft. Nina West!," accessed March 9, 2022, https://www.youtube.com/.

3   "Video excerpts from the San Francisco Gay Men's Chorus," July 1, 2021, https://www.youtube.com/.

4   Becket Cook provides a most insightful analysis of this in "We'll Convert Your Children," *The Becket Cook Show*, episode 3, accessed September 7, 2022, https://www.youtube.com/.

5   The San Francisco Gay Men's Choir released a statement excusing this video as parody, and this is at best a half-truth. It is more accurate to categorize it under the genre of persuasion: it seeks to persuade its listeners to sing and dance along in the normalization of homosexuality and transgenderism. Apparently, parental rights are the next pillar that gay male sexual

3

You exit electronics and head for the dry food section, and you have never been so relieved to see marshmallows in breakfast cereal in your entire life. You say yes to two large boxes when the children beg. You need only cereal, coffee, and bananas, so you scoot back home with your parcel and children. Nostalgia tugs hard at your heart. You ponder the past decade and its tumultuous metamorphosis.

This is real life, but it feels like you inhabit the pages of a dystopian novel. In sadness, you puzzle over the dethroned Christian luminaries and, with them, the parachurch ministries that once prominently featured those luminous names. Their heinous scandals serve as a stunning betrayal. You repent because you—and everyone around you—made heroes out of mere men and then watched them morph into heretics. Something sinister happened when you treated them like rock stars and started playing the groupie. And now that the genie is out of the bottle, there's no putting her back. Everything keeps changing, and even within your extended family, it feels like there is a spiritual civil war going on.

Welcome to our new world, where it feels like we are living at ground zero of the Tower of Babel.

The Tower of Babel

What does the Tower of Babel have to do with our current anti-Christian age? We read about the Tower of Babel in Genesis 11:

---

expression intends to topple. Why do I reject the genre of parody for this musical work? Parody, like all literary genres, selects content carefully. In no time during the historic gay-rights movement would gay men so boldly and openly celebrate pedophilia. That was the dirty little secret that they wished to conceal because the LGBTQ+-rights movement has historically wanted to downplay gay male affiliation with known pro-pedophilia groups like the North American Man/Boy Love Association (NAMBLA). After all, this kind of thing does not lend itself to the narrative that gay men are a victimized group in need of antibullying protection.

Now the whole earth had one language and the same words. And as people migrated from the east, they found a plain in the land of Shinar and settled there. And they said to one another, "Come, let us make bricks, and burn them thoroughly." And they had brick for stone, and bitumen for mortar. Then they said, "Come, let us build ourselves a city and a tower with its top in the heavens, and let us make a name for ourselves, lest we be dispersed over the face of the whole earth." And the LORD came down to see the city and the tower, which the children of man had built. And the LORD said, "Behold, they are one people, and they have all one language, and this is only the beginning of what they will do. And nothing that they propose to do will now be impossible for them. Come, let us go down and there confuse their language, so that they may not understand one another's speech." So the LORD dispersed them from there over the face of all the earth, and they left off building the city. Therefore its name was called Babel, because there the LORD confused the language of all the earth. And from there the LORD dispersed them over the face of all the earth. (Gen. 11:1–9)

The fall of the Tower of Babel is an action-packed biblical story showcasing God's powerful destruction of wicked men's evil plans. The futility of man's attempt to usurp God's will and glory is on full display here. The people wanted to build a city with a great tower; instead, God scattered them, and they fled. The people were confident that their tower would reach heaven; instead, it was so insignificant that God stooped low to find it. Envious of God's glory, the people wanted to make a great name and steal his glory for themselves; instead, they are known forever by God's naming their city Babel—confusion.

In pride, mankind attempted to reach heaven by building a tower. They strived in their own strength to come to God. God would have none of this and destroyed the tower—it collapsed like a toddler's Jenga stack.

From the biblical church's point of view, God's confusion of language and the scattering of his enemies was a good thing. Destroying the tower and confusing the language was God's way of protecting his people from false leaders and teachers. After God destroyed the Tower of Babel, those who opposed God had an even harder time finding and making allies. When miscommunication confounds evil, God's people see this as a blessing. But what does it mean when the chaos and confusion are within Christianity, not (only) external to it? "God is not a God of confusion," declares 1 Corinthians 14:33. If my enemies are Christ's enemies, and if Christ is not divided, why are enemy lines drawn within Christianity?

This book offers one simple answer: the world is in chaos, and the church is divided because we have failed to obey God and value his plan for how men and women should live. We foolishly believed that we could permanently extricate the gospel from the creation ordinance—that we could have the New Testament without the Old. We foolishly believed that personal piety and love for Jesus require no doctrinal integrity and no foundation in the Bible as God's inerrant, sufficient, and inspired word. We foolishly believed that we could reinvent our calling as men and women, defy God's pattern and purpose for the sexes, and somehow reap God's blessing. God's plan for men and women, the creation ordinance, is first found in Genesis 1. And it is central—not peripheral—to the gospel of Jesus Christ.

The Creation of Man and Woman

The creation of man and woman, also known as the "creation ordinance," is central, not peripheral, to the gospel. Found in Genesis 1:27–28, the creation ordinance is God's first covenant with man:

> So God created man in his own image,
>> in the image of God he created him;
>> male and female he created them.

> And God said to them, "Be fruitful and multiply and fill the earth and subdue it and have dominion over the fish of the sea and over the birds of the heavens and over every living thing that moves on the earth."

The creation ordinance rests on four matters:

- It is an ordinance (a law or an authoritative order).

- It is relational and noble: man made in God's image, man and woman made for one another. Man "is the image and glory of God, but woman is the glory of man. . . . In the Lord woman is not independent of man nor man of woman; for as woman was made from man, so man is now born of woman. And all things are from God" (1 Cor. 11:7, 11–12).

- It establishes a gender *binary*. A binary is an entity with two portions that make up one whole. A gender binary means that humanity is one entity that exists in one of two parts: male and female. Male and female, created by God's design for life on earth, will become male and female by God's

7

design in our eternal state in either heaven or hell and in the new heavens and new earth.[6] Adam's sin distorts and mars the goodness of God's created order, but it does not change what it means to be human.

- It reveals the rules and jobs given to Adam and Eve before the fall: marriage (between one man and one woman that features the life-giving blessing of children) and work (that requires stewarding the earth and having dominion over the creatures).

The creation ordinance not only describes how men and women are created distinctly and by God's design; it defines what it means to be human. When we dispense with the wisdom of the creation ordinance, we abandon the standard of God's intention for men and women, the purpose for masculinity and femininity, and the order that God has set for families and civilization.

The creation ordinance is also a covenant, a formal agreement between two parties and an obligatory declaration that is administered with sovereign seals and signs and blessings or curses. God created us to be in covenant with him. We were made for the covenant; the covenant was not an add-on after we roamed around for billions of years, presumably sprouting brains and legs.

Made in God's Image

The creation ordinance declares that mankind is made *in* God's image—not *as* God's image.[7] The image of God in us is not found

---

6 A helpful summary of what happens to people—believers and unbelievers—when we die is found in the Westminster Confession of Faith, chapter 32, "Of the State of Men after Death, and of the Resurrection of the Dead"; and in chapter 33, "Of the Last Judgment." G. I. Williamson, *The Westminster Confession of Faith for Study Classes* (Phillipsburg, NJ: P&R, 2004), 328–46.

7 Joel Beeke, "The Image of God," in *The Reformation Heritage KJV Study Bible* (Grand Rapids, MI: Reformation Heritage, 2014), 1733.

in the flesh of our human body, for God is "a most pure Spirit, invisible, without body, parts, or passions."[8] This means that as striking as the Sistine Chapel is, the image of God is not found on its ceiling in Michelangelo's artistry. That is merely crude paganism, beautiful and arresting as it may be.

If God's love for mankind is revealed in his creation of man and woman in his image, where do we find God's image in man? What exactly does it mean to be made in God's image? An image of yourself is what you see when you stand in front of a mirror. God is the object in the biblical creation account, and we are the reflection. Therefore, to reflect God's image accurately, we need to look at him through the mirror of the word of God illuminated through the Holy Spirit.

To repeat, we are made not *as* God's image but *in* God's image. We reflect the image of God, not by inventing what he wants for us based on our feelings or independent ideas for our lives and futures, but by looking to God through his word and growing in the knowledge of God, the holiness of God, and the righteousness of God (Eph. 4:24; Col. 3:10). Our authenticity comes from God and not from our feelings. Joel Beeke writes, "When man fell into sin, knowledge gave way to ignorance, righteousness to iniquity, and holiness to ungodliness."[9] God is holy, and therefore ignorance, iniquity, and ungodliness reflect our sin nature in Adam. The good news of the gospel is that when we put our trust in Christ and walk in his love and his commands, God's image in man is restored in knowledge, righteousness, and holiness. This restoration process proceeds from the powerful word of God being engrafted into a believing heart. Beeke describes the order by which God renews

8 Westminster Confession of Faith, 2:1.
9 Beeke, "Image of God," 1733.

his image in man: "First, we must acquire knowledge of the truth, which is imparted through the preaching of the Word (James 1:21)." Next, we do the will of God (Ps. 15:1; 1 John 5:3). And, finally, we "consecrate ourselves, soul and body, to serving God with loving reverence and godly fear."[10]

Male and Female

We are made in the image of God as *distinctly* men or women, and we are called to reflect that image in knowledge, righteousness, and holiness *as men and as women*. Some aspects of the gospel life are universal to both men and women. For example, we are all called to repent of our sin, put our hope in Christ, and live obediently. But because our creational design is different, some aspects of obedience to God are different. Wives are called to obey their husbands in the Lord (1 Pet. 3:1). Qualified men only are called to be pastors and elders in the church (1 Tim. 3:1–7; Titus 1:5–9). Brothers and sisters in the Lord show their love to one another by not leading each other into temptation, which means women are to conduct themselves with modesty, and brothers are to protect their sisters' reputations (Rom. 12:2; 1 Cor. 6:19–20; 1 Tim. 2:9). When we level creational differences between men and women, foolishly thinking that there is no vital difference between men and women, we disobey God. The disunity of our day reflects God's cutting down to size the tower of gender and sexual confusion that we have foolishly built.

Why Do We All Live in Babel Now?

We all live in Babel now because people exchanged the truth for lies and have codified these lies into the law of the land. It's a tragedy

10 Beeke, "Image of God," 1733.

that we embrace lies because we don't remember the truth. Paul describes three "exchanges" of truth for lies in Romans 1:21–28.

First there is the exchange of the Creator for the creature, or the exchange of God worship for idol worship:

> Although they knew God, they did not honor him as God or give thanks to him, but they became futile in their thinking, and their foolish hearts were darkened. Claiming to be wise, they became fools, and *exchanged* the glory of the immortal God for images resembling mortal man and birds and animals and creeping things. (Rom. 1:21–23)

Second is the exchange of truth for lies:

> Therefore God gave them up in the lusts of their hearts to impurity, to the dishonoring of their bodies among themselves, because they *exchanged* the truth about God for a lie and worshiped and served the creature rather than the Creator, who is blessed forever! Amen. (Rom. 1:24–25)

Third comes the exchange of natural sexuality (heterosexuality) for dishonorable passions (homosexuality):

> For this reason God gave them up to dishonorable passions. For their women *exchanged* natural relations for those that are contrary to nature; and the men likewise gave up natural relations with women and were consumed with passion for one another, men committing shameless acts with men and receiving in themselves the due penalty for their error. And since they did not see fit to acknowledge God, God gave

them up to a debased mind to do what ought not to be done. (Rom. 1:26–28)

These exchanges have a tragic order: (1) The exchange of the triune God for gods of our own making; (2) the exchange of truth for lies; (3) the exchange of the natural (heterosexuality) for the unnatural (homosexuality). A world that grows in its homosexuality and gender confusion is a world judged by God, given over to sin (Rom. 1:24), and increasingly barren and corrupt. I understand that this is not how people who call themselves "gay"—which I once did—understand the situation. But they would be better off if they did.

The world we inhabit is one that has completed all three exchanges in Romans 1. After these exchanges have been made, we are left with five lies that require biblical confrontation.

What are the five lies?

The Five Lies

Lie #1: Homosexuality is normal.

Included in this lie is the belief that homosexual orientation is true and immutable—fixed and never-changing. Homosexual orientation, a nineteenth-century Freudian invention (Sigmund Freud, 1856–1939), is an unbiblical category of personhood and an antagonist to the creation ordinance because it redefines sinful desire as something that defines who you are rather than how you feel. Lie #1 claims that the word of God doesn't apply to homosexual orientation because homosexual orientation represents a person's core truth. Some professing Christians believe that homosexual orientation is fixed, immutable (unchangeable), and part of God's creational and eternal plan. Some people believe that homosexuality is embedded in a person's identity.

We must ponder why God's attribute of immutability has been embraced by the LGBTQ+ movement as an attribute of homosexual orientation. God is immutable—God never changes. One theologian defines God's immutability as "that perfection in God whereby He is exalted above all."[11] But if you exchange the Creator for the creature, you impose God's attributes on man. When we hear "homosexual orientation is fixed and immutable—it never changes," this is only imaginable in a world that has already exchanged the worship of the Creator for the worship of the creature, of God for an idol. "Gay Christians" (an oxymoron if there ever was one) teach that you can't repent of who you are, how you feel, or even what you desire. They believe that homosexual orientation is morally neutral, separate from one's sin nature, cannot be repented of, and rarely changes over a person's lifetime. This is a lie.

Lie #2: Being a spiritual person is kinder than being a biblical Christian.

Unbiblical spirituality welcomes people exactly as they are or, at least, makes this promise. This is a religion that elevates being a "good" person over giving your life to Christ. To the unbiblically spiritual person, everything is one. Distinctions and hierarchies are called abusive, and true spirituality is supposedly found inside ourselves. This sort of spirituality, unbiblical spirituality, believes that everything in the universe supposedly shares in this divine power and unifying balance. Rules, divisions, and distinctions are violent, or so says the unbiblically spiritual person.

---

11 Geerhardus Vos, *Reformed Dogmatics: A System of Christian Theology*, trans. Richard Gaffin Jr. (Bellingham, WA: Lexham Press, 2012), 23.

In contrast, for the biblical Christian, there are two kinds of reality: God and creation. God is eternal, triune, personal, holy, loving, and separate from his creation. According to biblical spirituality, there are two kinds of people: those who love God and those who defy God. Even though we create our own problems by refusing to live by his laws, God provides the only solution through the Lord Jesus Christ. Pastor and theologian Peter Jones, founder of *TruthXchange*, offers the most helpful paradigm for comparing unbiblical spirituality to biblical spirituality.[12] While unbiblical spirituality self-promotes as kind and inclusive, it is in reality narcissistic and damning.[13]

Lie #3: Feminism is good for the world and the church.

Feminism began in 1792 with Mary Wollstonecraft's *A Vindication of the Rights of Woman*. As its title suggests, it sought to "vindicate," which means "to assert one's right to possession." And what rights needed possessing? Women needed to possess the rights to citizenship. Wollstonecraft sought rights for education and voting for women. Feminism has gone through four "waves" or phases since 1792, with the most recent wave so tied to the LGBTQ+ movement that now, in 2023, we cannot even define what a woman is or defend her right to exist—least of all to be noted as a citizen.[14] Feminism

---

12 "In one-ism, everything shares the same essence. In a word, everything is a piece of the divine. Two-ism believes that while all of creation shares a certain essence (everything apart from God is created), the Creator of nature, namely God, is a completely different being, whose will determines the nature and function of all created things." Peter Jones, *One or Two: Seeing a World of Difference, Romans 1 for the Twenty-First Century* (Np: Main Entry Editions, 2010), 17.

13 An unbiblically spiritual person becomes a narcissist with great ease. According to the *Huffington Post*, "Being a spiritual person is synonymous with being a person whose highest priority is to be loving yourself and others." Margaret Paul, "What Does It Mean to Be a Spiritual Person?," *HuffPost*, December 21, 2016, https://www.huffpost.com/.

14 Two incidents prove my point. First, Judge Ketanji Brown Jackson refused to define what a woman is during her Supreme Court hearing (truly ironic given that she was selected because

in the world is passè—it has been displaced by transgenderism. Feminism in the evangelical church, however, is alive and well. When the church sets itself up to follow the world and not to lead it, it necessarily lingers long with discarded trends and affections. Adherents of feminism believe the Bible has no bearing on gender roles, responsibilities, or requirements because the idea of men and women being made by God's design for God's purposes on earth is old-fashioned, silly, dangerous, abusive, and culturally driven. Some professing Christian feminists believe that Adam's headship is a consequence of the fall—and thus a sin. They claim that there is no biblical warrant for a married woman's submission to her husband and elders or for elders and pastors to be qualified men. Bible verses that call for a wife to obey her husband in the Lord, such as Titus 2:4–5, 1 Peter 3:1, 5–6, and Colossians 3:18, are "contextualized" and then dismissed.[15] Such feminists believe that feminism offers a corrective to Christianity because, without it, misogyny (the hatred of women) will run rampant with biblical

she is a black woman). See Jordan Boyd, "Judge Nominated to Supreme Court on the Basis of Her Sex Cannot Define Woman," *The Federalist*, March 23, 2022, https://thefederalist.com/. Second, Lia Thomas, a biological man who swam for the prestigious University of Pennsylvania men's swim team, came out this year as a trans woman and swam on the women's team where he won the 2022 NCAA Swim Championship. Fourth-wave feminists heralded this as a great victory for trans women. Everyone else interpreted this rightly as the end of Title IX, women's sports, and classical feminism. Brooke Migdon, "Lia Thomas: 'Trans Women Are Not a Threat to Women's Sports,'" *The Hill*, May 31, 2022, https://thehill.com/.

15 Brad Isbell, "Shall the Radical Contextualizers Win?," *Heidelblog*, February 24, 2022, https://heidelblog.net/. This article speaks more to the subject of homosexuality than feminism but is the most useful articulation of radical contextualization. To "contextualize" a passage of Scripture is to understand its binding command as relevant only in the ancient context in which it was written. This raises some obvious problems. If the word of God is only true in an ancient context and not applicable or binding on people today, then the Bible cannot be my guide to faith and life. If you are a contextualist, then you tend to read the Bible for its "moral vision," and you leave the concept of morality swinging in the wind of today's values.

support. Without feminism to the rescue, they argue, the church will unwittingly promote sexual abuse by giving perpetrators extreme and unchecked power and spiritual abuse by prohibiting a woman from using her gifts of teaching from the pulpit and assuming the roles of pastor and elder. This is a lie.

Lie #4: Transgenderism is normal.

People who believe in what is called "gender fluidity" also believe that sexual difference has no biological or ontological (original and eternal) integrity. Transgenderism is supposedly as normal for some people as freckles and a blue sky on a North Carolina summer day. Transgenderism maintains that there are more than two biological sexes and even more genders. The year 2022 boasts seventy-two genders and seventy-eight gender pronouns.[16] By the time you are reading this book, there may be ten thousand. What does this all mean? How did we get to a place in the United States where someone can walk into Planned Parenthood and, forty-five minutes later, leave with a prescription for powerful hormones that will leave her sterilized for life if taken over time?[17] We got here by believing the lie that transgenderism is normal—at least for some people.

Lie #5: Modesty is an outdated burden that serves
male dominance and holds women back.

People who believe this lie dismiss the virtue of modesty for Christian women. Having denied that men and women are different,

---

16 "What Are Some Different Types of Gender Identity?," Medical News Today, accessed May 21, 2022, https://www.medicalnewstoday.com/.

17 "We offer gender affirming hormonal care for patients 18 years and older at all of our health centers. You don't need to participate in therapy or provide information for a mental health provider to receive hormone therapy." "Gender Affirming Hormone Care," Planned Parenthood, accessed May 21, 2022, https://www.plannedparenthood.org/.

with different responsibilities, callings, and boundaries, those who reject modesty believe that calling women to a different standard of dress, speech, and conduct is oppressive. They deny that women owe their brothers the kindness of modesty. At the bottom of this is a feminist belief that it is not fair that women are different from men and that asking women to dress and behave with biblical modesty serves male dominance and holds women back. In the contemporary church climate, modesty has been replaced by exhibitionism.

Lies I Believed Even as a Christian

I want to confess right at the outset that I believed all of these lies as an unbeliever, but I continued to believe some of them for years into my Christian life. Because I know how sneaky and seductive each of these lies is, I needed to write this book. I woke up to realize that I was on the field running the ball in the wrong direction and wearing the wrong team colors.

1. Gender Dysphoria vs. Transgenderism and the Pronoun Question

For years, and even as a Christian, I used and defended what are called "preferred pronouns." This means that for those who were diagnosed as gender dysphoric or those who viewed themselves as transgendered, I willingly used the pronoun "she" to refer to a biological man and the pronoun "he" to refer to a biological female. I falsely believed that this would aid and abet my ability to bring the gospel to bear on these people's lives. I failed to distinguish between an illness (gender dysphoria) and an ideology (transgenderism). I falsely believed that this would be missional, exemplifying a gracious willingness to meet a person where she was, step into her shoes, and do nothing to escalate the anxiety of an emotionally unstable person. And perhaps before preferred pronouns were coded into federal law, the danger and clarity of the situation wasn't as evident.

My reason for changing my mind can be stated in two words: *Obergefell* (as in *Obergefell v. Hodges*, 2015) and *Bostock* (as in *Bostock v. Clayton County, CA*, 2020). Because of these two landmark Supreme Court cases, the former establishing gay marriage and the latter LGBTQ+ civil rights, we are no longer discussing terminology or vocabulary. Rather, we are talking about ideology and idolatry, which must be confronted in the case of the former and killed in the latter. After *Bostock*, we have nearly one hundred pediatric gender clinics in the US, when we used to have one. After *Bostock*, we have government schools putting LGBTQ+ propaganda in antibullying programs, where parents cannot exercise authority over their child by removing the child from them. After *Bostock*, we have ROGD (rapid-onset gender dysphoria) and nothing short of mass hysteria capturing the minds of our teenage girls. Christians must read the times. The gospel has been on a collision course with homosexual orientation and gender identity for about a decade, and the collision occurred in 2015 and 2020. During war, borders close. One border that must be closed to actual Christians is using people's preferred pronouns.

I have sinned in using transgender pronouns and claiming it as hospitable. I have come to see my use of "preferred" pronouns today as sin, pure and simple. Not only is it lying to people who are already being lied to by the world, but it also falsifies the gospel imperative of the creation ordinance, with its eternal binary of being created in the image of God as male or female and the command to live out that image-bearing within God-assigned sexual roles.

2. *Prioritizing LGBTQ+ Youth over the God Who Made Them*

My sin of lying against the creation ordinance through transgender pronouns reveals another sin: focusing on the girl lost to LGBTQ+ madness over the God who made her. By wanting to comfort the lost girl, I sinned in the pride that believed I could be more merciful than God. I sinned by using my personal experience over Scripture.

3. *Giving Biblical Meaning to LGBTQ+ Vocabulary*

My sin of prioritizing my personal history as a lesbian over Scripture bled into another sin—miscategorizing and then dismissing as dangerous all care efforts to promote healthy biblical sexuality. I did this by using language that the LGBTQ+ community had co-opted or invented, such as *homophobia*. For years I said things like, "Homosexuality is a sin, but so is homophobia." I defined *homophobia* as a wholesale dismissal of someone's soul, that is, of seeing some people as outside of the grace of God. But this is neither a truthful definition of sin nor a truthful definition of homophobia. A phobia is an irrational fear. It is not irrational to fear sin running rampant.

4. *Calling Reparative Therapy a "Heresy"*

In 2014 I wrote in a highly publicized article that reparative therapy "is a heresy, a modern version of the prosperity gospel. Name it. Claim it. Pray the gay away."[18] These rank among the most misguided words I have written as a Christian. I once believed that all change-allowing therapies harmed sexual strugglers by making promises that might not be delivered in this lifetime. But recent

---

18 Rosaria Butterfield, "You Are What—and How—You Read," The Gospel Coalition, February 13, 2014, https://www.thegospelcoalition.org/.

peer-reviewed studies have revealed that people are not harmed by change-allowing therapies even when they do not experience change in their affections.[19] By failing to distinguish "hurt" from "harm" I ran roughshod with overgeneralizations. The gospel message hurts our pride in life-giving ways, and for that I praise God.

The Necessity of Repentance

Sins spin webs of confusion. Repentance breaks those webs and replaces sin with clarity. But sin does real damage. I have done real damage. And repentance means more than saying you are sorry. According to Puritan Thomas Watson in *The Doctrine of Repentance*, true repentance is distinguished from counterfeit repentance by six ingredients:

1. Recognition of sin (Luke 15:17; Acts 26:18)
2. Sorrow for sin (Pss. 38:18; 51:17; Zech. 12:10; Luke 19:8)
3. Confession of sin (Neh. 9:2; 2 Sam. 24:17; Dan. 9:6; 1 Cor. 11:31)
4. Shame for sin (Ezek. 43:10; Luke 15:21)
5. Hatred for sin (Ps. 119:104; Ezek. 36:31; Rom. 7:15, 23)
6. Turning from sin (Isa. 55:7; Eph. 5:8)[20]

Because sin is a matter of the head, heart, and hands and corrupts our thinking, feeling, and doing, repentance is known by its fruit. Some believe (falsely) that because Christ has covered our sin and taken our shame on the cross, it means that we should have no consciousness of shame. Others (falsely) believe that repentance

---

19 Andrè Van Mol, "Even Failed Therapy for Undesired Same-Sex Sexuality Results in No Harm," Christian Medical and Dental Association, February 24, 2022, https://cmda.org/.

20 Thomas Watson, *The Doctrine of Repentance* (1668; repr., Carlisle, PA: Banner of Truth, 2012), 18.

just means saying you are sorry and then continuing on with no real change, business as usual.

The most dangerous and insidious misconception is from those who believe sin is only a matter of practice, not also internal desire. Oh, if only sin was so small an enemy as this! Theologian and pastor Mark Jones explains, "Sin is a parasite of the good; it feeds off of what God created. . . . Sin's nature is therefore understood as an ethical problem, not a physical problem."[21] The false belief that sin exists as a physical problem—and that it can be domesticated or stewarded for good—is not a biblical idea. It's hell-bound. Thomas Watson comments:

> Loving of sin is worse than committing it. A good man may run into a sinful action unawares, but to love sin is desperate. . . . To love sin shows that the will is in sin, and the more of the will there is in a sin, the greater the sin. Willfulness makes it a sin not to be purged by sacrifice (Heb. 10:26).[22]

Our language reveals the sins we love. The reason that loving our sin is worse than committing it is that we will commit the sins we love eventually. Repentance must go to the root—to the reckless, godless love of sin.

Confronting these five lies begins with repentance. Mine and maybe yours. Repentance gives us a clean slate, a deep fear of God, and the wisdom to go forward.

Along with repentance (which is a daily and lifelong practice), we must confront these lies with biblical truth.

---

21 Mark Jones, *Knowing Sin: Seeing a Neglected Doctrine through the Eyes of the Puritans* (Chicago: Moody, 2022), 41–42.
22 Watson, *Doctrine of Repentance*, 47–48.

The Necessity of Godly Confrontation

To confront something is not to reject, misrepresent, or mock it. Instead, a confrontation is an act of respect. To confront a deeply held belief involves recognizing the different points of view at play. It means knowing that there is a difference between acceptance and approval, which Pastor Ken Smith taught me decades ago and which I will address in the afterword. It requires us to take the side of the Bible's witness and to embrace Christ's point of view over and against anything and anyone that offers a different gospel. Your witness for Christ ultimately requires that you know Christ better than you know the world. (And this means that you are in the Bible more than you are on the Internet.) A confrontation finally concludes with accepting or rejecting a position—and encouraging others to do the same.

Godly confrontation does not include mocking derision.

Godly confrontation allows Christians to seek the truth, to pray to the God of truth, and to teach the truth. The truth may be hard to hear and will require many tears and much prayer. But Christians start with truth, and godly confrontation helps to reveal the truth.

Godly confrontation might seem naïve and overly simple, but that is because sin makes everything more complicated than it is. Sin creates more work for everybody. Our method for confrontation is found in 2 Corinthians 10:3–6:

> Though we walk in the flesh, we are not waging war according to the flesh. For the weapons of our warfare are not of the flesh but have divine power to destroy strongholds. We destroy arguments and every lofty opinion raised against the knowledge of

God, and take every thought captive to obey Christ, being ready to punish every disobedience, when your obedience is complete.

You might be wondering why we need to confront these lies. Wouldn't it be sufficient to leave well enough alone and build our faith on firmer foundations, leaving these lies to rot in their locations? Shouldn't we just distance ourselves from bad ideas and not take them head-on? Isn't the world just going to hell in a handbasket? If so, ought we not save ourselves and get out of Dodge?

Perhaps we could agree to disagree, turn a deaf ear to the conflict, and go about the business of our lives living peaceably (although deceptively) while we pretend that all is well when it is not? Perhaps we could argue for pluralism (where competing ideas stand side by side) or pragmatism (where practical solutions are valued over truth)? Or maybe we can take the valuable parts and reject the awful claims? Chew the meat and spit out the bones, if you will. Sometimes we wonder why we are in conflict with people who also call themselves "Christian." Can't we just focus on creating a gospel culture and not fret over the Bible, embracing the former as pure and the latter as corrupt?

The reason we can't do this is that none of these solutions honors God. Indeed, each and every one is a sin in its own right. Proclaiming the truth, living in humble obedience to the word, and professing faith in Jesus Christ is what honors God. We can't agree to disagree, and we can't split hairs because unconfronted lies work a little like air pollution: we breathe it in, and we never realize that we are ingesting it until it's too late. I don't believe that the Bible calls us to hopelessness or self-preservation in the face of evil. Just for the record, I don't even believe that the world is going to hell in a handbasket. I believe that the Lord Jesus Christ is King of the whole world, and his return to judge the living and the dead will be a triumphant celebration of a King returning to his kingdom.[23] But this does not mean that our King's triumphant return comes without conflict or that some of us won't lose our lives for the cause of Christ and his gospel. The good news of the gospel sends us into the heat of battle.

Unconfronted lies have made a big mess for us. They pervade our public culture (government schools, newspapers, social media) as well as those evangelical churches that have been taken off course. If our approach to dealing with the contention of these tough times involves telling or repeating lies to keep the peace, we are contributing to the problem. Why? Because lies cannot be tamed. Lies do not coexist with truth but rather corrupt it.

Something has changed, and we all can agree on that.

The rules of the game have changed.

The landscape has changed.

And it's harder now to be a Christian in the world.

Proverbs 22:28 says, "Do not move the ancient landmark that your fathers have set." But we look at the world and can barely find evidence that those landmarks ever existed. Sin has become grace, and grace has become sin. How did this happen and what should we do?

---

23 Postmillennialism teaches that the one thousand years of Revelation 20 is figurative and occurs prior to the second coming. We believe that there will be a time of immense worldwide blessing for the nations (which will be known as Christian nations) as well as a season where many people from ethnic Israel will come to Christian faith in vast numbers. It maintains that the Holy Spirit will draw millions of people to Christ through faithful gospel preaching, and Christ's return will witness a general resurrection of the just and unjust and the final judgment (Rev. 20:1–15). More information can be found in the following books: Loraine Boettner, *The Millennium*, rev. ed. (Phillipsburg, NJ: P&R, 1984); Kenneth Gentry, *He Shall Have Dominion: A Postmillennial Eschatology* (Chesnee, SC: Victorious Hope, 2021); Keith A. Mathison, *Postmillennialism: An Eschatology of Hope* (Phillipsburg, NJ: P&R, 1999).

*The Years of Our Lord 2015 and 2020: The Legalization of
Gay Marriage and the Codification of LGBTQ+ Civil Rights*

In June 2015 the Supreme Court of the United States redefined marriage. By judicial fiat, gay marriage became the law of the land. The court did not *expand* the definition of marriage to include gay couples. The court declared opposition to gay marriage a discriminatory act of "animus" (hatred). The court declared that denial of LGBTQ+ rights represents an attack on the human dignity of all people who use the letters LGBTQ+ to describe themselves.[24]

As we will explore in Lie #1, homosexual orientation became through this seismic shift a category of personhood. In other words, after *Obergefell* and *Bostock*, LGBTQ+ describes *who* someone *is* rather than *how* someone *feels*. Freudian ideas about sexuality replaced biblical ones and became the new and preferred anthropology, the study of what makes us human. This false idea of Sigmund Freud's has become a sacred value of American society. Freud believed that who you are is determined by your sexual desires. Freud, you may remember, also came up with a doozy of a list of other pseudoscientific stories, such as the Oedipus complex and a woman's supposed envy of the male sexual organ.

The biblical witness of the creation ordinance provides a radically different definition of what it means to be a person than what Freud and the world offer. Under Scripture, who you are is rooted in bearing the image of God. You are male or female image bearers of a holy God with specific responsibilities and blessings accruing from God's sexual design. But according to Freud, because your feelings are the fount of all truth, you are gay if you say so. (You are

---

24 Dale Carpenter, "Arguing Animus in the Gay Marriage Cases," *Washington Post*, February 10, 2015, https://www.washingtonpost.com/.

also trans if you say so, or a Christian if you say so, or a dragon, or a six-year-old girl trapped in the body of a fifty-two-year-old man.)[25]

You may not intend to invest the word *gay* with this much weight. But that doesn't make the problem go away, because the power of words is not located in our individual intentions. Once a word has become galvanized by a political cause and codified by legal force, it is no longer just a word but is now a *keyword*.[26] Just as a key unlocks a door, a keyword holds authority enforced by law. LGBTQ+ is an acronym, and it stands for a list of keywords. These keywords have become normalized and politicized by reenforcing their use with legal power. Take, for example, Peter Vlaming, a former Virginia high school French teacher who found himself in the crossfire of the transgender pronoun war. Vlaming refused to use transgender pronouns but graciously called students by whatever name they chose. This wasn't enough to appease the LGBTQ+ lobby. When Peter Vlaming was fired for avoiding pronoun use entirely, we see the difference between a *word* and a *keyword*.[27] A word can be exchanged for synonyms, but a keyword is implemented with religious exactitude. Mr. Vlaming was fired from his job not because he was incompetent but because he was noncompliant with pronoun laws. And while Mr. Vlaming's legal appeal is not finished, he is still out of a job.[28]

25 "'I've gone back to being a child': Husband and Father of Seven, 52, Leaves His Wife and Kids to Live as a Transgender Six-Year-Old Girl Named Stefonknee," *Daily Mail*, March 6, 2016, https://www.dailymail.co.uk/.

26 Raymond Williams, *Keywords: A Vocabulary of Culture and Society* (New York: Oxford University Press, 1983).

27 Teo Armus, "A Virginia Teacher Was Fired for Refusing to Use a Trans Student's Pronouns. Now, He's Suing His School District," *Washington Post*, October 1, 2019, https://www.washingtonpost.com/.

28 "VA Supreme Court Agrees to Hear Case of Teacher Fired over Pronoun Policy," *The Roanoke Star*, March 4, 2022, https://theroanokestar.com/.

When the evangelical church embraced LGBTQ+ vocabulary, the true gospel was exchanged for a false one. Ironically, this made the world much less safe for people who experience homosexual desires or gender confusion than it ever was before. A genuine Christian who experiences the indwelling sin of homosexual desire or transgenderism will find both the world that says, "Do what feels good," and a church that says, "You are a sexual minority and need a voice and platform in the church," as equally dangerous. Where is it safe to just repent of sin and be built up in the promises of God? Where is it safe to repent and flee from your sin and *no longer be gay or trans*?

Gay Christians tell you that they must "navigate" their homosexuality. But God equips you to overcome your sin. Why did it become wise for Christians to "come out of the closet" about their sin, to tell the whole world about their sin instead of repenting of it and seeking accountability from a pastor or elders and a few close friends? "Coming out of the closet" and describing yourself by sin will never help you to repent from it, flee from it, and be delivered from it. "Coming out of the closet" is a political act of celebration, pride, and solidarity with a cause that shares no substance with Jesus Christ.

The idea that you should always "come out" and share with everyone your sinful desires happened because homosexual desire was transformed from sin (which demands repentance) to a morally neutral category of personhood (LGBTQ+), which demands affirmation and celebration.

All atheistic paradigms of personhood hate the very people they claim to love by denying them soul care. Changing the definition of personhood is ungodly and unloving. It has led to all manner of lost souls, broken families, and theological heresy, with so-called Christian theologians declaring LGBTQ+ persons as the modern example of the biblical Gentiles.[29] Nothing is further from the truth. If anything, the LGBTQ+ lobby and the foolish self-proclaimed gay Christians who serve them have become more pharisaical in their practices than any other political movement in my lifetime.

And let's not forget that I was once a gay-rights activist and tenured radical professor.

This is the world that I helped create.

There is a world of difference between how you feel (recognizing and repenting from the sin of homosexual desire) and who you are (believing that you have a fixed and morally neutral homosexual orientation).

There is a world of difference between "struggling with your gender identity" and repenting of your sin.

To be sure, if you hear that someone is struggling with his gender identity, you need to stop right there and think that through. Sexual anatomy is a gift from God, and it comes with a purpose and a blessing. Because of sin, people need the redemption of Jesus Christ to experience the blessing in God's providence and calling. But even when sin clouds the reality of God's good plan, men are men and women are women, and even for those people who wish that they had a different sexual anatomy, the struggle is with the reality of physical and bodily truth. The struggle is with the sin of envy, not the God who made them.

His struggle is not with his identity. His struggle is with reality.

All this raises the question, Are people trapped in the modern invention of LGBTQ+ in need of parades, pep talks, and pronoun

---

29 Wesley Hill, "The Transformation of the Gentiles," Spiritual Friendship (website), accessed March 18, 2022, https://spiritualfriendship.org/.

stickers? Or is help to be found in biblical counseling, union with Christ, and the family of God? Do they need constant affirmation for all sinful feelings and even delusions? Should they seek change for sinful patterns and practices? Is sexual orientation fixed and unchangeable? Would not Christian faith and genuine soul care by a faithful pastor and church community go a long way toward growing in maturity and facing problems, repenting of sin and growing in grace? Are people who live apart from God's creation ordinance victims in need of civil rights or sinners in need of a Savior? Do we love our neighbor enough to tell the truth?

One of the great dangers that 2015 bequeathed is the idea that "how you identify" is true. If a boy identifies as a girl, we are told that it is true. If a woman identifies as a dragon,[30] we are told that it is true. And if a person identifies as a Christian, well, that must be true too. We are told that to question someone's profession of faith is a violent act of trying to read her heart. But John 14:15 suggests something else. Our Lord says, "If you love me, you will keep my commandments." The Bible says that we can observe with our own eyes if someone is following God's law (Matt. 7:16–17).

Unity in Christ's love emerges from unity in Christ's law. The world offers false beneficence in place of real care when it fails to use God's law to apply God's love. This is especially tragic in the context of transgenderism. The world says if your daughter wants to become your son, you must comply or she will kill herself. Her therapist asks, "Would you rather have a dead daughter or a living son?" But this isn't a valid question; instead, it's a manipulating one. It's also a no-win question. It places the blame for a potential suicide in a caregiver's refusal to believe a lie. It's impossible to give

---

30 "'Dragon Lady' Spends $75,000 to Transform into 'Transspecies Reptilian,'" *Toronto Sun*, August 16, 2019, https://torontosun.com/.

a good answer to a bad question, and Christian parents are tortured by this question daily and ought not to be.

What is the Christian answer to the disingenuous question, Would you rather have a dead daughter or a living son?

It's a hard answer.

If you are experiencing the desire to be or do something that God hasn't rightfully given you, whether this is coveting your neighbor's wife or your neighbor's gender, you are to cut *that* desire off (not your own body parts). The sin of transgenderism is actually the sin of envy. Envy will eat a person from the inside out. Appeasing envy will only make everything worse. Philippians 1:21 reminds us, "to live is Christ, and to die is gain." Giving the flesh the sin that it wants is not a Christian response to pain. Instead, we are called to die to sin.[31] Mark 8:34 says, "If anyone would come after me, let him deny himself and take up his cross and follow me."

The answer to the baiting question is found in the gospel. In the gospel, we have a Savior who has paid the penalty for us. He delivers us from temptation and evil. Jesus never encourages us to sin to preserve life. That convoluted idea is a lie from Satan. When God the Father grants to us his electing love, the Spirit unites us to Christ, bringing us out of spiritual death into newness of life. The bedrock of the Christian life is this: union with Christ means we can do all things through Christ who strengthens us (Phil. 4:13). Christians are beckoned first to die before we can live in Christ.

So when the atheistic therapist asks if you want a live son or a dead daughter, the answer is that all Christians want our children to be dead to sin and alive to Christ. If our child identifies as trans-

31 See Prov. 3:5–7; Matt. 10:37; Mark 8:38; Luke 9:23–25; 14:27–33; John 3:30; Rom. 6:1–6, 8; 12:1–2; 13:14; 1 Cor. 6:19–20; 15:31; 2 Cor. 5:17; Gal. 2:20–21; 5:24–25; Eph. 4:22–24; Col. 3:10; James 4:4; 1 Pet. 2:24.

gender, then, yes, the sin of envy and covetousness needs to be cut off, not the beautiful physical body that God graciously gave her.

Dying to sin and living to Christ was understood to be basic biblical wisdom until, uh, five years ago. Before the idea of "gay Christian" or "trans Christian" came into the church's vocabulary, sensible people understood that all believers must put a sharp knife through the heart of their choice sins every day.

Owing to the fact that there is an avalanche of scriptural evidence and comfort that speaks to any believer who is battling against sinful desires, no one should take seriously the manipulating question posed by LGBTQ+ therapists. The real question is, Whom do we believe? Confused people and their secular priests, or the God of all comfort and his eternal word? Christians struggle with all manner of sin, including the sin of wanting to reject bodily integrity and our responsibility to steward ourselves according to God's gift. No sin should shock us. We have a Savior who is mighty to save and to equip us to resist all manner of temptation. We show ourselves to be wicked barbarians if we sacrifice a true believer on the altar of LGBTQ+ and the secular psychology that defends it. If we sacrifice our children to the LGBTQ+ idol, we condemn them: "Those who make [idols] become like them; so do all who trust in them" (Ps. 115:8).

We Confront Lies with the Word of God

When it seems like we are living at ground zero of the Tower of Babel, when the whole world seems to have gone mad, we need to cling to Christ with courage, read and memorize our Bible with fervency, be active members of a faithful Bible-believing church with passion, sing psalms with joy, and pray for our enemies with humility. We need to be humble people, remembering that we were not created to be all-knowing. We don't need to be all-knowing, because God is. Christ alone can solve the problems we face today.

God calls us to live our Christian lives with courage, tell the truth, and fear God and not man. Can we with Jesus sing Psalm 118:6: "The LORD is on my side; I will not fear. What can man do to me?" I know. You can think of a long list of things the world can do to you. Your son, who calls himself Julie, won't talk to you. You will be fired from your job if you don't put a rainbow sticker on your door. Your neighbors will hate you when they learn that you believe in the God of the Bible. All of this may be true, and still this verse calls us to put things in perspective, specifically the Lord's perspective as seen in Hebrews 11, where we see firsthand that God uses our faith whether we live or die.

This is the faith story we like:

And what more shall I say? For time would fail me to tell of Gideon, Barak, Samson, Jephthah, of David and Samuel and the prophets—who through faith conquered kingdoms, enforced justice, obtained promises, stopped the mouths of lions, quenched the power of fire, escaped the edge of the sword, were made strong out of weakness, became mighty in war, put foreign armies to flight. (Heb. 11:32–34)

This is the faith story that terrifies:

Others suffered mocking and flogging, and even chains and imprisonment. They were stoned, they were sawn in two, they were killed with the sword. They went about in skins of sheep and goats, destitute, afflicted, mistreated—of whom the world was not worthy. (Heb. 11:36–38)

God records that both life and death, if done in faith, advance the gospel and give glory to God. Christians ought never despise suffering for Christ. And as we are seeing today and have seen throughout church history, all true Christians will suffer for the truth of Christ.

As we face inevitable suffering, we must pray for increased faith to endure to the end. We who believe the whole gospel must take care of each other, joining together in worship, prayer, and the practice of hospitality.

Let's turn now to the first prominent lie that our anti-Christian age embraces, the idea that homosexuality is normal. The normalization of homosexuality is the central controlling narrative of our anti-Christian age, so we must confront the question head-on.

Is it true? Is homosexuality normal?

LIE #1

———

HOMOSEXUALITY IS NORMAL

1

Once Gay, Always Gay?

If the LORD *of hosts*
had not left us a few survivors,
we should have been like Sodom,
and become like Gomorrah.

ISAIAH 1:9

I WAS NOT RAISED IN A CHRISTIAN HOME, and when I first
started attending church, I found myself bristling under the word
of God. It was patriarchal (and that was bad), and I was a feminist lesbian (and that was good). The Bible was outdated and untrustworthy, and I was progressive and kind. The Bible's narrative
worked from a worldview of totality and total truth, and I was
a postmodernist, a person who believed stories were fragmented
and arbitrary, like shattered glass. I was confident that the Bible
was androcentric (man-centered), heteronormative (promoting
heterosexuality, which I thought was a bad thing), and misogynist
(woman-hating). And I hated everything to do with the Bible, since
I was a women-centered, pacifist, lesbian vegetarian (and this was
all very good and moral, in my opinion). How in the world did

I end up with faith in the Jesus Christ of the Bible? And why did faith in Jesus change my loyalty such that I had to reject feminism and homosexuality—all of it?

The church that I first attended was pastored by Ken Smith, a Reformed Presbyterian pastor who was in his mid-seventies at the time. I was in this church because I trusted him. Our friendship was two years in the making when I stepped foot in church.[1] And in a Reformed Presbyterian Church of North America, there is no way to dodge the word of God. A heathen like me found no reprieve. There was never a Lord's Day when the pastor took some time off to let the interpretive-dance group use their gifts. Nope. Nor would there ever be a transgendered art show in the foyer of the church or a sexual minority bowling league.[2] The word of God was surround-sound, not only in the preached word but also in song, where psalms are sung a cappella and exclusively. I learned later that something called the "regulative principle of worship" (RPW) maintained this steady consistency.[3]

1 I describe this in *The Secret Thoughts of an Unlikely Convert: An English Professor's Journey into Christian Faith* (Pittsburgh, PA: Crown & Covenant, 2012).

2 One cannot say the same thing about a Midwest Presbyterian church that left the PCA in 2022. See Zachary Groff, "Trans Memorial in an Evangelical Chapel?," Reformation21 (website), Alliance of Confessing Evangelicals, March 6, 2020, https://www.reformation21.org/.

3 The regulative principle of worship understands worship of God as regulated by Scripture. The Scripture proof for it is found in Deuteronomy, where we find God's warning against idolatry and innovations from the world to worship God. The full passage reads: "You shall not worship the LORD your God [as other nations worship their pagan gods], for every abominable thing that the LORD hates they have done for their gods, for they even burn their sons and their daughters in the fire to their gods. Everything that I command you, you shall be careful to do. You shall not add to it or take from it" (12:31–32). Embraced by Reformed and Presbyterian churches, the regulative principle of worship declares that whatever is not commanded in Scripture is prohibited in worship, for the purpose of guarding against idolatry. While there are differences in how this principle is practiced among different branches of Reformed and Presbyterian churches, it is generally contrasted with the normative principle of worship, which welcomes anything that is not prohibited in Scripture. The regulative principle of worship not only sets a barrier to unbiblical worship practices, but

The first time I heard Psalm 113 was when I sang it along with others in corporate worship, and this psalm became a turning point for me. It was 1999, and I was sporting a butch haircut and extra piercings in my right ear—because back in the day, left was right (straight), and right was wrong (gay). I stood in a pew in the Syracuse Reformed Presbyterian Church awkwardly seeking a God whom I secretly hoped would accept me as I was. Floy Smith, the pastor's wife, stood at my side. Floy, a woman who could bridge worlds, brushed me with her shoulder before we started to sing. "God is making you his beautiful trophy, my dear," she whispered in my ear, the one with the extra piercings. Pastor Ken Smith told us to open our Psalters to Psalm 113A.

I jumped in with mouth open wide:

Praise Jehovah, praise the Lord!
Ye his servants praise accord;
Blessed be Jehovah's name
Evermore His praise proclaim;

---

it also sets a holy aesthetic in the church. As Pastor Barry York teaches, worship regulated by Scripture in turn regulates God's people. How and what you worship "regulates"—controls—you. While by no means a "magic bullet," the regulative principle of worship provides a much more useful tool to discern the seriousness of a conflict than that offered by the "theological triage" concept (Gavin Ortlund, *Finding the Right Hills to Die On: The Case for Theological Triage* [Wheaton, IL: Crossway, 2020]). The triage method categorizes issues into three tiers. First-tier doctrines are necessary for salvation (Trinity, incarnation, bodily resurrection of Christ). Second-tier doctrines are those theological convictions necessary for the long-term health of the church (administration of the sacraments and ordination vows). Third-tier contains biblical convictions that are matters of personal conscience that do not divide fellowship. Over time, the triage method easily places all second-tier matters into third-tier. And once ordination issues become third-tier, and once women are ordained to preach the word, it becomes the reason to make gay Christianity a third-tier issue. But the regulative principle of worship gives primary attention to anything that is out of God's order. Under the regulative principle of worship, human reason does not dictate priority for confrontation; God's word does.

Evermore His praise proclaim.
From the dawn to setting sun,
Praise the Lord, the Mighty One
O'er all nations he is high,
Yea His glory crowns the sky!
Yea His glory crowns the sky!
Who is like the Lord our God?
High in heav'n is His abode;
Who Himself doth humble low
Things in heav'n and earth to know.
Things in heav'n and earth to know.
He the lowly makes to rise,
From the dust in which he lies.
That exalted he may stand
With the princes of the land
With the princes of the land.
He the childless woman takes
And a joyful mother makes;
Keeping house she finds reward.
Praise Jehovah, praise the Lord,
Praise Jehovah, praise the Lord.

But before I realized what was coming out of my mouth, I was implicating myself into what I believed then was abusive male domination and institutional misogyny. I had a good chuckle over this. I summarily and thoroughly rejected this whole idea.

Like many things that have caught me in mid-leap, this psalm started on what I perceived to be safe ground. A song of praise to a God who must stoop to examine his creation; he lowers himself to examine the stars, the moon, and the sun. He makes no bones about his authority over creation, and then he makes dead bones live. He tells the mountains to stand, and they obey without back talk. He even bends low enough to build up men and women, extending love to the loveless, dignity to the depraved, and family to the refugee. But the crescendo verse brought praise to a halt for me. I choked in mid-verse:

> He the childless woman takes
> And a joyful mother makes;
> Keeping house she finds reward.
> Praise Jehovah, praise the Lord,
> Praise Jehovah, praise the Lord.[4]

That psalm stuck with me like a backache all throughout the service and beyond. Its outdated embrace of patriarchy was unthinkable! I had warred against patriarchy for decades. As the daughter of a feminist, I took up my destiny with pride. Even more than my lesbian identity, my feminist identity grounded me in everything that I valued. I wasn't a man hater. I had women friends who were sexually partnered with men. In college I had boyfriends and even called myself heterosexual. And I celebrated male-female relationships that valued unity, interdependence, and service. I lamented male-female relationships that called for a woman's submission, even if voluntary. My feminist worldview/religion declared any male-female sexual relationship that rejected sameness (the idea that men and women are interchangeable) and called for a wife's submission to her husband foundational to rape culture. What God called good, I called rape.

4 *The Book of Psalms for Singing* (Pittsburgh, PA: Crown & Covenant, 1973), selection 113A.

The whole verse was unthinkable. "Keeping house she finds reward"? Absurd! How could anyone find reward as a homemaker, where no one can regard and celebrate her work? I even struggled to understand what this verse could mean. Would anyone aspire to work at home as a homemaker? Wasn't that the 1950s default employed to keep women enslaved to men? Wasn't homemaking a sign of failure? In my feminist playbook, a homemaker failed to do essential and valuable things in the world. I observed church members I respected singing this line without shame, and I shook my head. When asked, "What do you want to be when you grow up?" what girl answers, "Homemaker"? Apart from the people in this small church, I realized that I didn't know any homemakers on planet earth.

After the service, I was still fuming over the verse. I jumped to the hope that it was just a bad translation or a vivid literary metaphor—one that needed some serious reining in. And so I asked the pastor's wife. And then I asked the elders' wives. And then I asked some other trusted women in the church.

No one in this church apologized for this verse, and no one dismissed it as an overextended metaphor.

Instead, Floy and the other women I asked told me that every word of God is good. This line was both metaphorical *and* material. It spoke of real women reflecting their relationship to Jesus by their resemblance to Jesus. It captures the covenant promise God gave to Abraham and Sarah (Gen. 17:15–21; Isa. 54). My friends told me plainly that a mother finding reward in her home portrays God's compassion on the solitary. These women reminded me that Scripture interprets Scripture. They told me that these verses highlighted the complementarity of husbands and wives in a harmony of obedience that pointed to the second coming of Christ. The sense and purpose and beauty of this verse had to be read in the context of Genesis 1:26 and 3:16, they said. Floy told me that this verse did not prohibit women from having a job outside of the home, but it did mean that any outside job needed to build up and not tear down the family. I pondered this. I had colleagues at the university who lived apart from their husbands and children for six months of the year. I had one colleague whose daughters and husband lived halfway around the globe. My colleagues at the university often chose professoriate over progeny. A lectern at a research university was valued over all else.

Floy suggested that I situate Psalm 113 in the context of the creation ordinance. So with the help of faithful Christian homemakers, I started to study these passages. I read Genesis 1:27: "So God created man in his own image, in the image of God he created him; male and female he created them." I beheld the dignity of this verse, that both men and women derive their image from God. I beheld how far short my feminist worldview stood in relation to God's word. The order of creation made the point: the sexes are equal in essence and different in social roles. Everything in my body and brain screamed, *Wrong!* Even so, a whisper in my heart craved covering by God and the covenant of church and family.

Then my sisters walked me through Genesis 3:16, God's curse on Eve: "To the woman He said: 'I will greatly multiply your sorrow and your conception; in pain you shall bring forth children; your desire shall be for your husband, and he shall rule over you'"(NKJV). This verse was not easy to untangle. It became more manageable when I read it next to the parallel verse: "Sin lies at the door. And its desire is for you," God tells Cain, "but you should rule over it" (Gen. 4:7 NKJV). The literary echoes exposed how sin distorted everything—including relationships between husbands and wives. It started to make sense that sin's entrance into the world produced a collision of wills within marriage. I wondered, Which came first? God's love followed by Adam plunging the world into sin? Or violence and male dominance followed by a Christianity that institutionalized stupidity, myopia, and misogyny? I wondered, Which story is true? The feminist one or the biblical one? Is a wife's submission to her husband part of the blessing of creation or part of the curse? Where (if anywhere, I thought) does my lesbianism fit into a biblical paradigm?

Over time, as the Holy Spirit was working on my heart and mind, I started to see the logic in God's love and God's order. And if God's love came first—because God himself has no beginning and no end—then God's law could not be some 1970s rallying cry or some 1950s cultural trap. Instead, God's law is presented as a logical and obvious interpretation of what total depravity reveals about my heart. The sin that Adam imputed to all would vex our will to do what God wants—both personally and relationally. And what does God want? He wants his firstfruits—men and women—to cherish and triumph under his creation ordinance. Even as I railed against Psalm 113, some deep part of me recognized God's word as good—truly, uniquely, separately good. God's word was real as rain to me, even as I tried to push it away. And God's word started a war in my heart that needed to be fought to completion. His word made clear that a wife's submission in the Lord to her godly husband is part of the creation order, like it or not. (And I didn't.)

What did this mean for me as a lesbian in a committed relationship?

Was I just an outsider looking in?

What does this mean for Christian women who are single?

Psalm 113 raised questions that demanded answers.

Psalm 113 did more than make me reflect on culture. It pressed me to see my lesbianism in the light of both Scripture and feminism. Lesbianism was my sexual identity and my sexual preference. (I never did call lesbianism my sexual *orientation*. I was a nineteenth-century scholar after all, and I knew that sexual orientation was embedded in Freudianism, which was not exactly feminism's friend.) Sexual orientation also seemed to lean on the idea that homosexuality was an illness that needed a cure. I believed it was an informed choice—and part of normal sexual fluidity. The late lesbian poet and essayist Adrienne Rich, in her essay, "Compulsory Heterosexuality and Lesbian Existence," perfectly captured my understanding of why I was a lesbian—and the path that led me there.[5]

But feminism was my worldview *and* religion. I didn't just find women sexually attractive; I found the whole worldview of queer theory and feminism inspiring, meaningful, and life-giving. I believed in a world where distinctions and hierarchies of any kind must be eliminated so that the sacred and divine nature of people could be finally realized. My life as a lesbian seemed to invite me to participate in something deeper and larger than my small world and good for the future of the world. It gave me a team jersey and a position on the field. But Psalm 113 said something else entirely. If Psalm 113 was true, then I was heading in the wrong direction. Like a cancer patient weighing therapies, I feared the cure as much as the disease.

But as I sang Psalm 113, my priorities and values seemed to be wrong, wrong, wrong. Scripture whispered from the inside, and feminism shouted from the bleachers. Lesbianism reflected how I felt. But as a thinking person, I realized that lesbianism was more than a

5   Adrienne Cecile Rich, *Compulsory Heterosexuality and Lesbian Existence* (London: Onlywomen Press, 1981).

set of feelings and desires. Can a person be a lesbian and a Christian, in desire and deed? Psalm 113 said no. Lesbianism in light of Scripture is a rejection of men in general and the creation ordinance in particular. Lesbianism rejects the creation cosmology—the nature of the universe. Calling lesbianism good and holy meant denying that God planted the seeds of the gospel in the garden. That made me think. If lesbianism in light of Scripture is a rejection of the creation ordinance, then I can't have my lesbian identity and Christ.

While meditating on this psalm, I considered how my homosexuality was tightly woven into certain feminist predispositions that, while not sinful in themselves, served me well as a lesbian. I exuded boldness and strength rather than gentleness and kindness. Christians are, of course, called to be bold and strong, but the ease with which I applied these attributes became something of a setup for me, a setup for sin and not submission. My feminist worldview valued boldness and strength and regarded gentleness and kindness as weaker virtues, reserved for only safe spaces, and dangerous in any patriarchal hierarchy. I pondered this. Again, sisters in the Lord were there at my side, reminding me that the fruit of the Spirit calls for "love, joy, peace, patience, kindness, goodness, faithfulness, gentleness, [and] self-control" (Gal. 5:22–23). Christians sure are a mixed bag of unusual virtues, I thought.

I went back and forth like this for months, asking the same questions of both communities, my church community and my lesbian one. I respected women from both places, and I listened intently and weighed their answers.

I straddled two incommensurable worlds. They represented not just different sides of a coin, but different coins. We were not all in the same forest looking at different trees from different angles. We were in different forests altogether.

46

It was utterly and completely shocking to realize that my lesbianism was truly a sin. How in the world does one do battle with something that just feels like normal life? My friends from the church talked about biblical patterns of addition and subtraction, about repentance and grace.

I was starting to see that if I intended to do battle with my flesh—that is, if I intended to do battle with the sin of homosexuality—this required embracing God's intent for me to live out all the attributes of the fruit of the Spirit, not just the ones that came easily to me. Godly womanhood started to appear not as a cookie-cutter recipe but as a particular application of God's grace to me, with the word of truth molding the clay of my heart. I started to pray in earnest, with Bible open and pen and notebook in lap. I started to pray that God would make me a godly woman.

Sometimes this prayer would wrap me in cold fear, and I would get up from the chair and look at myself in the mirror.

My butch haircut and piercings seemed to mock every word.

I told no one about this prayer.

The women in the church continued to encourage me to search the scriptures for answers. They firmly believed that the Bible was a living book and that it knew me better than I knew myself. They reminded me that godly womanhood does not erase a woman's strength or identity; rather, it applies God's grace to me. The women in my church told me that God intended to make me a godly woman and that I indeed would recognize myself as he conformed the clay of my heart and life to his will.

And so it was that Psalm 113 changed my life. I looked into its mirror, and I saw how short I had fallen from God's will. God used the offense of God's word for the good of my soul.

The afternoon that I broke up with my lesbian partner was a dark one. Uttering words of defeat felt like walking underwater. Margaret collapsed in tears and called me every name in the book. I was pushing through a weight that I could not explain. I felt miserable before the breakup, and I felt miserable after. And so did she. After the breakup we started the painful process of dividing up a shared life—dogs, dishes, and a house on the lake. My church friends carried me through this. They didn't meddle, but they also didn't leave me to figure it out all by myself.

And then, a few years later, Psalm 113 changed my life again.

After my conversion, I noticed my affections changing. It wasn't instantaneous—like a combustion—but union with Christ was something that I could perceive growing inside me. I started to embrace my role as a single Christian woman and a member of the Syracuse Reformed Presbyterian Church. I didn't stop cold turkey feeling like a lesbian. Not at all. But I did register lesbian desires as sinful acts in need of repentance, not morally neutral attributes of my identity or person. No one told me to pray the gay away. Because every sermon told me to drive a fresh nail into every sin every day, no one needed to. I started to commit to memory the Westminster Shorter Catechism:

Question 35: What is Sanctification?
Answer: Sanctification is the work of God's free grace, whereby we are renewed in the whole man after the image of God and are enabled more and more to die unto sin and live unto righteousness.

Dying and living, growing in sanctification and looking to Christ, embodied the Christian life.

Instead of lesbianism being who I was, I now understood it as both a lack of righteousness and a willful transgressive action. I was no victim. I was no "sexual minority" needing a voice in the church. I needed to grow in sanctification—just like everyone else in the church. I learned that we repent of sin by hating it, killing it, turning from it. But we also "add" the virtue of God's word. It is light that changes darkness. The Bible calls us to mortify (kill) and vivify (enliven). I realized that Christians are given a new nature, yet we have sin patterns that we need to kill, to be sure. Colossians 3:9–10 puts it like this: "You have put off the old self with its practices and have put on the new self, which is being renewed in knowledge after the image of its creator." This passage told me that I am a Christian and that lesbianism is part of my biography, not my new nature, regardless of how I feel inside. The biography of my life as a lesbian is from the short and early chapters of my life, and there is no reason in heaven and earth for me to keep reliving and rereading those chapters. Progressive sanctification is real.

The Lord had both changed the affections of my heart and beckoned me to embrace my role as a godly woman. One afternoon while having tea and Bible study with Floy, I asked her what I should do with my life. I was thinking about this question in a comprehensive and philosophical way. Floy answered in predictable feet-on-the-floor practicality. Floy suggested that I look around for young mothers in the church who needed help and offer to make some meals, do some dishes, help with toddler story time and folding laundry. I took her advice.

My only experience with babies and small children at that time was what I learned in their homes. I had never held a baby in my arms until this time in my life. Nevertheless, I discovered that I loved helping new mothers. Mothering was a fascinating job, not terribly unlike being a research professor: you must do one thing at a time well, and you must have flexibility and good humor as you carry on. Soon, I found myself at home in the world of holding babies and entertaining toddlers and cooking meals for families. I learned so much during that time. I learned that I loved to watch children grow—in physical and spiritual ways. It amazed me that I could perceive the Holy Spirit working in the lives of some very small children. I understood why Jesus wanted to have children around him. A child who loves God and knows that Jesus has forgiven his sins was a marvel to me. Nothing is more precious to behold. It seemed strange to me that young mothers welcomed my company. It seemed even stranger when they asked me for advice! These women in the church wanted me—*me*—to pray for them and sing psalms to their children. I had no idea until this experience that I was a nurturing person and a gentle woman. I took up my role as an older friend with a glee that surprised me. I was fascinated by how their households worked, by how much skill went into keeping a home and homeschooling children.

After I had poured out my heart to God, begging him to make me a godly woman, he gave me another desire: to be a godly wife to a godly husband and to submit to him, help him in his work, and, if God willed, to be a mother of children. A season fraught with strife and turmoil—including a failed engagement—followed,[6] and then I met Kent Butterfield. The Lord knit our hearts together, and Kent proposed marriage.[7] I have been married to Kent for over

---

6   I discuss this in *Secret Thoughts*.

7   I share this personal history with you not because I am trying to win an argument using my personal feelings and experiences. It is the word of God alone that witnesses to the truth. I dated men in college and assumed that I would one day marry a man and have a family. In graduate school, when I met my first lesbian lover, I felt like I had come home to myself. Lesbianism felt normal and natural for me. And then I met the Lord and started

two decades now, and the Lord has used Kent more than any other person on earth to show me God's love and purpose. Kent is my husband, but he is also my pastor. The Lord knows that I am a weak woman, and in his perfect plan, I have been married to my good and godly pastor for almost as long as I have been a Christian. My own life story of conversion and sanctification, of healing and transformation, merged with biblical marriage. No one had ever wanted to protect me before the Lord brought Kent into my life.

Our engagement forced many decisions. One was what to do with my professional life. I wanted to be Kent's helper, but was that what God wanted for me? Was it right or wrong to leave my profession as a tenured professor at a prestigious research institution? Would it not be a greater win for the kingdom of God to have a tenured professor in the world than to have another homemaker in church?

I stood at the mouth of three divergent paths, three opposing life directions, three mutually exclusive options. The one that I walked in would unmistakably shape me. I could return to Syracuse University as a tenured professor of English. I could stay at Geneva College and apply for a position in administrative leadership. Or

---

to do battle with the sin of lesbianism. I realize that some people reading my story may be quick to dismiss it, since I "only" lived as a lesbian for a decade. I'm grateful that the Lord gave me a way of escape and that I was not trapped in that sin for any longer than I was. I narrowly escaped and have the Lord and my church to thank for that. I am daily grateful that the Lord brought me to repentance. I realize that for some faithful Christians, the battle against homosexual lust is harder and longer than mine. The Lord knows how hard desires of the flesh are, and how it feels like you have a civil war going on inside of you. The apostle Paul gives us these words of comfort: "The desires of the flesh are against the Spirit, and the desires of the Spirit are against the flesh, for these are opposed to each other, to keep you from doing the things you want to do" (Gal. 5:17). In other words, the battle is part of the victory. My generation of lesbian came out of the paradigm reflected by the late poet Adrienne Rich—that heterosexuality was compulsory and therefore many women's lesbian lives were erased. She made a full case for this in *Compulsory Heterosexuality and Lesbian Existence*.

I could marry Kent Butterfield and become a homemaker and a church planter's wife.

The first path was familiar.

The second path was recognizable.

The third path was unimaginable.

Immediately, well-intended people—Christian brothers and sisters—started to weigh in.

How could a smart cookie like me turn away from the university work the Lord had already prepared me to do? God called me to work, not sit at home and bake cookies, for goodness' sake! Isn't it sinful *not* to use my gifts? What about the books I would never (presumably) write? One brother asked, "Why can't you be a professor, dean, or university president, and Kent be the stay-at-home dad?" As one sister put it, "Do you really need a PhD in hermeneutics to change diapers?"

On May 19, 2001, Kent and I were married. Kent's work moved from a church plant in Virginia to secular work to a small Reformed Presbyterian church in North Carolina. Unable to bear children of our own, the Lord allowed us to adopt four, including two out of foster care at the age of seventeen that we adopted five years apart.

Yes, it was very hard to give up my professional life. Yes, I needed to unlearn habits and learn new skills to be a church planter's wife. During the early days of the church plant, my first job Lord's Day morning was to clean the restrooms at the Purcellville Community Center, where we met for worship. Saturday night at the community center was open men's basketball. This may explain something about the state of the restrooms on Lord's Day morning. I took up my lot Psalm 84:10–style: "I would rather be a doorkeeper in the house of my God than dwell in the tents of wickedness."

At the time of the writing of these words, the ages of my children span sixteen to thirty-four. The older children (thirty-four and twenty-nine at the writing of this book) broke the cycle that had held them in dangerous crisis, and the younger children (nineteen and sixteen at the writing of this book) are thriving as strong Christians, covenant members of our church, hard workers in school and in their jobs. I spend my days homeschooling my children and teaching other students in my Christian homeschool co-op. I have spent joyful years with my grandson, even homeschooling him during the Covid shutdown. One afternoon at the park, pushing grandson Ben on a swing in the garden as we counted cardinals, I realized something simple: I had many things to do (like write this book), but nothing more important than taking care of my children and grandson. God has made the path straight for me. And God has also allowed me to write books and speak to a hostile culture about our powerful and gracious God. My hands and heart are full and overflowing.

Taking care of my children provides a weight, a way to balance and measure the other good things to which God calls me. My husband provides a covering and a boundary. God has blessed and imbued both my roles in caring for my husband and children such that my life has balance and momentum, borders and a shield. Far from holding me back, my role as a submitted wife to a godly husband has given me liberty and purpose.

Psalm 113 has carried me full circle. Decades ago I railed against patriarchy and the Bible, seeing submission of any kind as a recipe for abuse and belief in the integrity of this ancient book as something for dupes and idiots. Today I believe with all my heart and mind that the only safe place in the world for a woman is as a member of a Bible-believing church, protected and covered by

God through the means of faithful elders and pastors and, if God wills, under the protective care of a godly husband.

My life is open to scrutiny. One of the fair criticisms of my choosing the role of a submitted wife over and against a tenured professor is that my life commitments fortify biblical patriarchy.

Guilty as charged.

But let's be clear. I don't embrace biblical patriarchy because I think men are good. On the contrary, the sinful nature that we all inherit through Adam is lethal in the bodies and minds of all men. I embrace biblical patriarchy because men are *not* good (Jer. 17:9). Because men are not good, I am grateful to have godly men around who can defend and protect me against the roaming ravages of evil men who truly are wolves.

I learned that being owned by Christ does not mean that once you declare yourself a Christian, everything you think, feel, say, and do is magically baptized with God's approval. Our works (including our intentions, desires, and thoughts, as well as our deeds) do not merit God's justification. Second Corinthians 5:21 declares, "For our sake he made him to be sin who knew no sin, so that in him we might become the righteousness of God." For Christians, Jesus Christ became sin (took on the stain and the punishment of what we deserved) so that we could become righteous by his grace (our righteous standing before God is all because of what Christ did). I learned that justification by grace alone comes down to this: How do I know that I am a true Christian, especially in a world of faith deconstructions and deconversions (formerly known as "apostates")? How do I make my calling and election sure (2 Pet. 1:10)? The doctrine of sanctification does not mean that I am a passive recipient of grace. No true believer is. Sanctification is a gift of God's grace, but only when we participate in our own sanctification are we renewed in the image of God. Our obedience, then, reflects the integrity and authenticity of our faith. Our obedience is a duty and a joy. If this is not the case, we have reason to worry about the state of our soul.

I share with you my story because I come to Christ through the lived experience of having been radically changed by his atoning blood. I have been redeemed, which means that I do not have to pay my debt of sexual sin, because Christ paid it for me. Christ became my propitiation—a sin offering that deals not only with my guilt but also with the wrath of God directed against me. I now have peace with God. As Paul says, "Since we have been justified by faith, we have peace with God through our Lord Jesus Christ" (Rom. 5:1). Peace with God is not a fleeting, subjective feeling but an objective reality.

If the Bible is true, how did contemporary Christianity get all turned around? I believe that the church started to import unbiblical ideas about who people are and what the world is like, and those unbiblical ideas distorted the gospel message itself.

In the 1990s, when I worked as one of the newly minted tenured radicals, the concept of intersectionality was introduced. Intersectionality moved from the ivory towers to the evangelical church, and it is playing a significant role in reshaping contemporary thinking—both in society and in the church. We are living in the tragic era when the world is leading the evangelical church—a sign of judgment and curse, and not of God's approval and blessing.

2

What Is Intersectionality?

Then Pilate said to him, "So you are a king?" Jesus
answered, "You say that I am a king. For this purpose I was
born and for this purpose I have come into the world—to
bear witness to the truth. Everyone who is of the truth
listens to my voice." Pilate said to him, "What is truth?"

JOHN 18:37–38

A FEW YEARS AGO, during an open question-and-answer session
on a college campus, a student accused me of hate speech.[1] She
referred to something I described in my lecture, the time when,
in 1998, I was in my kitchen confessing to my transgender friend
Jill that I was starting to believe that the gospel is true, that Jesus
is alive, and that we are all in trouble.

The student approached the microphone and blurted, "That's
hate speech! When you described your transgender friend putting
her hand over yours as you shared your new faith, you mocked her!"

"How?" I asked.

---

1   To protect privacy, names and distinguishing features of the people and situations in my
    illustrations have been changed.

57

"You said, 'Jill's large hands covered mine.' *You actually said that she had large hands!*" The student felt she had made her point as firmly as possible and that I was guilty as charged.

I paused, perplexed, and asked, "So, it is hate speech to say that Jill's hands are large?"

The student jumped at the microphone and shouted, "Of course it is!"

"Jill stands six foot two without heels," I explained. "I'm five two. My hands barely cover an octave on the piano. Compared to mine, Jill's hands are large. Large is a descriptive adjective."

The student, nonplussed by a brief grammar lesson, tossed her own hands in the air in exasperation with me and declared, "Transgender women are hurt by such insensitive comparisons to bio women. It's hateful."

Me: "Why is it hateful to say Jill's hands are large?"

Her: "This is what leads LGBTQ+ people to suicide!"

Me: "But the size of Jill's hands is measurable, objective truth."

Her: "Who cares about your truth? Your truth isn't my truth! Your truth hates my reality!"

———

How did we get to a place where it makes sense for a person to reject truth not because it's false but because it hurts? How did we get to a place where we label people as knowable primarily by their political and social group, as if that is their truest and most indelible virtue? Under what worldview could my words be responsible for someone's suicide, but the genital mutilation that allows a biological man to masquerade as a woman can cause celebration and affirmation?

The answer is *intersectionality*, an analytical tool introduced in humanities and social science departments in US universities in the 1990s. Intersectionality creates a grand story, a metanarrative, out of oppression. It maintains that the world is made up of power struggles, and that white, male, heterosexual patriarchy must be destroyed to liberate those who are oppressed by it. It understands the biblical complementarity of husbands and wives as perverted and "weaponized." It believes that if we can expose the myriad ways in which people suffer down to the smallest detail and then rearrange the power oppressions, we can change the storyline of a person's history (of oppression) and destiny (of liberation). Suffering in the world of intersectionality has been reframed by the "dignitary harm" clause of the *Obergefell v. Hodges* decision, the 2015 Supreme Court decision that legalized same-sex marriage in all fifty states.

Today, failing to affirm LGBTQ+ rights is considered an act of harm. The Revoice movement, a gay Christian movement that falsely claims biblical orthodoxy, maintains that failing to honor a person's homosexual orientation and identity is spiritual abuse. Today, even in the church, it seems, accepting someone without approving her is to reject her. The LGBTQ+-rights movement declares no such thing as acceptance without approval. They tell us silence is violence. They tell us tolerance is the emotion of the oppressor because to tolerate people means you also have the power to reject them. Intersectionality has redefined what it means to harm someone, moving the concept of harm from material to psychological, from real to imagined.

Under intersectionality, liberation depends on the power of voice. It works like this: when we allow those with a hefty load of intersections (perhaps a transgender person of color who is deaf, poor, incarcerated, and overweight) to have a larger voice in culture and simultaneously require those with white, male, heterosexual privilege to remain silent, we supposedly tear down the walls of violence. How exactly such walls collapse, no one can tell me. Intersectionality maintains that who you truly are is measured by how many victim statuses you can claim—with your human dignity accruing through intolerance of all forms of disagreement with your perceptions of self and world.

Let's be clear: God condemns real injustice. God knows that certain groups—widows, orphans, the poor—require special care, and he commands us to care for them (Heb. 13:1–3). God condemns the sin of partiality (James 2:6). Certainly the most horrific forms of betrayal and sin against the vulnerable are those committed within families and churches, when the very people called by God to protect the small and weak become their captors and predators. And the Bible already teaches us how to advocate for justice. But we need to apply what God has revealed in his word.

The question must be asked: Can intersectionality serve the gospel? Should we add intersectionality to the gospel to arrive at a better way of loving our neighbor? Several churches and parachurches say yes and offer sensitivity training to help make the church a supposedly friendlier place, especially for "sexual minorities." The idea that comes on the back of intersectionality is that homosexuality is not a sin but rather an orientation. So we must ask the question, Is this true?

Pastor and professor Denny Burk has helpfully identified the two most prominent ways that intersectionality works at cross-purposes with the Bible. First, it offers an unbiblical view of human identity (such as homosexual orientation), and, second, it produces social fragmentation.[2]

---

2 Denny Burk, "Two Ways in Which Intersectionality Is at Odds with the Gospel," Denny Burk (website), July 19, 2017, https://www.dennyburk.com/.

Intersectionality fails to distinguish between morally neutral categories of lived experience (race and ethnicity) with morally charged ones (homosexuality and transgenderism). Because intersectionality lacks a biblical category of sin, it instead multiplies sins of its own making. Because it lacks a biblical category of repentance, redemption, or grace, its good intentions cannot stop it from punishing the good and celebrating the evil. Because it rejects the creation ordinance and a biblical definition of human identity, it has no concept of what it means to grow in knowledge, righteousness, and the holiness of Christ.

Intersectionality increases human fragmentation and division. This is ironic, because when it first appeared in US universities in the 1990s, the hope was that it would challenge the idea that dominant and oppressive social groups are easily identifiable. Instead, it multiplied social groups and attributed to them an invented reality, leaving us with a culture of identity politics on steroids.

Contradictions to the creation ordinance violate both love of neighbor and common sense. Intersectionality claims to create community, but the community it creates is fractured, victim-minded, angry, and inconsolable. This is the exact opposite of the community created by the fruit of the Spirit (Gal. 5:22–23). When intersectionality joins forces with the gospel, it leaves us with an immature faith, a false hope, and a deceptive vocabulary.

Intersectionality confuses a biblical understanding of mercy and justice with an unbiblical one.[3] Biblically speaking, sin causes

---

3 Upholding justice is included in what John Calvin (1509–1564) saw as the "third use" of God's law. The first use of the law is as a mirror: it mirrors God's righteousness and reflects our sinfulness. The second use of the law is to restrain evil by punishing evil and rewarding good. The third use of the law is doing what is pleasing to God, and this includes hospitality

suffering. We sin because we are sinners, not because we are victims. Widows, orphans, and the poor need soul care too. And people who are sinned against need a savior to save them from their sins as well. The order of sin and suffering matters. Miss the point or change the order and you have bypassed the entire gospel.

As Elizabeth C. Corey has pointed out, the departure point for intersectionality is a debatable but never debated set of ever-expanding personal qualities that constitute identity and personhood: age, race, class, sex, sexuality, gender identity, weight, attractiveness, feelings, phobias—the list goes on and on.[4]

Intersectionality sets us out in the wrong direction, and heading the wrong way is a great way to end up in the wrong place. This is the path of gay identity in the church. This is the unintended fruit of intersectionality in the church. The church's embrace of intersectionality as an analytical tool was intended to give voice to the voiceless. But the victimized identities that emerge from intersectionality are perpetually immature and in constant need of therapy and affirmation. Because of the nature of the beast, several false positives are breaking out. Breakouts of "rapid-onset gender dysphoria" among young women prove this point.[5] Gone are the days when feminists valued empowerment and strength; intersectionality requires life support.

Two cultural movements have combined to create a world that believes that lesbianism is normal: the uncritical use of intersec-

and mercy ministry. See *Reformation Study Bible*, ed. R. C. Sproul (Orlando, FL: Reformation Trust, 2015), 273.

4   Elizabeth C. Corey, "First Church of Intersectionality," *First Things*, August 2017, https://www.firstthings.com/.

5   Lisa L. Littman, "Rapid Onset of Gender Dysphoria in Adolescents and Young Adults," *Journal of Adolescent Health* (February 1, 2017), https://doi.org/10.1016/j.jadohealth.2016.10.369.

tionality as a tool to empower people who perceive themselves to be victims, and the uncritical use of homosexual orientation as a category of personhood. Let's turn now to chapter 3 and ask, What exactly is homosexual orientation? And how does it fashion gay Christianity?

What Are Homosexual Orientation and Gay Christianity?

Woe to those who call evil good
and good evil,
who put darkness for light
and light for darkness,
who put bitter for sweet
and sweet for bitter!

ISAIAH 5:20

Those whom I love, I reprove and
discipline, so be zealous and repent.

REVELATION 3:19

HOMOSEXUAL ORIENTATION IS a man-made theory about anthropology, or what it means to be human. It comes from atheistic worldviews that coalesced in the nineteenth century in Europe. Homosexual orientation is not a biblical concept, nor can it be manipulated in the service of Christian living. Sigmund Freud and Charles Darwin (1809–1882) both contributed to the general idea of sexual orientation, the idea that human beings are oriented—aimed, directed, pitched—by sexual desires, understood as an internal, organic drive over which we have no control. Freud understood sexuality as a reflection of who a person is, and Darwin situated it in the survival of the species. Neither Freud nor Darwin accepted the Bible's mandate that sexuality is under God's divine order for his created purposes. The actual phrase "sexual orientation" became the twentieth-century articulation that who you are is determined by the objects of your sexual desire. Under the worldview of homosexual orientation, homosexuality is a morally neutral and separate category of personhood, rendering the homosexual a victim of a world that just doesn't understand sexual variance.

The Bible defines personhood in the creation ordinance, as we have discussed, and situates sexual desire and practice in the context of the sexual pattern of male and female. We understand that the sin that entered the world with Adam malformed the human heart and corrupted human desires, and this of course includes sexual desires. After the fall of Adam, all manner of perversion and depravity entered the human bloodstream, including homosexuality. And after Adam, the natural pattern of man and woman in the covenant of biblical marriage has been under direct assault by the unholy practice of sinful desires (including adultery and pornography). But under the creation ordinance, heterosexuality is the only natural pattern.

A movement began in 2002 that helped support the lie that homosexual orientation is a God-blessed category of humanity. That movement gave moral credence to homosexuality by making the claim that the Bible condones—indeed, even blesses—homosexual sin, either at the level of practice (dubbed "Side A" gay

Christianity), or at the level of identity ("Side B" gay Christianity). The gay Christian movement—Side A or B—presents a false religion, a different religion from biblical Christianity. Side A rejects the Bible as inerrant, infallible, sufficient, and authoritative, while Side B rejects the biblical doctrines of sin, repentance, and sanctification.

Sadly, the broad evangelical church fell for Satan's bait and endorsed gay Christianity, whether on Side A or B. I will explain the origin of these terms later in this chapter, but suffice it to say for now that without the evangelical church's endorsement of gay Christianity, we would not be in the confusing mess we are in today. The witness of the evangelical church on the subject of homosexuality expresses more corporate sin than saving grace.

As I noted earlier, sexual orientation, a secular concept, began in the nineteenth century. You will not find the concept of sexual orientation in the Bible. Instead, the Bible locates sexuality in the creation ordinance as a covenant between one man and one woman. "One man and one woman" can be captured by the word *heterosexuality* and reflects the goodness of God's creation. Biblical sexuality is natural, God-blessed, and procreative. The goodness of heterosexuality is found in our unique and distinct biology as men and women and the procreative power God gives, while its holiness is found in the covenant of marriage. In contrast, homosexuality is unnatural, sinful, and barren. But what about when heterosexuality is practiced sinfully, as in pornography or adultery? Even when heterosexuality is used in the service of sin, the sin is in the practice, not the pattern.

The Bible addresses clearly and unequivocally the sexual sin of homosexuality in a variety of places:

You shall not lie with a male as with a woman; it is an abomination. (Lev. 18:22)

If a man lies with a male as with a woman, both of them have committed an abomination; they shall surely be put to death. (Lev. 20:13)

For this reason God gave them up to dishonorable passions. For their women exchanged natural relations for those that are contrary to nature; and the men likewise gave up natural relations with women and were consumed with passion for one another, men committing shameless acts with men and receiving in themselves the due penalty for their error. (Rom. 1:26–27)

Do you not know that the unrighteous will not inherit the kingdom of God? Do not be deceived. Neither fornicators, nor idolaters, nor adulterers, nor homosexuals, nor sodomites, nor thieves, nor covetous, nor drunkards, nor revilers, nor extortioners will inherit the kingdom of God. And such were some of you. But you were washed, but you were sanctified, but you were justified in the name of the Lord Jesus and by the Spirit of our God. (1 Cor. 6:9–11 NJKV)

The law is not made for a righteous person, but for the lawless and insubordinate, for the ungodly and for sinners, for the unholy and profane, for murderers of fathers and murderers of mothers, for manslayers, for fornicators, for sodomites, for kidnappers, for liars, for perjurers, and if there is any other thing that is contrary to sound doctrine. (1 Tim. 1:9–10 NKJV)

Biblically speaking, the sin of homosexuality is a verb, not a noun: it manifests itself in action either at the level of desire or practice or both.

According to the American Psychological Association, sexual orientation is "an enduring pattern of emotional, romantic, and/or sexual attractions to men, women, or both sexes."[1] *Sexuality* has become a term that encompasses sex acts and romantic feelings and everything in between. How did we get here? How did sexuality become intertwined with personhood? Does sexuality explain how I feel or who I am? These are the questions that the modern concept of sexual orientation answers.

Sexual orientation was one of Germany's cutting-edge "scientific" ideas, and it has quickly made its way into the modern world. Its effect was to radically resituate sexuality from its biblical/creational context to something entirely new: personal identity. Suddenly, your sexual feelings define who you are rather than your last name, status, class, and profession. Freud was—intentionally or not—suppressing the biblical category of being made in God's image, male and female, and replacing it with the psychoanalytic elevation of feelings and emotions. In both intent and word choice, Freud took aim at the Bible's authority to call out sin and prescribe gospel grace. This was no innocent move. Throughout his career, Freud maintained that belief in the God of the Bible was a "universal obsessional neurosis."[2]

This new Freudian concept of sexual orientation was a predictable extension of the German Romantic movement that shaped the worldview of the nineteenth century. The Romantic period is

---

typified by an uncontested embrace of personal experience, not merely as self-expression or self-representation, but also as the way in which we know truth (epistemology). For the first time in the history of the world, personal feelings were now believed to be the fount of truth. Romanticism introduced the idea of "my personal truth"—and with this concept, we lost all standards by which to measure objective truth. Anyone who disagrees with "my truth" is now a bad actor or an oppressor, not merely someone with whom I disagree.

In 1774 Johann Wolfgang von Goethe wrote a suicide narrative entitled *The Sorrows of Young Werther.* For the first time in the history of Western culture, a novel put forward the idea that suicide was an expression of self-empowerment. The novel spawned a rash of suicides, not unlike the way anorexia in the 1980s and transgenderism in the 2020s captured the cultural imagination through art and culture.

When we have a revolution in thinking about what it means to be human and a new worldview that rejects the category of sin, it often results in isolation and self-murder.

The nineteenth-century category of sexual orientation reflects Romanticism's claims on truth, redefining men and women from people who are made in God's image with souls that will last forever to people whose sexual perversion and gender confusion define, liberate, and dignify them. Nothing is further from the actual truth. Indeed, while the Christian maintains that image-bearing is what sets apart humans from animals, the nineteenth century ushered in a new measure of man—one in which sexual desires, self-conceptions, and practices are defining of person-hood. In this climate, the idea of a homosexual orientation was born, and it served to create a fictional identity that robbed people of their true one: being made in the image of God with creational purposes.[3]

The history of sexual orientation raises the question, Is heterosexuality as "fallen" as homosexuality? The biblical answer is no. But author Greg Johnson, in his book *Still Time to Care*, advocates an unbiblical response. He believes that heterosexuality is as fallen in its very nature as homosexuality. Johnson writes:

Heterosexuality is being drawn to people of the opposite sex. People—as in plural, more than one. And that's the problem. It seems to me that the polygamy of heterosexual sexual desire—or more technically, a polyamory of polyeroticism—is also disordered. Heterosexuality as experienced this side of the fall is drenched in sin.[4]

Johnson confuses here pattern with practice. When the Bible regards heterosexuality as natural and homosexuality as unnatural, it refers to its pattern. When the Bible regards heterosexuality as procreative and homosexuality as barren, that refers to its practice's logical consequences. Thus, heterosexuality is natural in pattern and practice, and homosexuality is unnatural and perverse in both. Can one use the gift of heterosexuality in a sinful way? Of course. That a practice may be stewarded sinfully does not change the reality that the pattern is natural and good.

Because Johnson rejects the natural and good pattern of heterosexuality, he believes that there is no point or hope in striving for

3 A portion of this was taken from Rosaria Butterfield, *Openness Unhindered: Further Thoughts of an Unlikely Convert on Sexual Identity and Union with Christ* (Pittsburgh, PA: Crown & Covenant, 2015), 94–96. Used by permission of Crown & Covenant.
4 Greg Johnson, *Still Time to Care: What We Can Learn from the Church's Failed Attempt to Cure Homosexuality* (New York: Zondervan, 2021), Kindle, loc. 139.

it. Johnson writes, "There is no reason to believe that the ordinary progress of spiritual growth would involve the replacement of sinful homosexual temptation with sinful heterosexual temptation."[5]

Since to Johnson homosexuality and heterosexuality are equally fallen and sinful, he goes on to explain, tongue-in-cheek:

> Our pastoral response to believers with fallen heterosexual orientations should be grounded in grace. We don't need to set up a bunch of ex-straight ministries to help you sisters and brothers be cured of your unwanted attractions to other people's spouses. . . . I don't tell straight men they're not real Christians for identifying as straight, even though that typically means attractional polygamy. So long as they recognize that it's disordered, I don't get too worried. If my (gay) internal pull is disordered 100 percent of the time, perhaps theirs might be disordered 90 percent of the time?[6]

The problem with this analysis is that it is disingenuous. Heterosexuality is, as M. D. Perkins writes, "a necessary description of the relationship in which sexual expression can rightly occur—according to nature and God's law."[7] To reject God's law is to reject God's love.

Decades ago, when I first met Ken and Floy Smith, started reading the Bible for my own understanding, and tried to come to terms with my homosexuality, I was grateful that Ken made knowing Jesus my primary task. Even when I wanted to derail him about

5 Johnson, *Still Time to Care*, loc. 140.
6 Johnson, *Still Time to Care*, loc. 140.
7 M. D. Perkins, *A Little Leaven: Confronting the Ideology of the Revoice Movement* (Tupelo, MS: American Family Association, 2021), 20.

gay rights and feminism and everything under the sun, he kept me focused on my need for salvation. His point was this: one step at a time. My sin of unbelief was my most foundational sin. I needed to repent and turn. After I came to Christ, I started meeting with Floy weekly so that Floy could disciple me on what it meant to be a woman of God. In theological terms, Ken and Floy were following the pattern of Scripture: justification (God's free grace that imputes the righteousness of Christ) must come before sanctification (growing to be more like Jesus as the Holy Spirit indwells, rebukes, and calls to repentance and new life).

Gay Christianity

Like the secular LGBTQ+ movement, the gay Christian one operates under the notion that homosexuality is "normal" and that calling it a normal variance is kindness. Gay Christianity believes that sexual orientation accurately organizes humanity into fixed, morally neutral expressions of sexual desire. Side A is "gay-affirming," meaning that it invents biblical support for gay marriage and full inclusion of people who identify as LGBTQ+ in the leadership and membership of the church.[8] Side B is "nonaffirming" of gay sex. Additionally, it elevates celibacy and singleness as God's highest calling while heartily embracing homosexual orientation. This embrace of homosexual orientation places some cognitive dissonance within the unstable category of Side B theology. On the one hand, it wants to be seen as biblically traditional, but on the other, it wants to participate in gay culture (including gay Pride parades) and bring gay culture to the church. Side A errs on its handling of Scripture, rejecting inerrancy, sufficiency, and inspiration. Side

---

8 Christopher Yuan, *Holy Sexuality and the Gospel: Sex, Desire, and Relationships Shaped by God's Grand Story* (New York: Multnomah, 2018).

B errs on its handling of matters of salvation and sin, forgetting that the first word of salvation is *repent*—"Repent," declares Jesus, echoing John the Baptist, "for the kingdom of heaven is at hand" (Matt. 4:17). Side B redefines gay sin merely as sexual action and denies that sin acts with affections, feelings, attractions, and desire. Both Sides A and B believe that homosexuality is fixed and that the gospel might change people in smaller ways but never in the deep matters of sexual desire.

Side A and Side B

Pre-*Obergefell* leaders of the Side A gay Christian position included Justin Lee, *Torn: Rescuing the Gospel from the Gays-vs.-Christians Debate*;[9] Matthew Vines, *God and the Gay Christian: The Biblical Case in Support of Same-Sex Relationships*;[10] and James V. Brownson in *Bible, Gender, Sexuality: Reframing the Church's Debate on Same-Sex Relationships*.[11] Brownson offers the most scholarly defense of gay-affirming Christianity.

In 2001 Lee created the Gay Christian Network (rebranded in 2018 as Q Christian Fellowship) as a support group for gay Christians. Vines created the Reformation Project, the purpose of which is to "advance LGBTQ inclusion in the church."[12] Brownson

9   Justin Lee, *Torn: Rescuing the Gospel from the Gays-vs.-Christians Debate* (Nashville, TN: Jericho), 2012. Christopher Yuan's review of this book is a must-read for faithful Christians: "Rescuing the Gospel from the Gays-vs.-Christians Debate," The Gospel Coalition, January 7, 2013, https://www.thegospelcoalition.org/.

10 Matthew Vines, *God and the Gay Christian: The Biblical Case in Support of Same-Sex Relationships* (New York: Random House, 2014). R. Albert Mohler Jr. edited a useful booklet entitled *God and the Gay Christian? A Response to Matthew Vines* (Louisville, KY: SBTS Press), 2014.

11 James V. Brownson, *Bible, Gender, Sexuality: Reframing the Church's Debate on Same-Sex Relationships* (Grand Rapids, MI: Eerdmans), 2013.

12 The Reformation Project, https://www.reformationproject.org/.

invented the biblical interpretation that would support all this political activism. The gospel, according to gay Christianity, features a Jesus who loves you just as you are. He asks you to repent of sins of injustice, materialism, and lack of love, but he has nothing to say about your homosexuality. Side B Christians don't believe that homosexual sexual practice is "God's best" for you, but that won't stop them from going to your gay wedding or celebrating milestones like gay Pride marches with their gay "brothers and sisters." The most intimate connection for the gay Christian is born through shared same-sex attraction.

Both Lee and Vines use an egalitarian framework for interpretation, one that fully embraces women as pastors and elders in the church and makes the case that what is hermeneutically true for women in the pulpit is also hermeneutically true for people who identify as LGBTQ+ in the church. Egalitarianism is the highway to LGBTQ+ church leadership, as a faulty interpretation that endorses sin in one context is imported wholesale to another. Where Vines is an exclusive advocate of gay affirmation (believing that God blesses your homosexual identity, culture, sexual activity, and relationships), Lee tried to include Side B gay Christianity in a Side A conference. Such inclusivity no doubt cost him something—after all, Lee did this even as he advocated strongly for Side A as biblical.[13]

In contrast, Vines sees no room for such inclusion and throws down the gauntlet in his book's conclusion: "As more believers are coming to realize, [affirming same-sex sexual relations as moral] is, in fact, a requirement of Christian faithfulness.[14] Did you catch that? Vines believes that supporting gay sexuality is a "requirement

---

13 Lee, *Torn*, 221–54.
14 Vines, *God and the Gay Christian*, 178.

of Christian faithfulness." According to Vines, gay sex (and all the sinful sensibilities that surround gay sexuality) is normal and blessed by God. To Vines, to reject gay Christianity and gay sex is simply anti-Christian.

Vines's hell-bound presumption lurches the church from (1) believing the clear word of God, which calls sinners to repentance and faith in Christ, to (2) tolerance for those who don't, where different sides of a position agree to disagree and come together on shared goals, reducing the gospel to a self-care movement, to (3) rejection of the clear word of God, where nothing except exclusive and wholesale support of all things LGBTQ+ will be accepted.

Brownson lends credence to Vines's boldness. Brownson advocates for a progressive reading of Scripture, one where our biblical interpretations match social moral standards. Brownson's denomination, the Reformed Church in America, has affirmed sexual orientation as a category of personhood and encouraged "coming out." As of this writing, the RCA's booklet *Christian Pastoral Care for the Homosexual* says this: "The homosexual must be accepted in his homosexuality. If this is not the case, he is left with the choice of leaving the fellowship, wearing the mask of heterosexuality, or being contemptuously condemned."[15] Brownson employs a method of Scripture reading that highlights the moral "vision" or "trajectory" rather than what the text says.

Brownson explains that he came to his gay-affirming stance in no small part because his son came out as gay. Brownson writes, "The church is faced with gay and lesbian Christians

---

15 Reformed Church in America, *The Church Speaks: Papers of the Commission on Theology, Reformed Church in America, 1959–1984*, Historical Series of the Reformed Church in America 15 (Grand Rapids, MI: Eerdmans, 1985), 262. Reprinted in Brownson, *Bible, Gender, Sexuality*, 12.

who exhibit many gifts and fruits of the Spirit and who seek to live in deep obedience to Christ. Many of these gay and lesbian Christians seek not to suppress their sexual orientation but rather to sanctify it."[16] We see here that in Brownson's theology, sanctification doesn't mean "the work of God's free grace, whereby we are renewed in the whole man after the image of God and are enabled more and more to die unto sin and live unto righteousness."[17]

In Brownson's invention of Scripture, there is no dying to sin and being renewed by the Holy Spirit to live unto righteousness. Instead, *sanctify*, in Brownson's paradigm, means "domesticate." Brownson believes that if you support gay marriage, then homosexuals will not be in sin. The fault is Scripture and society, and the responsibility is for the church to change the meaning of Scripture to be more inclusive. What Brownson means when he writes about living in "deep obedience to Christ" is baffling, since Brownson has dispensed with the law of God, which is the only objective standard by which we measure obedience to Christ.

To repeat, if Side A gay Christianity errs in its misreading of Scripture, Side B gay Christianity errs in its mishandling of matters pertaining to sin and salvation. Both Side A and Side B are false teaching that mishandles the gospel's message. If we cannot repent of sin at the root of desire, we aren't repenting according to the Bible's clear guidance. Jesus's words are instructive, that anger in your heart is murder (Matt. 5:21) and that lust is adultery (Matt. 5:27–28). And if we believe that the Bible is corrupt but Jesus is true, we are disobeying the clear teaching of Jesus. John records this word-picture of the glorified Christ in the book of Revelation:

16 Brownson, *Bible, Gender, Sexuality*, 11.
17 See the Westminster Shorter Catechism, Question 35.

"He is clothed in a robe dipped in blood, and the name by which he is called is The Word of God" (Rev. 19:13).

The sticking point for the gay Christian is the authority and trustworthiness of Scripture and the necessity of repentance. Repentance requires the six ingredients that I outlined in the introduction. If you recall, I said that those steps distinguish true repentance from counterfeit repentance. Here they are again:

1. Recognition of sin.
2. Sorrow for sin.
3. Confession of sin.
4. Shame for sin.
5. Hatred for sin.
6. Turning from sin.[18]

Because sin is a matter of the head, heart, and hands and corrupts our thinking, feeling, and doing, repentance is known by its fruit. Thomas Watson goes on to say that in the life of a true Christian, while we cannot "see" faith (and therefore we cannot see into the heart of others), we can see repentance.[19] And if we don't see repentance, we have no reason to believe that there is faith.

The single most compelling pre-*Obergefell* leader of Side B gay Christianity is Wesley Hill, author of *Washed and Waiting* and *Spiritual Friendship*, cofounder of the Internet community bearing the same name, and supporter of Revoice, the gay-supporting movement and conference notedly briefly in the last chapter.[20]

18 For supporting Scripture references, see page 20.
19 Thomas Watson, *The Doctrine of Repentance* (1668; repr., Carlisle, PA: Banner of Truth, 2012), 18.
20 Revoice was founded by Nate Collins and supported by Wes Hill and Greg Johnson and others. Its carefully crafted mission maintains that LGBTQ+ is a legitimate identity, that God's

Wes Hill has been fighting and preaching and teaching the subtle and dangerous idea that some Christians are sexual minorities who need a voice in the church because homosexual desires, if not acted upon, can be sanctified for the cause of Christ. Hill is a compelling writer, often tugging at the heartstrings of his reader. To Hill, our sinful desires make us suffering victims to be pitied, not transgressors against God who need greater repentance. For Hill and other Side B gay Christians, homosexual desire is primarily a problem of unanswered prayer. The homosexual is primarily someone who suffers, says Hill, not someone who sins.

This idea is seductive because it is half true. Yes, we do suffer for our sins. But when we get the order wrong, we get the gospel wrong. We suffer because we sin. Sin comes before suffering.

So while we often do suffer for our sins, this does not make our responsibility for sin disappear. Sin is still sin—a transgression against God's law, an act of moral treason. This definition stands whether we suffer because of our chosen or unchosen sin. Because God hates sin, God calls us to hate our sin without hating ourselves, which is every Christian's life lesson.

Wesley Hill starts in the right place, that homosexuality, for many, is a consequence of the fall of Adam. In this way, it was unchosen. But Hill departs from the Bible's witness when he concludes

---

people can bear a category of condemning sin without reproach, and that sanctification is insufficient to grow believers into the likeness of Christ. Its mission statement is: "To support and encourage gay, lesbian, bisexual, and other same-sex attracted Christians—as well as those who love them—so that all in the Church might be empowered to live in gospel unity while observing the historic Christian doctrine of marriage and sexuality." The best way to support self-identified gay Christians is to lead them to repentance; gospel unity is not based on issues but on theology; the creation ordinance does not call us to merely "[observe] the historic Christian doctrine of marriage and sexuality." True biblical sanctification is not passive or free-floating. It is active and rooted in justification. The counterfeit sanctification of the gay Christian movement seeks to domesticate sin, not mortify it.

that unchosen sin is something that requires not repentance but sympathy, or that being given a new nature in Christ (Eph. 4:24) means that the believer is tossed to and fro between the old and the new, between Adam and Christ. No! Homosexuality may be part of my biography but it is not part of my new nature. God commands born-again Christians, those who are a "new creation [because] the old has passed away" (2 Cor. 5:17), to "put off" our old self and "put on" our new self (Eph. 4:22–24). Once born again, I can never see homosexuality as part of my essence or nature, because I am a new creation by God's regeneration. While homosexuality arises out of my sin nature, once redeemed, I am no longer in Adam but in Christ. When I sin or desire to sin, as a new creation in Christ I am now acting against my new nature. Sexual sin is a bear because of the body memories that it leaves in its wake, but body memories are part of my biography, not my new nature in Christ. If I believe that the gospel leaves me hanging in the middle, helplessly straddling between two natures as Side B gay Christianity proclaims, sometimes in Adam and sometimes in Christ, I do not understand the gospel.[21] Hill concludes that LGBTQ+ "Christians" are victims who make up a sexual minority in the church, not sinners in need of repentance and restoration. Furthermore, Hill considers his homosexual orientation a blessing and a doorway to ministry:

> I want to explore the way my same-sex attractions are inescapably bound up with my gift for and calling to friendship. My question, at root, is how I can steward and sanctify my homosexual

---

21 An outstanding sermon that sets forth the power of the gospel and the deep change it creates is one delivered by Pastor Aldo Leon, Pinelands PCA, Miami, FL, entitled, "A Sermon from Ephesians on Identity," February 21, 2022, https://presbycast.libsyn.com/.

orientation in such a way that it can be a doorway to blessing and grace.[22]

In another section, Hill writes:

> In my experience, at least, being gay colors everything about me, even though I am celibate. It's less a separable piece of my experience, like a shelf in my office, which is indistinguishable from the other shelves, and more like a proverbial drop of ink in a glass of water: not identical with the water, but also not entirely distinct from it either. Being gay is, for me, as much a sensibility as anything else: a heightened sensitivity to and passion for same-sex beauty that helps determine the kind of conversations I have, which people I'm drawn to spend time with, what novels and poems and films I enjoy, the particular visual art I appreciate, and also, I think, the kind of friendships I pursue and try to strengthen.[23]

Wes Hill is in direct contradiction to Scripture. When someone is converted, the indwelling sin of homosexuality must be repented of and mortified, even if it does not entirely disappear. It exerts the same kind of temptation that the Israelites experienced in wanting to return to Egypt in the wilderness. Temptation is to be fought through grace. But that does not mean that sinful temptations should ever be whitewashed or miscategorized. Sin is our enemy, not our friend.

Gay Christianity is born from the same "gay pride" of its fallen secular host.

22 Wesley Hill, *Spiritual Friendship: Finding Love in the Church as a Celibate Gay Christian* (Grand Rapids, MI: Brazos Press, 2015), 78–79.
23 Hill, *Spiritual Friendship*, 80–81.

Wes Hill teaches that the celibate gay Christian is righteous in his gay "sexual orientation," which, he says, is fixed and morally neutral. This is false teaching.

Since 2018, even Reformed and confessional churches have been made into war zones through a false teaching promoted by the Side B gay Christian organization called Revoice.[24] Featuring workshops on everything from cuddling to "queer treasures in heaven,"[25] Revoice is Side B on steroids.[26] Faithful pastors and teaching elders in our Reformed and confessional denominations brought biblical truth to bear on the false teaching of Revoice but to no avail.[27] Side B gay Christianity is fanatically deceived in believing that homosexual orientation provides a cover and excuse for the sin of sexual desire and lust. It has continued to destroy the peace and purity of the church as well as mar the dignity of the gospel.

The Revoice movement adds some additional contours to the Side B gay Christian movement that bear exploration.

1. Revoice founder Nate Collins invented the idea of "aesthetic orientation" in order to soften the stigma of homosexual orientation. Collins says:

> If we are to speak of an aesthetic orientation and use it to differentiate between gay and straight, we would say that both gay men and straight women are, for example, less aware (in gen-

---

24 See R. Albert Mohler Jr., "Torn between Two Cultures? Revoice, LGBT Identity, and Biblical Christianity," Albert Mohler (website), August 2, 2018, https://albertmohler.com/.

25 See Perkins, *A Little Leaven*.

26 The best analysis of this movement is Perkins, *A Little Leaven*.

27 See R. Scott Clark's excellent summary, "Johnson to the PCA: 'Merry Christmas. Here Is a Lump of Coal for Your Stocking," *Heidelblog*, December 22, 2021, https://heidel blog.net/.

eral) of the beauty of feminine personhood than straight men or lesbian women. These general patterns that we discern in the way people experience the beauty of others are now the basis for distinguishing between straight and nonstraight orientations, rather than an impulse toward sexual activity.[28]

Notice how Collins sweeps away the category of sin: homosexual orientation to Collins is just one of many morally neutral aesthetic orientations. This sets up a tension in Revoice: sometimes it's about the sex they can't have (which makes them suffering victims), and other times it's not about sex at all.

2. Revoice avoids words with origins in the Bible, like *born again*, and denies progressive sanctification's power over sexual orientation. Collins writes:

> How is gayness related to the fall? And what does gayness look like when it is redeemed? Christians have traditionally used terms like sin, temptation, and healing to answer these questions, all of which are found in various texts of Scripture. My suspicion, however, is that we could provide more specific, and potentially more meaningful, answers to these questions if we broaden our search for descriptions of gay people's experience beyond terms explicitly found in Scripture.[29]

Did you catch this? Personal experience is "more meaningful" than God's word. Hope is not found in change but in visibility as gay people in the church.

---

28 Nate Collins, *All but Invisible: Exploring Identity Questions at the Intersection of Faith, Gender, and Sexuality* (Grand Rapids, MI: Zondervan, 2017), 150.
29 Collins, *All but Invisible*, 190.

3. Revoice believes coming out of the closet as gay will destroy the shame of its sin rather than solidify it. The feelings of shame, according to Revoice, are not the result of a tender conscience responding to God's holy call on my life, but rather, a lack of public affirmation.[30] Borrowing from Wesley Hill's article "Shame and the Reflex of Non-Recognition," shame is the discomfort of being misunderstood. But the Bible records shame for sin as a good and necessary impulse that compels us to flee to Christ and repent of sinful desires.

4. Revoice denies the power of progressive sanctification to change sinful sexual patterns. It questions whether the removal of homosexuality through the glorification of a believer would be a good thing. Wesley Hill, in a blog post entitled "Will I be Gay in the Resurrection?," says:

> If it's also true that Christ's return means I'm to be "healed" of my homosexuality, then will my entire personality undergo a complete overhaul? To go back to [Francis] Young's language above, if I'm to be "perfected"—meaning I won't be gay anymore—well, I can't imagine that that wouldn't make me into someone who is almost completely different than the person I am now, and that thought isn't exactly a hopeful one.[31]

Greg Coles, in a blog post entitled, "You Don't Need to Pray That God Makes Me Straight," writes:

> I've stopped praying to be straight. In fact, most of the time, I've stopped wanting to be straight. If you offered me a choice today

---

30 Wesley Hill, "Shame and the Reflex of Non-Recognition," Spiritual Friendship (website), March 4, 2014, https://spiritualfriendship.org/.

31 Wesley Hill, "Will I Be Gay in the Resurrection?," Spiritual Friendship (website), March 10, 2016, https://spiritualfriendship.org/.

between a Wonder-Pill-That-Makes-Gay-People-Straight and a Tylenol, I'd take the Tylenol. . . . One of the reasons that I've stopped praying to be straight: It's possible to be heterosexual without honoring God, and it's also possible to honor God without being heterosexual.[32]

This trend among Revoice advocates poses a serious question: In what religion would you reject God's promise of glorification so that you may retain your gayness? Not the Christian one.

My critique of Revoice begs for a godly alternative, and I will supply that here. It's simple: be a member of a true church, leave gay culture for Christian living, and get the help you need from your church and, if needed, from a good counselor. My alternative has a multipronged approach.

1. *Worship God in a true branch of a Bible-believing church.* True worship is your guardrail against apostasy and unbelief, including the apostasy and unbelief of the gay Christian movement. See 2 Chronicles and the righteous reign of King Hezekiah, who cleansed the temple and restored true worship.

2. *Apply the means of grace to your daily life.* The "means" are channels by which the grace of God is ushered down from heaven for your life, your help, your comfort, and your growth in godliness. Through them, the Holy Spirit enables believers to receive Christ and to apply Christ in all hardships of life. Reformed and Protestant churches understand these means as instruments of God's grace to include the word, the sacraments, and prayer.[33]

---

32 Gregory Coles, "You Don't Need to Pray That God Makes Me Straight," Center for Faith, Sexuality and Gender, September 15, 2017, https://www.centerforfaith.com/.

33 Nicholas T. Batzig, "What Is a Means of Grace?," *Tabletalk*, June 2020, https://tabletalk magazine.com/.

3. *Deal with sin in God's way—repent and walk in the light.*
This includes repentance and growth in grace, but it may also include therapy and counseling. Biblical counseling as well as other methods may be used of God to help.[34]

The religion of gay Christianity, Side A or B, is not a branch of the Christian faith. Specifically, gay Christianity is different from biblical sexuality in that it teaches:

1. *A different understanding of biblical personhood.* Homosexual identity is Freudian, not biblical, as we have seen. It denies the creation ordinance and being made in the image of God (Gen. 1:27–28).

2. *A different understanding of scriptural authority, temptation, desire, and redemption.* In the Gospel of John we read that "Scripture cannot be broken" (John 10:35). Among other things, this means that the word of God is truer than our feelings, including our feelings of sexual desire. The gay Christian's investment in personal victimization replaces the truth of God's word with the manipulation of feelings.

3. *A different understanding of sin: original, actual, and indwelling.* Psalm 51 reveals that the Christian must fight even unchosen sin. To the gay Christian, if that unchosen sin

---

34 Good counseling can be helpful even if you do not achieve all of your counseling goals. Andrè Van Mol writes, "Swiftly on the heels of his 2021 study showing sexual orientation change efforts (SOCE) 'strongly reduces suicidality' and that restrictions on SOCE may 'deprive sexual minorities of an important resource for reducing suicidality, putting them at substantially increased suicide risk,' sociologist Paul Sullins's new peer-reviewed analysis revealed, as per its title, an 'Absence of Behavioral Harm following non-efficacious Sexual Orientation Change Efforts: A Retrospective Study of United States Sexual Minority Adults, 2016–2018.'"Andrè Van Mol, "Even Failed Therapy for Undesired Same-Sex Sexuality Results in No Harm, Finds New Study," Christian Medical and Dental Associations, February 24, 2022, https://cmda.org/.

falls under the category of homosexual orientation, then it registers as a vulnerability, not a sin.[35]

4. *A different understanding of the centrality of the cross.* The blood of Christ does not make an ally with the sin it crushes on the cross, ever.

5. *A different understanding of justification and sanctification.* The Bible locates our sanctification in our justification, not in any notion of good works stemming from how we "steward" our sexual orientation.

6. *A different understanding of God's holiness.* God's holiness cannot abide with sin, including our sexual sin.

The fact of the matter is that sinners need to change their behaviors, attitudes, and affections, and change starts with repentance for sin. Only God can make dead bones live, so sanctification must find its root in justification—the reality of being a born-again Christian. In repentance and new life in Christ, we grow in holiness.

We never become holy in the sight of God because we are victims who blame him and the church for our sin.

---

35 "What Is 'Sexual Orientation' and Is It a Helpful Category?" Revoice, March 16, 2020, https://revoice.us/.

4

Why Is Homosexuality a Sin When It Feels Normal to Some People?

IF HOMOSEXUALITY IS YOUR indwelling sin, what does *change* mean—what exactly does it mean to be made a new person in Christ? There is no place in Scripture where we see the gift of saving faith bestowed on people unaccompanied by rigorous change to and within them. That change is due to the cross of Christ and the redemption that flows from his resurrection. But that truth is a contested issue. Advocates of gay Christianity tell us it is the church that must change. Yet that is not what Scripture says.

Scripture calls us to repent of all sin, including unchosen sinful desires. Colossians 3:5 calls the believer to change not just outward behavior but the evil desires that fuel it. The Bible teaches that sin "insinuates itself into our motives, designs, objects, thoughts, prayers, and every action, sleeping and waking."[1] Genesis 6:5 and

---

1 Sarah Hawkes, "September 11," in *Seasons of the Heart: A Year of Devotions from One Generation of Women to Another*, ed. Donna Kelderman (Grand Rapids, MI: Reformation Heritage, 2013).

Mark 7:20–23 bring to light that our sinful nature drives corruption deep into the cavernous desires of our hearts. And Ephesians 4:22–24 calls for the transformation of our inner being to conform to Christ's righteousness. At the same time, the Bible compassionately reveals that all true Christians feel this inner war: "The desires of the flesh are against the Spirit, and the desires of the Spirit are against the flesh, for these are opposed to each other, to keep you from doing the things you want to do" (Gal. 5:17).

But sin no longer defines us, as the apostle Paul reminds us: "You also must consider yourselves dead to sin and alive to God in Christ Jesus" (Rom. 6:11). Our call is not to despair but to hope in Christ and to drive a fresh nail into our choice sin every day (Col. 3:1–5). Because of what Christ did on the cross, believers are no longer in bondage to sin, although it still knows our names and addresses. While we are no longer enslaved to our sin nature (Christ has covered us in a robe of righteousness and has taken our sin upon himself), sin still resides in our patterns of thought and must be daily—sometimes hourly—battled with. For believers, the beloved children of God who know the Father's electing love and the Son's ransom and the Spirit's comfort, sin no longer rules us. And because sin no longer rules us, homosexuality is not a fixed feature of our humanity. Rescue is found in the gospel.[2]

The Antidote to Gay Christianity

Union with Christ is the central privilege of the Christian faith and the antidote to gay Christianity. You can't place your life's meaning in Christ and in sin at the same time. And even if you

---

2   Peter Jones, "Still Time to Care about the Whole Gospel," Truthxchange, March 2, 2022, https://truthxchange.com/. Includes excellent resources for counseling. Help is also available from the Association of Certified Biblical Counselors, https://biblicalcounseling.org.

believe that you are just using the category of *gay* as a plain way of describing your feelings, you must remember that *gay* is a keyword, not a neutral one. *Gay* is no longer just one of many vocabulary terms. *Gay* is not a terminology choice. *Gay* refers to our nation's reigning idol.

The central privilege of the Christian faith, the one that keeps you in God's will and his love even when it hurts, is union with Christ. It is the single most extraordinary privilege a believer has. It explains how Christ both redeems your future and heals your past. At the moment that God the Father calls you,[3] adopts you,[4] and justifies you, your heart is regenerated, and you are born again. The Holy Spirit forges with you an unbreakable, spiritual, irreplaceable, and eternal union with Christ. This union is better than the one that Adam had in the garden, when he walked and talked openly with God prior to the fall. Adam's union depended on his obedience; our union depends on Christ's obedience, being, and character. We don't measure up. Christ measures up for us— and this is what we mean when we say that believers are united to Christ by faith. Although all believers have this union, if you do not exercise your faith—build it up, make it strong, depend upon it, engage in all the means of grace as often as possible—the blessings of it might not flourish as God intends. When union with Christ is not enjoyed, the cares of the world sneak up and steal our joy in the Lord and weaken our faith.

---

3 Westminster Shorter Catechism, Question 32: "What Benefits do they that are effectually called partake of in this life?" Answer: "They that are effectually called do in this life partake of justification, adoption, and sanctification, and the several benefits which in this life do either accompany or flow from them." See also Rom. 8:30.

4 Westminster Shorter Catechism, Question 34: "What is Adoption?" Answer: "Adoption is an act of God's free grace, whereby we are received into the number, and have a right to all the privileges of the sons of God." See also John 1:12; Rom. 8:17; 1 John 3:1.

Understanding the believer's union with Christ is so important to anyone dealing with persistent sexual sin. If homosexuality is a persistent sin, you should find comfort in these verses:

> Do you not know that all of us who have been baptized into Christ Jesus were baptized into his death? We were buried therefore with him by baptism into death, in order that, just as Christ was raised from the dead by the glory of the Father, we too might walk in newness of life. For if we have been united with him in a death like his, we shall certainly be united with him in a resurrection like his. We know that our old self was crucified with him in order that the body of sin might be brought to nothing, so that we would no longer be enslaved to sin. For one who has died has been set free from sin. Now if we have died with Christ, we believe that we will also live with him. We know that Christ, being raised from the dead, will never die again; death no longer has dominion over him. For the death he died he died to sin, once for all, but the life he lives he lives to God. So you also must consider yourselves dead to sin and alive to God in Christ Jesus. (Rom. 6:3–11)

> He chose us in him before the foundation of the world, that we should be holy and blameless before him. (Eph. 1:4)

> But God, being rich in mercy, because of the great love with which he loved us, even when we were dead in our trespasses, made us alive together with Christ—by grace you have been saved—and raised us up with him and seated us with him in the heavenly places in Christ Jesus, so that in the coming ages he might show the immeasurable riches of his grace in kindness toward us in Christ Jesus. (Eph. 2:4–7)

The truths found here stand between you and Satan. If you are God's chosen vessel, you are dead to your homosexuality and alive to Christ. If this sounds impossible, you might not have a good understanding of the basics of the gospel.[5] There is nothing impossible about living out your citizenship in heaven here on earth.

Union with Christ is this dynamic and supernatural power that God gives his redeemed people, but you cannot have union with Christ if you have made an identity out of anything else. Union with Christ demands that Christ has exclusive claims on his redeemed people. Indeed, you do yourself great harm if you insist on holding two forms of self-representation—sexual and spiritual. Both forms of self-representation compete for the same thing: your loyalty, your heart, your sense of self, your faith.

Homosexual identity is incompatible with union with Christ because there is no dual citizenship for a Christ follower. A Christ follower has a single mission. She does not bow down to the idol of sexual-orientation identity. Idols cannot be added and stirred to the melting pot of ideas and made peace with. Instead, idols must be publicly repented of. Like Nehemiah, we must take ownership of our nation's sins and publicly repent of them. We must stand in our union with Christ and against the idea that sexual identity encompasses personhood. Personal identity is not in the eyes of the beholder. Our humanity is not in our feelings. Our sense of

---

5 "An overrealized eschatology transfers the Christian's hope from the coming age to this present life, placing expectations on God that he does not place on himself. The Christian Scriptures are much more measured about what we should expect during this brief lifetime." Greg Johnson, *Still Time to Care: What We Can Learn from the Church's Failed Attempt to Cure Homosexuality* (Grand Rapids, MI: Zondervan, 2021), Kindle, no loc. Since he cites no scripture that supports his position that God does not sanctify the born-again believer, allowing him to overcome his persistent sin patterns, this reader is left wondering to what god he refers. Johnson uses personal testimony in place of God's word to make his case.

self is not in our sin. It is in Christ, held in God's hands, framed by Christ's death and resurrection. The only way you can hate your sin without hating yourself is through union with Christ.

What If It Feels Right?

People ask, How can homosexuality be a sin if it feels natural to some people? From a biblical point of view, homosexuality is a sin that belongs to our fallen nature—the one everyone is born with. That sin nature is why homosexuality can feel normal and natural to some people.

When Adam sinned at the fall, all his posterity inherited a sin nature. A sin nature is a human inclination toward sin, a bent for darkness, a longing for something that God hates. Because Adam committed his sin as our covenant head, the sin nature we inherited is ours to overcome. We can't blame Adam. Far from making us innocent victims of Adam's foolish choice, our sin—even when it arises from some unconscious place within—condemns us:

> Do you not know that the unrighteous will not inherit the kingdom of God? Do not be deceived. Neither fornicators, nor idolaters, nor adulterers, nor homosexuals, nor sodomites, nor thieves, nor covetous, nor drunkards, nor revilers, nor extortioners will inherit the kingdom of God. And such were some of you. (1 Cor. 6:9–11 NKJV)

The Bible paints the picture starkly: those who reject the idea of Adam's covenant headship and the responsibility of learning to repent of all sin that flows from our sin nature reject everything to do with God's covenant, including his salvation and covenant blessing.

John 3:18–19 puts it this way: "Whoever believes in him is not condemned, but whoever does not believe is condemned already. . . . And this is the judgment: the light has come into the world, and people loved the darkness rather than the light." In other words, genuine Christians repent of all sin (including the sin that feels natural and good) because they trust Jesus more than they trust themselves. We manifest our faith by believing that the Bible is truer than our feelings. This is what authentic faith in Jesus Christ looks like.[6]

Biblically speaking, holding to the false view that you can be gay (in desire or practice) and a Christian is self-deception, but we live in a culture that has embraced and lives under this deception, which only serves to deepen the deception.[7]

Total depravity, fallen nature, unable to please God without faith, unable to fight sin with the grace of Christ—these are sober thoughts. But if you are in Christ, it means that you have the King of the universe praying for you, receiving you to the throne

---

6 The Heidelberg Catechism Questions 6–8 offer additional insight into unchosen sin and man's responsibility to repent of it. Question 6: "Did God then create man so wicked and perverse?" Answer 6: "By no means; but God created man good (Gen. 1:31), and after His own image, in true righteousness and holiness (Gen. 1:26–27, Col. 3:10, Eph. 4:24), that he might rightly know God his Creator, heartily love Him and live with Him in eternal happiness to glorify and praise Him (Eph 1:6, 1 Cor. 6:20)." Our image-bearing of God is compromised by sin and restored by repentance unto life. Doing what feels right when it contradicts biblical teaching brings upon us God's wrath, not his love.

Question 7: "Whence then proceeds this depravity of human nature?" Answer 7: "From the fall and disobedience of our first parents, Adam and Eve, in Paradise (Gen. 3:6, Rom. 5:12, 18–19); hence our nature is become so corrupt that we are all conceived and born in sin (Psa. 51:5)."

Question 8: "Are we then so corrupt that we are wholly incapable of doing any good and inclined to all wickedness?" Answer 8: "Indeed, we are (Gen. 6:5, Job 14:4, Job 15:14, 16), except we are regenerated by the Spirit of God (John 3:5, Eph. 2:5)."

7 Charlie Rodriguez with Paula Rodriguez, For Those in Peril: A Call for the Church to Speak Truth to the State (Dallas, TX: Tanglewood, 2021). This book is very helpful in identifying and repenting of corporate sins.

of grace, building you back up when you fall, forgiving your sins, and holding you in perfect union until he takes you to glory. It means that in our faithlessness and unbelief, we cannot do good because our works are tainted by idolatry and sin. If God created us for his glory, then works apart from faith will not be counted by him as good, even if they serve and promote social kindness. The common grace that allows an unbelieving doctor to work hard in helping people heal is not the saving grace that bestows God's electing love upon him, no matter how many people he has helped. This is the hard truth of what biblical faith says.

The Bible offers the true way out for those with loved ones trapped in this fanatical deception that maintains gay is who you are (not just how you feel).

Indoctrination, Empathy, and the New Religion of Homosexuality

Peter Jones makes the case that homosexuality is not a secular concept but, rather, a pagan one.[8] Homosexuality is actually a new false religion.

In pagan concepts of the sacred, everything is divine. "God" is internal and part of us, not external to us. Everyone is part of the same sacred and divine power, and if we stand together in political protests, we can channel this divine power for social good. And that, from the pagan standpoint, is what real spirituality is. Every religion leads to the same good path, and therefore all religions are one.

In a Christian concept of the sacred, God is separate from creation. God is eternal, triune, and personal. He made us and takes care of us, but he is also separate from us. There are also two kinds

---

8 Peter Jones, *Whose Rainbow? God's Gift of Sexuality: A Divine Calling* (Ontario, Canada: Ezra Press, 2020).

of people in the world: those who know Christ and those who don't. Those who love Christ also love his law. No gray area exists. Spirituality means that we worship and serve the Creator, and we serve one another in love and care. We all will worship something: God or ourselves, the Creator or idols.

In a pagan paradigm, the problem is that we have failed to achieve unity with other people, and the solution is that we need to look within ourselves to find the power and love to change. In a biblical paradigm, the problem is that we have rejected God's authority by refusing to obey the Bible as it is written. We disobey his laws, and we don't like his solutions. What is his solution? The solution is to look to God for repentance and accept the sacrifice of Jesus for us.[9]

Homosexuality is inherently pagan, where men see themselves as god and everything shares the same essential nature. In my own experience in the gay community, same-sex couples often resembled each other more and more over time. While a similar observation might be made for heterosexual couples, there is a very big difference between the two. In a homosexual relationship, the resemblances between the partners reflect a barren narcissism. In a biblical marriage, growing in one flesh reflects God's complementarian

---

9 A helpful way to understand the paganism of homosexuality is through Peter Jones's articulation of Oneism (nonbinary) and Twoism (binary). He writes, "In Oneism the world is self-creating and self-explanatory, sharing the same substance, whether matter, spirit, or a mixture, to be worshipped as divine or of utmost importance. . . . All distinctions are eliminated, and everything has the same worth. . . . Twoism believes the world is the work of a personal, transcendent God who creates *ex nihilo* and is not constrained by or dependent on the creation or any pre-existing conditions. God's free act of creation displays his transcendence and sovereignty. No human analogy is adequate to 'explain' the mystery of this unique Creator. There are two kinds of existence—the Creator who is uncreated and everything else, which is created. We worship as divine the unique, distinct, personal, triune Creator, who wove distinction throughout creation." Jones, *Whose Rainbow?*, 64.

design. Right-leaning and gay-identifying English social critic Douglas Murray, ironically, confirms Jones's observation:

> Sex between men dissolves otherness into sameness . . . in a perfect suspension: there is nothing that either party doesn't know about the other. If the emotional aim of intercourse is a total knowing of the other, gay sex may be . . . perfect because, in it, a total knowledge of the other's experience is, finally, possible.[10]

In a fascinating add-on, Murray goes on to show how the self-referential (dare I say, narcissistic) aesthetic of gay sexuality is ultimately self-defeating: "But since the object of that knowledge is already wholly known to each of the parties, the act is also, in a way, redundant. Perhaps it is for this reason that so many of us keep seeking repetition as if depth were impossible."[11] These last words— "as if depth were impossible"—should haunt all of us who have loved ones trapped in the sin of homosexuality. Indeed, repetition as well as affirmation is a constant requirement for the homosexual sinner, even though we are all "without excuse" (Rom. 1:20).

The only way out of the ever-damning homosexual repetition, the constant hunger for the elusive depth of knowing and being known, is repentance for sin, even repentance for a sin that feels natural. And after repentance must come renewal—which requires a complete break with all sinful patterns and the people and entertainment venues in which these patterns lurk. It all comes down to this: Do you trust your feelings, or do you trust the word of God? Do you perceive your feelings through the word of God, or do you

---

10 Douglas Murray, *The Madness of Crowds: Gender, Race, and Identity* (London: Bloomsbury, 2019), 49.
11 Murray, *Madness of Crowds*, 49.

perceive the word of God through your feelings? Do your feelings know you best, or does the God who made you? True Christians believe God's word over their feelings. Paul explains this in Romans 3:4: "Let God be true though every one were a liar." Indeed. The whole world is guilty before God, and jollying people out of this truth only condemns them more.

What Jones identifies as paganism and Murray as a longing for depth of knowing brings us to our next key term, *empathy*—a word that has shaped the imaginations of those swayed by the LGBTQ+ agenda. *Empathy* means standing in someone else's shoes. In a world where kindness is the most important virtue, empathy is the highest manifestation of this love. But is empathy always a good thing? Is empathy ever dangerous? When did empathy become more virtuous than sympathy?

Do We Need Empathy or Sympathy?

Empathy is a relatively new word; it didn't enter our language until the twentieth century. The dictionary defines *empathy* as "the power of mentally identifying oneself with (and so fully comprehending) a person or object of contemplation."[12] When people say, "My thoughts and prayers are with you," they are likely referring to the power of empathy, which holds that if you mentally identify with something or someone, you comprehend (apprehend with your senses) their pain. And your ability to feel with them helps break the isolation of their experience, which in turn helps them heal. My dictionary contrasts *empathy* to *sympathy*: "Pity is feeling sorry *for* someone; empathy is feeling sorry *with* someone."[13] If you pity someone, you are observing

---

12 *The New Shorter Oxford English Dictionary on Historical Principles*, vol. 1, ed. Lesley Brown (Oxford, UK: Clarendon Press, 1973), s.v. "empathy."

13 *New Shorter Oxford English Dictionary*, s.v. "empathy."

some identifiable and objective problem experienced by that person. Being the object of pity means that something is terribly wrong, and something must be done about that. Sympathy identifies an objective problem and seeks an objective solution.

The character of Satan in John Milton's magnificent *Paradise Lost*, a seventeenth-century epic poem that boasts ten thousand lines of iambic pentameter, has a word for us about this matter of pity. In the poem, the character of Satan says, "The mind is its place, and in itself / Can make a Heaven of Hell, a Hell of Heaven. . . . / Better to reign in Hell than serve in Heaven."[14] In other words, Satan would rather be anything but pitied. Rather than be the object of pity or the agent of prayer to God, calling out to him for mercy and begging him for the grace to repent, the fallen angel would rather play mind games, somehow "making" an imaginary heaven out of a real hell. The seventeenth-century poet John Milton helps us ask the twenty-first-century question, Do people in real trouble benefit from pity or empathy? Do people in real trouble need real help (sympathy)? Or do they just need to reframe their troubles?

In contrast to *empathy*, *sympathy* is an old word with an old history. It describes "the quality or state of being affected by the suffering or grief of another; a feeling or expression of compassion or condolence."[15] Sympathy recognizes a problem that someone else has, and sympathy grieves and longs for a solution. This means that when your daughter comes home from college and tells you that she is a man named Rex, you ought to feel sympathy, because something is terribly, dreadfully wrong with your daughter.

---

14 John Milton, *Paradise Lost*, vol. 4, ed. Rebekah Merkle (Moscow, ID: Logos Press, 2015), lines 255, 265.

15 *The New Shorter Oxford English Dictionary on Historical Principles*, vol. 2, ed. Lesley Brown (Oxford, UK: Clarendon Press, 1973), s.v. "sympathy."

But LGBTQ+ propaganda wants you to feel empathy instead.[16] LGBTQ+ propaganda wants you to reframe your point of view, not help fix your daughter's problem.

While empathy is not always unwarranted, we are never called to empathize with sin. In this context, empathy puts you squarely into Milton's satanic paradigm—the mind is so powerful that it makes a reality of its own will.

Author Joe Rigney has traced the movement in this term, *empathy*, and he suggests that while empathy certainly has a place in our lives, we all tend to use the term selectively.[17] We empathize with perceived victims only. (Who, for example, wants to empathize with a murderer or rapist?) Selective empathy is one of the key contributors to tribalism and polarization. To Rigney, empathy is dangerous because if the highest form of love is standing in someone else's shoes, no one is left standing in a place of objective truth. If someone is drowning in a river, jumping in with him may break up his loneliness, but having two drowned people produces an even greater problem. Sympathy allows someone to stand on the shore, on the solid ground of objective truth where real help might be found. Empathy's intent is good—connecting with another person in pain. But when the person in pain needs to be rescued, empathy leads to alienation. This constant state of alienation reiterates the false idea that there is no real

---

16 In modern and surrealist literature, empathy always leads to alienation. That point is made clear in Franz Kafka's brilliant *The Metamorphosis* (1915). Gregor Samsa wakes up one morning to discover that he has transformed overnight into a "monstrous vermin"—a six-foot cockroach. No one can understand him. His sister tries, and her empathy fails and crumbles into alienation and murder.

17 Joe Rigney, "The Enticing Sin of Empathy," Desiring God (website), May 31, 2019, https:// www.desiringgod.org/. See also Joe Rigney, "Do You Feel My Pain? Empathy, Sympathy, and Dangerous Virtues," Desiring God (website), May 2, 2020, https://www.desiringgod .org/.

help available and that all we have is loneliness—the autonomous individual seeking meaning in his own pain.

Words matter. And we are living in a world that has become a war of words. Christians are called to be peacemakers, not passive dupes in this war. Words do more than communicate ideas; they shape our imaginations. Change the words, and you change the world. And Jesus is still the Word made flesh. Jesus is also our high priest who offers us sympathy, not empathy:

> Since then we have a great high priest who has passed through the heavens, Jesus, the Son of God, let us hold fast our confession. For we do not have a high priest who is unable to sympathize with our weaknesses, but one who in every respect has been tempted as we are, yet without sin. Let us then with confidence draw near to the throne of grace, that we may receive mercy and find grace to help in time of need. (Heb. 4:14–16)

This matchless description of the person and work of Jesus invites us to a place so perfect that it exceeds our imagination: the throne of grace. Jesus is prophet, priest, and king, but this passage in Hebrews focuses our attention on his priesthood—Jesus as man's representative before God.

The Need to Know Jesus

Any Christian struggling with homosexuality needs to know the resurrected Jesus, the Son of God, as high priest. Jesus is fully man and fully God, which is fully a mind-boggling mystery. God loved us so very much that he gave us Jesus (John 3:16), and Jesus fulfilled the terms of our ransom. Jesus obeyed the law perfectly, and he did this as a man. Jesus died a shameful death on the cross, taking ownership and making payment for the sins of all his people for all of time. Puritan John Flavel wrote:

> Christ Jesus set himself wholly apart for believers. We may say, "Lord, condemnation was yours, that justification might be mine; agony was yours, and victory mine; pain was yours, and ease is mine; agony was yours, and victory mine; the curse was yours and the blessing mine; a crown of thorns was yours, and eternal life mine!"[18]

Jesus loves his people more than we can ever understand this side of eternity.

The resurrected Jesus is our high priest, and he sympathizes with our weaknesses. Christ's sympathy is far greater than human empathy because God is able to do more than reframe our troubles. He can cure us of all our infirmities. He offers us sympathy, not mocking or shame. Even if we are suffering because of our sin, Jesus does not heap shame on us. He calls us to come boldly to him. He is the great physician who knows our sin disease better than we do. His power to resist temptation was real. Christ fought sin as a man. His fight was not a sham. His hunger and want and temptation were real. And to his people, Jesus is offering real healing, real cure. But his terms are not what we would expect. Jesus suffers with us, but Jesus does not sin with us. He will cure us on his terms, which include stepping into the power that his resurrection offers to fight sin every day of our life on earth. His power to resist temptation is given to us by grace.

18 John Flavel, cited in *Voices from the Past: Puritan Devotional Readings*, ed. Richard Rushing (Carlisle, PA: Banner of Truth, 2009), 62.

Sometimes we just want someone to say that we are okay just the way we are. But that is not what Jesus offers. Are we willing to be healed on Jesus's terms? Or are we insisting that Jesus heal us on our own terms?

John 5 records a story of a man who had to confront this problem head on. He had been paralyzed for thirty-eight years, lingering by the healing waters at the Sheep Gate. He trusted that the water would heal him, and he was waiting for someone to put him in. But day after day, week after week, month after month, and year after year, no one did. Then Jesus arrived. But Jesus didn't put him in the water either. Instead, in sympathy, Jesus asked him a question: "Do you want to be healed?" (John 5:6).

Let that linger for a moment. Do you want to be made well? Do you want to be made well on Jesus's terms or your own? Does the Christian who calls himself gay want to be made well on God's terms?

Importantly, the sick man didn't take offense at this question, as perhaps someone like the rich young ruler might have (see Luke 18:18–25). After all, why would the man be sitting there for decades if he didn't want to be made well? The question was meant to reveal that Jesus heals on his own terms, not ours. For the man to be healed, he needed to embrace the terms that Jesus was going to set.

The paralyzed man answered, "Sir, I have no one to put me into the pool" (John 5:7). True enough. While we don't know what was happening in the man's heart as he looked up at Jesus, we do know that he embraced the terms that our Lord offered. We know this because of two things. First, when Jesus said, "Get up, take up your bed, and walk" (5:8), the man obeyed. He trusted that he could do what God asked of him through the power of Jesus. And what is the power of Jesus? It's grace. Unmerited favor. Jesus gives us the power to do that which we could not imagine or do on our own terms. We obey in grace. But this is not passive; it still requires trust and faith and grit and strain and action on our part. Trusting Jesus is an action. Accepting Jesus's terms of sympathy means abandoning our own notions about how we need to be helped. It means doing what he says.

The second matter revealing the now-healed man's heart happens in the next scene. The very next time Jesus encounters the man, he is in the temple. The setting implies something important—the man knows that God has healed him. (Whether he was worshiping, the text does not say.) Jesus approaches the man and says, "See, you are well! Sin no more, that nothing worse may happen to you" (5:14). We know that not all suffering is the consequence of active sin, but Jesus's words imply that this man's sin was. So we know from this encounter that the man received Jesus's terms in two ways, in active obedience (5:9) and in repentance (5:14). Both his active obedience (walking, after thirty-eight years of paralysis) and his repentance (receiving Jesus's gentle rebuke), as well as his evident change and healing, suggest that this man needed the saving grace of our high priest.

Tempted without Sin

The resurrected Jesus was tempted as we are, yet without sin. Jesus was conceived by the Holy Spirit and born of the Virgin Mary (Luke 2:34–35). He was fully man, and during his earthly ministry, he felt hunger and thirst and pain. But Jesus had no sin—no sin from Adam and no sin from his own action. So the perversions that have become part of the sinful story of modern life were not things that Jesus experienced. Jesus did not experience sexual lust directed at either men or women. If he did, he could not save us, because the Lamb of God that takes away the sin of the world could not sin in nature, desire, or deed.[19]

This is where people get tripped up. On the one hand, our generation does not want to talk to a perfect man. We want to talk to someone who sins the very same way we do. If we have an accountability group for the same-sex attracted, we want it to be led by someone who fails like we do. Why do we prefer to go to someone who experiences our sin? Likely it is because we feel that such a person will not make us feel bad. Because we are sinners, we feel safe with people who sin the same way we do.

But Jesus sympathizes with us, in both our weakness and our sin, as the example from the paralytic in John 5 suggests. Part of his sinless nature involves not mocking us for our sin. Jesus sympathizes with us and offers us healing and repentance and forgiveness— on his terms, not ours. Jesus gets us out of the rut of the self-help group and offers us something far greater than human empathy.

Come to the Throne of Grace

The resurrected Jesus calls us to come boldly and with confidence to the throne of grace. Because Jesus did not sin, we can go to the throne of grace. The throne is called one of "grace." One Puritan said that God gives us grace because he is good, and mercy because we are miserable. We need both grace and mercy, and Jesus calls us to come boldly. Have you sinned—again? Repent quickly and come boldly. On the throne is our living high priest ready to help. He does not mock or criticize. He receives our repentance, and his forgiveness and the power of his resurrection strengthen us to obey.

19 Denny Burk, "Is Homosexual Orientation Sinful?" *Journal of the Evangelical Theological Society* 58.1 (2015): 95–115.

All who have been justified by God the Father can come to the throne of grace. Those who have already been justified receive grace and mercy to obey the Lord with joy and to grow in sanctification. You cannot justify yourself. But you can cry out to the Lord for his mercy to pardon and justify you. God is faithful to hear your cries, for a broken and contrite heart he will not despise (Ps. 51:17). But all of this must be on God's terms, as outlined in the Bible. The terms of the gay Christian movement, rooted in Freud and Darwin and Marx rather than in Jesus and Paul and Scripture, will not heal you or help you. It will dig you further in sin and confusion.

God teaches us by contrasts: wheat and tares, sheep and goats, saved and lost. In Paul's epistle to the Christians in the Roman colony of Philippi, Paul calls us to imitate him and model our life after other mature Christians. Paul warns against innovation:

> Brothers, join in imitating me, and keep your eyes on those who walk according to the example you have in us. For many, of whom I have often told you and now tell you even with tears, walk as enemies of the cross of Christ. Their end is destruction, their god is their belly, and they glory in their shame, with minds set on earthly things. But our citizenship is in heaven, and from it we await a Savior, the Lord Jesus Christ, who will transform our lowly body to be like his glorious body, by the power that enables him even to subject all things to himself. (Phil. 3:17–21)

This passage contrasts a mature believer walking in grace and an unbeliever or pretend Christian who worships her own desires (entertainments, hobbies, or lusts) and is consumed with earthly matters. The mature Christian life is one of constant fleeing to the throne of grace for mercy, grace, and forgiveness of our sins. Our fight with sin ends at our death, when we are glorified; perfection only comes at the resurrection (1 Cor. 15:12–28). Paul's phrase, "the power that enables him even to subject all things to himself," echoes the messianic Psalms 8:6 and 110:1. Because our citizenship is in heaven, we don't want to perjure our Christian lives by framing them in categories of sin. The thought puts shivers down the spine of a Christ follower, or, along with Paul, tears. To follow an enemy of Christ in her walk away from the truth is suicide. Don't even toy with it.

Gay Christianity—Side A and Side B—is false teaching. Both Side A and Side B beliefs are the ugly stepchildren of the bereft idea that homosexual orientation is a true mark of humanity. How sad indeed for someone who is already weighed down by sin to be denied the true remedy for the problem. That is what gay Christianity does. It denies the sexual sinner repentance and immerses her in the futile task of trying to domesticate her sin. Trying to deal with sin in your own flesh is what Pharisees always encourage. Jesus speaks to this: "Woe to you, scribes and Pharisees, hypocrites! For you travel across sea and land to make a single proselyte, and when he becomes a proselyte, you make him twice as much a child of hell as yourselves" (Matt. 23:15).

We must flee from this false teaching and embrace the word of God. The word of God—the Bible—is different from every other book on the planet. The word of God is sanctified, which means it is a "set apart" book. It is different in both what it says and what it is. But this forces simple questions that we each must answer individually: Are we willing to be instructed by God's word? Do we believe that God's revelation reigns over our own will and reason? Or is it the other way around for us?

The sixteenth-century French Reformer John Calvin declared, "Let us not hear [God's revealed word] as if it were subject to our judgment but let us subject our understanding and minds to it and receive it without calling it in question, for *otherwise we will willfully make war against God and lift ourselves above him.*"[20] To answer this charge from Calvin, we need to do some heart searching and some Bible searching. We need to address what the word of God is and what the word of God does, because if the Bible is false, flawed, semitrue, or just true in the red letters, then none of it is true. If you aren't convinced of that, then the minute the Bible crosses you, that part you will declare an ancient bias and no longer binding.

Albert Mohler wrote, "For a full moral reversal to take place, three conditions must be met. The first is this: what was condemned must be celebrated. The second is that what was celebrated must now be condemned. And, third, those who will not join in the celebration will be condemned."[21] Christians live under this third category now.

To summarize, the claim of a fixed homosexual orientation is Freudian pseudoscience. It finds its roots in atheistic rejections of the creation ordinance. For reasons only Satan may know, gay Christianity uses homosexual orientation as its bedrock definition for personhood. Gay Christianity—Sides A and B—is a different religion from biblical Christianity, with different understandings of human origin and endings, biblical authority, centrality of the cross, sexual ethics, means of grace, how one is justified before a holy God, and the holiness of God.

Theology doesn't save us. We are saved only by the electing love of the Father and the mercy of the Son, so there are true believers

20 John Calvin, *365 Days with John Calvin: A Unique Collection of 365 Writings of John Calvin,* ed. Joel Beeke (Carlisle, PA: Day One, 2008), October 1 entry; emphasis added.

21 R. Albert Mohler Jr., "The Briefing," Albert Mohler (website), February 23, 2017, http://www.albertmohler.com/.

who affiliate with gay Christianity to their own harm. But one thing is clear. False religions operate through the diligence of false teachers, whose master, Satan, never sleeps.

> If Satan is always awake, it is dangerous for the Christian at any time to be spiritually asleep, secure and careless. . . . The saint's sleeping time is Satan's tempting time.[22]

The evangelical church has been asleep to the dangers of gay Christianity, even though we have witnessed scandal, sin, and debauchery. Some have overlooked obvious dangers in order to be winsome and not discourage weak brothers and sisters. But because we are not more merciful than God, this strategy has backfired. Gay Christianity is false teaching.

The false teaching of gay Christianity is one part of a larger problem. Let's turn now to Lie #2, where we will explore why many of our neighbors believe that being a spiritual person is kinder than being a biblical Christian.

---

22 William Gurnall, cited in *Voices from the Past*, 358.

LIE #2

BEING A SPIRITUAL PERSON IS KINDER THAN BEING A BIBLICAL CHRISTIAN

5

Where Is God—in an Ancient Book or in Me?

The word of God is living and active, sharper than any
two-edged sword, piercing to the division of soul and
of spirit, of joints and of marrow, and discerning the
thoughts and intentions of the heart. And no creature
is hidden from his sight, but all are naked and exposed
to the eyes of him to whom we must give account.

HEBREWS 4:12–13

A FEW YEARS AGO, I lost a friend to an unbiblical marriage and to a struggle between two worlds: the world of unbiblical spirituality and the world of biblical faith.

Jessica was a strong Christian and on fire for the gospel. But she met a man who fed her the lie that being a spiritual person is kinder than being a biblical Christian. Whether she believed the lie or just loved the man, I do not know.

Jessica had just turned forty and was on the rebound from a broken engagement (with a man who claimed to be a Christian but did not act like one). She shifted quickly from her broken engagement to a short-term mission field in a poverty-stricken land. When she returned from the field, she resumed her work as assistant director of small groups and women's counseling at her faithful church.

She felt that her entire life was out of sorts, like many women who try to pick up the pieces after a broken engagement and then return from overseas. Giving her heart to a man who broke it had shattered all her hope of ever being married. Seeing brutal poverty on the mission field and then having no spiritual resources to deal with what seemed to be daily unanswered prayer had broken her. Having seen real suffering on the mission field led her to wonder if her relatively comfortable life back home could possibly be God's will. She could depend on three meals a day and go to Target on a whim, but the people she'd left behind with promises of prayer could no sooner imagine the privileges of her world than they could walk on the moon. Jessica was tender to the Lord and shaken by what she had lost, both in her personal life and in her missionary experience.

Jessica's faith was shaken, to be sure. Sometimes she would wake up in the middle of the night in a panic attack, thinking she heard moaning from a child's hunger. She wondered what God was doing (or not doing) in the lives of poor people she'd left behind. There was a lot to take in.

Jessica had returned home just before Christmas. Her church was in a joyful pitch, and there was so much organizing and celebrating to do. She was busy, but no one (including me) realized how heavy her heart was and how the bright Christmas lights and frenzied motion of the Christmas season dug a hole in her heart.

And then Jeremy came along.

Jeremy was a perpetually nice guy with a steady desk job and a loyal personality. Raised by Christians but not one himself, Jeremy could understand Christian lingo. He said he could never suspend his imagination sufficiently to believe in the God of the Bible. He also hated the way that the Bible seems to put life into such a small box. So black and white. So harsh. Jeremy majored in pluralism—listening to as many points of view as there were people to express them.

Jeremy said he was spiritual, but not Christian. He liked a little Buddha and a little Carl Jung, and he didn't like rules, hierarchies, or anything that started with "Thou shalt not."

God was inside him, he said, and that was all he needed. "Kindness to all" was his motto.

He saw no point in being judgmental to people by using the morality of the Bible against their will. He was open-minded, and he believed that his gay friends should have whatever privileges he had. He was a supporter of Planned Parenthood and staunchly defended a woman's "right to choose." He cringed when Christians denied evolution. He tried to live by the Golden Rule. And he thought that the Christian category of sin was the way that one group of people exercised their unearned privilege over another. He believed that Christian churches—including the one that his parents and Jessica attended—were filled with spiritual abuse. He learned that last tidbit in a sociology class in college, and it made sense to him. Jeremy valued his public-school education and believed that it helped him see life from all points of view without having to pick one. The only people with whom he found himself at odds were Christians who believe that the Bible is true. He dismissed them as small-minded bigots. They were the only people on the planet who really annoyed him. Although he loved his parents and older brother, he put them in this camp, and it drove a wedge between them. Especially during Christmas.

Jeremy and Jessica became friends. Jessica said Jeremy was the best listener she had ever met. He was the only one who could understand why she felt so out of sorts after her broken engagement. And he agreed that God had not answered her prayers for the poor children she tried to save while on the mission field. He confirmed that Christmas was all glitter and no gold. He put life in this perspective: Do your best and leave the world a better place than you found it. The credit goes to you for your hard work, not some cultural invention that we call Jesus.

Just when Jessica couldn't handle one more letdown, her dad was diagnosed with cancer. Her mom was a faithful prayer warrior, but Jessica wasn't sure God was even listening to her anymore. She would rather live with her feet on solid ground than believe one more empty promise from anyone, least of all the God she had followed since she was four. She felt betrayed, abandoned, and left out in the cold. Her Christian friends told her to pray more, which just made her feel worse. Jeremy told her not to pray to God anymore. All it was doing was getting her hopes up. Jeremy said that fate would have its course and that he would be there for her on the other side, no matter what.

Her father went through chemotherapy and radiation through the dark of winter. He lost 50 pounds and all his hair.

Jeremy tried not to eat meat or kill bugs. He valued pantheism and pacifism. He believed that every creature has a divine power within, and strongly felt that spirituality is something we all hold in our hearts. Being open-minded, Jeremy believed that all religions have something to teach. It grieved him that religion divides people, for he believed that if only we could bring all the religions of the world together, we could behold real spirituality. If only we could remember that we are one with the universe, perhaps we could achieve world peace.

Jeremy was a rock to Jessica. He stuck with her through all of the heartache. And when her father recovered from cancer, he broke down in tears, and they cried together. Jessica knew she was supposed to thank God for her father's cancer remission, but she just couldn't get herself to do this. Her father's life—like the lives of the children she left in poverty—seemed to lack rhyme or reason. She was glad that her father was one of the lucky ones. But luck just seemed to make Jessica more anxious. So arbitrary. Life felt cold and purposeless. And God? Well, he seemed either distant or fickle.

Jessica knew she was not supposed to fall in love with an unbeliever. But she couldn't help it. She prayed that God would intervene if he did not want her to marry Jeremy. He didn't, and Jessica took Jeremy's proposal as a blessing.

Jeremy and Jessica got engaged.

Her Christian friends and pastors and parents counseled against it.

One night, two months before the wedding, Jessica brought Jeremy to our home for dinner. We enjoyed pleasant conversation about work and wedding plans.

After dinner, the children distributed Bibles to everyone at the table, and Kent turned in his Bible to where we had left off the night before, to Luke 14:26–33. When I saw the text that we would be studying, I broke out in a cold sweat, but Kent was nonplussed. He does not modify the Bible passage for the guests at the table. Kent asked for the Lord's blessing on our understanding of this text, and then he began to read:

Now great crowds accompanied him, and he turned and said to them, "If anyone comes to me and does not hate [Jeremy almost jumped out of his seat at this] his own father and mother and wife and children and brothers and sisters, yes, even his own life, he cannot be my disciple. . . . For which of you, desiring to build a tower, does not first sit down and count the cost, whether he has enough to complete it? Otherwise, when he has laid a foundation, and is not able to finish, all who see it begin to mock him, saying, 'This man began to build and was not able to finish.' Or what king, going out to encounter another king in war, will not sit down first and deliberate whether he is able with ten thousand to meet him who comes against him with twenty thousand? And if not, while the other is yet a great way off, he sends a delegation and asks for terms of peace. So therefore, any one of you who does not renounce all that he has cannot be my disciple." (Luke 14:25–33)

Jeremy was breathing heavily and starting to twist the left side of his moustache between his thumb and index finger. Jessica leaned over and said, "Honey, we don't have to stay. Let's just go." But Jeremy didn't want to be placated. Mr. Steady-Eddy flew the coop and into a rage.

"How can you follow a God who tells you to hate?"

Jessica was mortified and started to apologize for Jeremy.

Kent said, "Jeremy, do you want to know how Christians interpret this passage?"

"No! I don't want any of your hate spewed my way!"

Visibly shaking, Jeremy bolted from his chair, turned to my children, ages ten and thirteen at the time, and said, "I'm really sorry for you, that you had to have people like these as parents. Don't believe them!" and he charged out of the room.

We sat in stunned silence. Jeremy returned for Jessica, and Kent asked him if he was willing to hear how we interpret this passage. Kent stood stoically and said, "The words of the New Testament—including the word 'hate' here—are translated from Greek. Luke uses hyperbole—exaggeration—to make a comparison about the order of loyalty for all Christians. I think if we slowed down and talked this out, it would help you to understand it before you reject it."

Jeremy wouldn't sit down, but he did listen. Kent went on:

This is Jesus's loyalty test. Disciples of Christ are called to love him first before others, and to love him deeply and without reservation, so that from the world's point of view, it looks like hate or rejection of everyone else. From the world's point of view, our love for Jesus looks excessive, because we are not prioritizing things the way the world does. Of course we love our children and our spouse and our neighbors. But we love them less than we do the Lord. "Hate" in this passage can be translated "love less."

Kent stopped, giving time to Jeremy to respond.

Jeremy, shaking, said, "This is vile, fanatical hate speech that you are spewing at me! That's legalism and fundamentalism!" And then turning to Jessica, he said, "You will be my 'Jesus,' Jess. I promise to love you unreservedly so that by comparison I hate all else, including these false gods!" Turning to our children, Jeremy shouted, "Don't believe a word of this garbage!" and then he ran out the door and sat in the car, waiting for Jessica.

We asked Jessica to take a deep breath and take a long look at the man she was going to marry. God had just given her a clear picture.

Jessica knew the Lord.

Jessica knew what she was rejecting.

In tears, she apologized to Knox and Mary. Her apology was sincere. She knew that Jeremy's words were violent and wrong and should have been directed to me or Kent—if they were going to be directed to anyone—but not the children. In the end, Jessica followed Jeremy. She walked out the door, and we have never seen her since.

After Jessica left, Kent turned to our children, and we started to discuss what had happened. Children in a pastor's home often receive the anger and rejection of the world long before they are ready. But this was the first time anyone had come at them in a verbal rage. Jeremy had clearly told them to defy Christ and their parents. It was one of the first times that the cold hand of pure evil had descended upon them.

We found out that night that this brought the high stakes of faith into focus. Knox and Mary had just made professions of faith and joined with our church in the covenant of church membership. The youngest children in a family made up of adoption and foster care, they have older adopted siblings who bear the scars of child abuse, parental neglect, and atheism.

Knox and Mary were shaken up, to be sure. They had not witnessed an adult so out of control. They also loved Jessica and intuitively perceived she was marrying a petty man.

Kent also pointed out that while we were reading the Bible in its literary context to make sense of the word *hate*, it was Jeremy who was reading it literally, as though words just operate like so many wooden planks on a dock. It was interesting to ponder. Jeremy was accusing us of being literalists, but in truth we were reading the passage in its fullest meaning.

It was a lot to ponder for all of us. How many people reject Jesus, the Word made flesh, because he is buried in a false interpretation of Scripture? How many people follow a paper-mache Jesus, created by cutting away the words of Scripture that offend? While you can't be saved by your theology, you can be taken dangerously off course by an unbiblical one. It reminded us to beg Jesus in prayer to keep our hearts firmly rooted in his word. Without the word, our anchor, we are all tiny rowboats tossed in a tempestuous storm.

After washing the dishes and walking the dogs and playing a few family rounds of Uno, Knox said he was scared for Miss Jessica. Kent said, "When we love Jesus first, we love others safely. When we love others first, we don't love others safely. I'm scared for Miss Jessica too, so we need to keep praying for her."

It's Still All Very Personal

As you know, I lived for a decade as a lesbian feminist-activist English professor. The world we live in now is the one I helped create. This has caused more dark nights of the soul than I can count. That the Bible was a violent, groundless book composed of illegitimate sources and structures was a foundational idea for me when I was an atheist lesbian. When I met Pastor Ken Smith and he told me that every word of the Bible is true and that the Bible validates itself, I said, "Let me get this straight. You have one book that defends itself on the grounds of its own truth claims—which is, at best, a circular argument—and meanwhile I have fifty people in my office that call this absurd foolishness, right?"

Ken, never one to be discouraged by atheism, said, "Right! So, let's get together tonight, and I will make my case."

We did. Ken gave me his lecture "A Summary of the Bible."

That night was a watershed for me. I was not converted then, but Ken's lecture made me realize something—the Christian faith depends not on what my lesbianism meant but on what the Bible is and says. My conversion hinged not on what my flesh craved but on who Jesus is. Who Jesus is and what the Bible is are inseparable. Jesus is alive, and so is the Bible. And that is what set it apart from all the other books on my shelf that denied him.

A tiny crack of light opened, and I couldn't stop looking at it, wondering if there was more to behold, wondering if Jesus had a little light left over for me, and wondering what my life would look like if I walked toward it.

We live in a world that believes being a spiritual person is kinder than being a biblical Christian. At first it might sound like "being a spiritual person" and "being a biblical Christian" could be two versions of the same thing. Christians are filled with the Holy Spirit, not the spirit of the age. The difference between "being a spiritual person" and "being a biblical Christian" lies in content, not emphasis. Biblical faith starts and finishes with a distinct God who is set apart from us and who made us. And this truth stands in opposition to the values of our world. Christ's word makes kingdoms rise and fall. It proclaims truths and exposes lies. It offers salvation and perfect peace.

What Is the Difference between Unbiblical Spirituality and Biblical Faith?

Peter Jones contends that we are not dealing with secularism—unbelief. If we were, that would be easier to dismantle. Instead we are dealing with competing religions. In *The Other Worldview: Exposing Christianity's Greatest Threat*, he says that it is not only the lack of genuinely converted Christians in the church but also the destruction of Christian culture that has made our world unsafe, unsavory, and unrecognizable: "Many of the traditional plausibility structures that gave life meaning and significance under Christian influence in the West are unrecognizable:

1. Morality is relativized by varied (and often contradictory) personal or social conventions.
2. Honesty means being true to one's inner commitments and longing more than to external expectations or objective facts.
3. Acceptable models of sexuality and family allow various combinations of persons and genders.
4. Marriage is often functionally indistinguishable from mutually convenient cohabitation.
5. Motherhood is celebrated in the same breath with abortion on demand."[1]

Peter Jones and I are not recommending returning to the good old days (whenever that was). We are not recommending that we go backward. We are recommending reformation and repentance.

The new, unbiblical spirituality has deep roots in paganism but also in materialism. Jones writes, "Spirituality has become a do-it-yourself life hobby that blends ancient Eastern practices with modern consumer sensibilities."[2]

---

1 Peter Jones, *The Other Worldview: Exposing Christianity's Greatest Threat* (Bellingham, WA: Kirkdale Press, 2015), 4.
2 Jones, *The Other Worldview*, 5.

What Happens When People Dress Their
Christian Faith in Pagan Clothes?

As Western culture moved from secularism to paganism, as opposition to the Bible and to Christ moved from antireligion to competing religion, something strange happened. Well-meaning Christians started to see conformity to culture as missional: "Emergent church leader Kester Brewin, for example, believes we must admit 'our dependence on [our] host culture' and 'open ourselves to . . . and adapt to it,' recognizing its 'essential goodness.'"[3] Somehow, and for some reason, we inhabit a divided evangelicalism, one that seeks conformity to the world over hearing the word from God. It seeks acceptance. It is this kind of paganism—one that wears the clothes of Christianity—in which many of our daughters and sons are lost (for now).

What makes one child's faith stand against the world and another fall in conformity to it? The word of God is our answer. And the word of God is an answer of hope. Jesus is our hope, and he is not done with any of us. He is not done with me or you or Jessica or the loved one who is on your heart as you read these words. The gospel doesn't just make us nicer versions of ourselves. The gospel gives us a new nature and the power to live for the glory of God. Paul says, and we say with him, "I am not ashamed of the gospel, for it is the power of God for salvation to everyone who believes, to the Jew first and also to the Greek. For in it the righteousness of God is revealed from faith for faith, as it is written, 'The righteous shall live by faith'" (Rom. 1:16). God provides the righteousness, not only the attribute of perfect righteousness but applied righteousness through Jesus Christ's perfect life and atoning death.

3 Jones, *The Other Worldview*, 140.

This righteousness goes from faith to faith and only from faith to faith. The power of Christ's atoning blood is imputed only through faith, and it ensures that peace with God forever makes everything right—even when our whole world is falling apart.

6

The Bible Knows Me Better
than I Know Myself

ON MAY 8, 1997, Pastor Ken Smith of the Syracuse Reformed Presbyterian Church wrote a letter to one notorious Dr. Rosaria Champagne, lesbian professor of English and women's studies at Syracuse University. It would turn out to be the first contact in a friendship that would forever change my life. He wrote this letter in response to an editorial I wrote, which appeared in the *Syracuse Post Standard*, titled, "Promise Keepers' Message Is a Danger to Democracy."[1] I later learned that one of the elders of the church slapped my editorial down on Ken's desk and declared, "We need to shut this woman up!" Ken reportedly replied, "Well perhaps Floy and I should invite her to dinner." The rest is, as they say, history.

Ken's first contact with me was his May 8 letter. In it, he said:

---

1 Rosaria Butterfield, "Promise Keepers' Message Is a Danger to Democracy," *Syracuse Post Standard*, April 15, 1997, A-9. Also see Anne M. Stiles, "Prof. Decries 'Promise Keepers,'" *Crimson*, October 24, 1997, https://www.thecrimson.com/.

Dear Ms. Champagne,

It was with keen interest I read your "Comment" in the paper re Promise Keepers. For quite a number of years now I have had a concern for what has been and not been happening with men in our culture; so I too, have had a keen interest in this movement inspired by Bill McCartney.

Coming to Syracuse from Pittsburgh, I have a friend there who recently participated in Promise Keepers when it visited Pittsburgh. As a woman, she could not be a regular attender; but because of her keen interest, she volunteered. I thought you might like to read what she wrote about her experience. She and I have had some intense conversations about the relationship of men and women—not always agreeing—but always maintaining respect for one another. Anyhow, I send this along [articles written by Ken's friend] as grist for the mill.

Could I inquire of you about a question I have had since coming to the City? How can I as a local minister interested in university students encourage an acquaintance with the Bible? From what I have observed, most university students are woefully ignorant of simply what the Bible says. Their opinions are largely forged by the comments—true or not—of others when it comes to the content of the Bible. So, how then can they appreciate Western literature with all of its allusions to Scripture? And in terms of English majors, how can they become better educated in this book that has no doubt had more influence on our culture than any other single volume? That is my concern.

Would you have any suggestions? For example I have a presentation which I have actually given in university classrooms on "A Book Review of the Bible." It takes about 30–40 minutes to present; and its purpose is to acquaint persons with the central theme of the book. Would that be admissible in an English class?[2]

Ken's letter concluded with an invitation to discuss this more fully in person.

I was intrigued by everything in Ken's letter. I didn't know that there existed in the land of the living a "true believer" who just wanted to have an honest discussion and not manipulate me. I had never read the Bible, and yet I, like the students he referred to, had no trouble critiquing it. I took that as a helpful rebuke. And as I was embarking on a book project criticizing the Bible and its followers for hating people like me, I realized that Ken Smith could be very helpful to me. I realized that Ken Smith could be my unpaid research assistant. I wanted to hear his lecture for myself, and I wanted to read the Bible through his eyes, understanding what assumptions and ideas he brought to the text.

I picked up the phone and called his office. Ken was warm and engaging, and I approached our upcoming meeting, which was to include a meal, with anticipation. One meal led to many, many more. After a few months into our friendship, Ken asked me again about delivering a lecture to my students. I told him that I never present material to my students that I have not fully reviewed first, and I asked him if he would deliver that lecture to one student—me. He responded with characteristic warmth and joy, and we set a date for Ken Smith to deliver to me his lecture, "A Summary of the Bible."

I selected a date where I was sure to have the house to myself—not an easy feat when you live communally. I served a

2 Personal correspondence from Pastor Ken Smith, May 8, 1997, quoted with permission from the author. Ken Smith's lecture, "A Summary of the Bible," was transcribed by his daughter-in-law, Vicki Smith, and is used with permission from the author.

fresh lettuce salad and poached salmon from the Syracuse Fresh Seafood Market. After dinner, I brought Floy a steaming mug of peach tea. Floy loved peach tea, and I would later learn that she loved it in the dead of winter and heat of summer with equal affection. Ken pulled out his lecture, and I pulled out my pen and notebook. He began:

> The Bible begins with these words: "In the beginning God created the heavens and the earth," Genesis 1:1. We can therefore call this creation. According to the Bible there actually was a beginning, a beginning of time and space, so one can really know the historical origin of things.

From the get-go it appeared that I was going to disagree with everything Ken said. So I drew a line down the center of my notebook page and launched the two-column note-taking system I employed for unfriendly ideas. The left column was reserved for what Ken said and the right column for what I believed. Ken went on:

> Now this most basic verse in the Bible states more. It makes plain that at the time of the beginning, God existed. He is in fact eternal. So at the outset, the Bible tells us that we live in what has been called the supernatural reality. Everything there is, in other words, cannot be judged on the basis of simply the material or physical. God the Father, God the Son, and God the Holy Spirit existed before the beginning, and it was this Trinity who decided to create. In fact, the first chapter of Genesis tells us they actually conferred during the process.

In my column I wrote: "Yikes" and "This is nuts" and "What would Marx say?" I also wrote a big question mark next to the idea that the Trinity existed in the Old Testament. Wasn't Jesus born in the New Testament? And I thought the Holy Spirit only came into existence after Jesus's death. If I thought this lecture was going to be some kind of free-for-all about homosexuality being a sin, I was dead wrong. I found this lecture singularly more offensive. Ken continued:

> So the Bible begins therefore by asserting God's reality and that it was He who originated the material universe. In so doing, it also answers a question troubling many persons: the question *Who am I?* Rather than being just a "speck of protoplasm float-ing on a sea of meaninglessness," as one man described himself, man, according to the Bible, is a creation of God. The Bible says he was made in God's image! Man really is somebody! And as such he first of all has immeasurable value and worth! He is not a zero. Besides worth, he also has purpose and responsibility. God designed man with something particular in view, and man despairs unless he fulfills it.

Ken made a point to tell me that "man" refers to "man and woman" and reminded me that I was not to take offense to common sense. Nothing makes me want to take offense more than someone telling me not to take offense. I could conjure up prepared responses that illustrated my disdain and rejection of everything Ken Smith was saying. I scratched heated notes. As I searched my heart, I realized that I felt something deeper than disdain—Ken's words made me feel guilt and shame and disgust. It took a year of Bible reading to make the link between being told that I have immeasurable worth and my violent internal sense of shame. After a year of Bible reading with repentance, my heart, head, and soul began to arrive at a fragile consensus. The lecture continued:

> So, God began by creating the first man, Adam, and the first woman, his wife, Eve, and He put them in a beautiful place called the garden of Eden. Here this first couple enjoyed their worth and purpose before God. It really was paradise!

In the right-hand column of my notes, I wrote, "What is my worth and purpose before God?" No one had ever asked me such a question. I didn't even know that such a question had an answer.

> Now God had certainly showed that He loved man, but He also wanted the man to love Him. God is personal after all. He is living. He can be known, communicated with, loved. So God arranged for man to choose to show his own appreciation and love for his Creator. What He did was this: He placed a tree in the garden and made it "off limits." He told Adam not to eat any of the fruit from it. It wasn't that there was something wrong with the tree. God wanted Adam to choose to obey Him, and this was man's test. To eat of the tree would be to choose to disobey God and go "independent," or just do his own thing. God warned him that if he chose to eat from it, Adam would certainly die. To disobey God is to choose death. Man's created purpose was to love and serve God. Would he choose to obey or disobey?
>
> The Bible tells us plainly that under the temptation of Satan, a rebellious and fallen angel appearing as a talking snake, Adam and Eve willfully chose to eat of that tree! Instead of choosing to love God, they chose their own way. They rebelled against God. And that is the record of how sin historically came into

the world. Man, by his own choice, had brought down on himself and all his descendants the consequences of his rebellion, about which God had warned him: guilt, shame, misery, and ultimately death. And even the ground would suffer the effect of God's curse on man for sin.

In my reaction column, I wrote, "Why so many binary oppositions?" Binary oppositions—black and white, either/or—these were the opposite of postmodern thinking. My thinking at the time was postmodern: everything was a shade of gray, everything was nuanced and contextualized and subjective. Ken's lecture made clear that what I called "personal autonomy," the Bible called "sin." I bristled.

Now the whole story could have ended here. God could have pulled off a "cosmic abortion" and just started again. But His plan was to establish another arrangement or "covenant" by which He would rescue a people for Himself in a restored kingdom. We catch a glimpse of that plan in figurative language in Genesis 3:15, where God said He would bring this all about through the seed of the woman who would crush the head of the serpent. And that is what the whole rest of the Bible is about: how God would do it! So our first parents, Adam and Eve, were given a promise of hope.

How intriguing, I thought. Ken believes that Adam and Eve were actual historical people, like George Washington and Rosa Parks! I realized that the only thing I knew about Adam and Eve was what John Milton said about them in *Paradise Lost*. Probably not the most useful reference in this context, I decided.

This promise of the seed was first spoken in the presence of Adam and Eve. Later God renewed it to Noah, the man who built the ark at the time of the great flood. Then one of his descendants, a herdsman named Abraham, received it even more specifically. God told him that through his seed all the nations of the earth would be blessed. Abraham had a son named Isaac, to whom the promise came, and Isaac had twin sons, Jacob and Esau, and the promise went to Jacob, whose name was later changed to "Israel." Jacob had twelve sons, and the promise went to Judah, and we know his descendants popularly as "Jews." So, God made clear that through the children of Israel this seed—or specifically, anointed one, the Messiah—would eventually come.

Wow, I thought. Ken talks about these events in the Bible as if they are true. He treats the Bible like real history.

Now when one begins to read the second book of the Bible, Exodus, the children of Israel have gone down to Egypt because of a famine, but now after four hundred years they have become a nation of probably over two million. The problem was they had become enslaved to the Egyptians and were in great distress. But God had not forgotten His promise. He raised up a man named Moses, and Moses with God's help led that nation out of Egypt. But first they sacrificed a lamb, sprinkled the blood on the doorposts so that the angel of death coming on Egypt would pass over that home. That became an annual memorial called "the Passover." Then they miraculously crossed the Red Sea and came to a craggy peak called Mount Sinai. There on Sinai, a place you can visit today, God called

Moses up to meet with Him, and on that historical occasion God gave Moses His law, or what is commonly called the Ten Commandments.

This law came from God, whom the Bible describes as holy, pure, good, and everything right. The law reflects His character. And so we know that there is after all a right and a wrong. It is because God is. And what is compatible with Him is right or righteous. What is not is wrong or wicked. But when man now looks at this law of God and compares himself to it, he suddenly realizes he is not holy. He doesn't have that kind of character. He is in fact un-Godlike. Why is it that man gets angry and loses his temper, gets depressed, is self-centered, discontent, and full of hate, murder, and war? The answer is: man is, in fact, a law breaker, not a law keeper! Like Adam and Eve, he has chosen his own independent way apart from God. He is a sinner! While it is difficult for us to admit this, nonetheless it gives a plausible answer to the question, What am I like? The Bible simply says man has become a rebel against God and His law, and so he suffers the consequences.

There was no one in my life who said such things. Through simple deduction, Ken was telling me that I was a sinner, that I was wicked, and that I was a rebel. I thought religious folks believed that "god" (whatever that meant) was in my heart. Ken's presentation stood in such contrast to everything I believed that I wondered who was right. I was disarmed.

Now some people seem to think that God gave the Ten Commandments so that by obeying them they could find favor with God and go to heaven. Actually, this is not true. God had delivered them from Egypt, not by their efforts, but by His gracious love represented in the Passover. They were now God's delivered people! God gave His law to Moses in Exodus 20 so His people . . . could know what God desired of them. They failed to live up to those commandments, proving what the New Testament says, "For by the law is the knowledge of sin" (Romans 3:20).

So how could such sinful persons hope to be able to worship and serve such a holy God? To answer that dilemma, God included with the Ten Commandments another part of His law which showed how sinners under the condemnation of death could find acceptance with Him. Since the first sin committed by Adam had brought death as its curse, so it would only be through death of sacrifice that God could accept man and his worship. . . . While it still may sound strange to many people, the Bible shows us that God's character includes justice. Sin must be punished by death. So God gave careful instructions about offering sacrifices, including a tent as a place of worship, sometimes called the tabernacle, and including an altar for offering sacrifices and priests to offer them. When a person offered a sacrifice, he laid his hands on the steer, or sheep, or birds, symbolizing the guilt passing on to the animal, and so the animal must die as a substitute for the worshiper.

I never thought about what animal sacrifices in the Old Testament symbolized. It had never occurred to me that God demanded a payment for sin. I thought God just looked away if we did the best we could and lived life with integrity. The idea that justice always demands payment made sense but also felt harsh. I shuddered to think about all of those innocent animals who died as sacrifices for sin.

When one begins to read the New Testament, he discovers something is really new! The promised one is coming! Born of a young teenager named Mary, He was supernaturally conceived in her by the Holy Spirit as announced by an angel. Joseph, to whom she was engaged, also got a similar message so he did not have to think she had been unfaithful when she became pregnant. So this is the way God's Son came into the world. God the Father, God the Son, and God the Holy Spirit had arranged or "covenanted" that it would be God's Son who would offer himself to come as the "seed" of the woman, exactly in line with the way the prophets in the Old Testament had foretold. Joseph was instructed to name the baby "Jesus," for "He would save His people from their sins" (Matthew 1:21). So it happened. He was born in Bethlehem and grew up in Nazareth in his step-father's carpenter shop, and there He spent the first thirty years of His earthly life.

So Ken also believed that a virgin can have a baby and that angels are real. That's a lot to swallow.

At thirty Jesus began to carry out His specific purpose in coming into the world. A man named John, nicknamed "the baptizer," introduced him. One day, John pointed to Jesus and said, "Behold! The Lamb of God who takes away the sin of the world!" (John 1:29). That title may sound strange unless one remembers what we said about the necessity of sacrifices or death for acceptance with God. Remember that Passover lamb in Egypt? The significant thing about this statement is that God Himself in history was sending His Son Jesus into the world to be His sacrifice for sin! God was indeed carrying out His promise or covenant through the seed of the woman. . . . One could also say it this way: God Himself would offer a sacrifice to save His people from eternal death. He would indeed restore them to His eternal fellowship.

The words "God Himself in history was sending His Son Jesus" made clear that Ken was saying this was *the* history of the world. And unlike all of the histories that we postmodernists discussed—women's history, postcolonial history, Western history, African-American history—this history found in the Bible seemed to claim that it unified them all. This made me suspicious. How could one history bind all people together? And, I wondered, how do I (and do I?) fit in here?

Everywhere Jesus went, He went about doing good. Where Adam had failed to love God and obey Him, Jesus as true man was perfectly responsive to doing God's will. He served God by choice. He kept the Law of God perfectly! No flaws! He was in the sight of God truly righteous. And God was thoroughly pleased with Him. But beyond keeping the Law, Jesus showed that He had come from God by the miracles he performed. He healed the sick, cured cripples, gave sight to the blind, hearing to the deaf, and on certain occasions, raised persons from death. Everything about Jesus' life and service pointed to God. He was, in fact, God come in the flesh! And as such He would accomplish for us what Adam had forfeited.

I really didn't understand why Ken kept talking about God the Father now that Jesus was in the world. I had been raised in the Roman Catholic Church, and I knew the sign of the cross meant, "In the name of the Father and of the Son and of the Holy Spirit," but the Trinity was so confusing. I had mostly attended Roman Catholic schools, but I hadn't thought about God in years. And now I was not just across the table from someone who wanted to talk about God in a theoretical way—no, Ken and Floy had a real faith, and it was clear that their faith had a real object, the God of the universe. While I didn't understand what they believed, it was evident that they believed something real and vital and true.

But Jesus also preached. He told people about God, about themselves, about the world, and about why He had come. He showed by His love and concern that people—men, women and children—had worth and value; but yet He spoke plainly to them of their sin against God and His judgment awaiting them. He bluntly told people, "Repent!" He not only invited them to turn from self-centeredness and pride and find forgiveness with God through Him. He exposed self-righteous religion as a farce. He spent time with the social outcasts and gave them hope through His love for them. When people heard Jesus, they heard truth. So, many came to Him in faith. But lawbreakers do not naturally like to hear someone pointing out their sins, especially when it's true, and even if it is God himself saying it. So you might imagine what happened.

At this point in Ken's lecture, I was riveted. When Ken said, "He told people . . . about themselves," I felt a palpable sense of solid ground beneath my feet. I wondered, does God know me? Does God know me better than anyone? Could this be true?

The religious leaders stirred up the crowds against Jesus, drummed up false charges against Him, and pressured the Roman governor Pilate to sentence Him to death. . . . At a place called Calvary, on a hill outside Jerusalem's walls, Jesus was nailed to a cross and left to die. And Jesus willingly suffered that horrible death, which included . . . punishment in hell. That is why He had come after all. While His murderers, both Jews and Gentiles, thought they were rid of Him, their plot fell right into the plan of God. In fact, they became the means by which God's sacrifice for sin, the Lamb of God, the real Passover lamb, had been offered. He died and was buried. Yet three days later, Jesus miraculously came back to life! He rose from the dead! He finished what He had come to earth to do.

I pondered this. Jesus suffered in hell? I remembered this from the Apostles' Creed, but I had never understood that if he was really our Passover lamb, he would have to go to suffer the wrath of God for the payment of sin. I had always thought of the death of Jesus as a horrific murder, not a purposeful ransom. And where, I wondered, do I fit in to this story? Ken kept lecturing.

So here we have the heart of the Bible's message. One passage says it like this: "For I delivered to you first of all that which I also received: that Christ died for our sins according to the Scriptures, and that He was buried, and that He rose again the third day according to the Scriptures" (1 Corinthians 15:3–4). This focal point of history—the death, burial, and resurrection of Jesus—points out the answer to man's question, What do I need? Of all the things man thinks he needs, the Bible says his basic need is to be brought back into a right relationship with his Creator, God. Without that, he is doomed and unfulfilled. So it is of first importance to recognize in the life and death and resurrection of Jesus how God calls us into this right relationship with Himself. According to the Bible, it is only through Jesus.

The focal point of history is the death, burial, and resurrection of Jesus? I thought the focal point of history is the oppression of people of color and violence against women. Can history have two focal points? What do I have to reject in order to believe that the focal point of history is the death, burial, and resurrection of Jesus?

> What then does God call on us to do? Certainly He does not tell us just to be good and save ourselves? No, He calls men, women, and children and the whole world to come to Jesus as their sacrifice for their sin. In fact, He commands it. God offers mercy and forgiveness to every sinner who looks to Jesus's death on the cross as the completed sacrifice for his sin and offenses against Him. And when we accept that mercy and lean by faith on Jesus as our substitute, we are in fact turning away from our self-centered, sinful lifestyle back to obeying God with our whole life and escaping eternal judgment. That's why Christians speak of "being saved." Jesus becomes both our Savior and our King. His will becomes our concern, just like it had been with Adam before he sinned. By faith in Jesus, we live in a restored relationship with God!

There it is—"being saved," the need to be a born-again Christian. In my lesbian, feminist world, there was no category of people more hated and despised than this one.

But let's finish the story. A short time after Jesus rose from the dead, He returned to God the Father in heaven. And the Bible states that He is there today, alive and ruling by His Holy Spirit, whom He sent to live in His people. As His disciples watched Him ascend into the clouds, two angels appeared and told them, "This same Jesus, who was taken up from you into heaven, will so come in like manner as you saw Him go into heaven" (Acts 1:11). And this means that Jesus will, in time and space, come to earth again.

Jesus as King sounded pretty frightening to me. I thought Jesus was for personal encouragement and Sunday-morning community. Did Ken really believe that Jesus was the King? Of the whole world?

Unlike His coming as a baby, however, this time He will come with power and splendor. And the Bible says that everyone will see Him. We don't know how all of that will work out, but we know from the Bible that He will come, and everyone will appear before Him for a final judgment. In John 5:28–29, Jesus said it this way: "The hour is coming when all who are in the graves will hear His voice and come forth—those who have done good, to the resurrection of life [or what the Bible calls heaven], and those that have done evil, to the resurrection of condemnation [or what the Bible calls hell or eternal death]."

Are heaven and hell real places? I wondered.

So when a person considers, "What is going to happen to me?" the Bible is clear. He is going to meet Jesus Christ. And Jesus Christ, God's appointed King, will pronounce judgment. Those persons who have put their trust in Jesus as their sacrificial substitute and submitted to His rule will enjoy everlasting life with God and His people in what the Bible calls "new heavens and a new earth," His new paradise (2 Peter 3:13). In fact, according to Jesus's word in John 5:24, persons believing in Jesus won't even need to wonder about it, because he says such a person "shall not come into judgment, but has passed from death into life." So a believer in Jesus receives eternal life the moment in time when he believes.

On the other hand, those who neglect or refuse Christ's sacrifice for sin, persisting in their own self-trust and rebellion against God and His word are choosing a terrifying future. They are consigning themselves to an eternal hell under God's anger. Revelation 20:14 calls this "the second death" and a "lake of fire." No words can fully convey the pain and remorse of having to live with one's self forever, alone, separated from everyone, God-forsaken. It's like refusing to kill that Passover lamb and putting the blood on the door. The death angel does not pass over, but destroys with eternal death.

Ken was done, and he put his manuscript back into a folder. Floy looked at me with compassion and said, "Well dear, this is a lot to take in, I know." My notes from that night don't record anything else. But I remember that when Ken and Floy left and I was home alone, walking my dog in a dark Syracuse night, I wondered what my life would be like if I believed what Ken had said. But at this point in my life, there was no room to believe it, because I already believed other things, and those others things left no room for Jesus. My complex belief system was important to me. I wasn't a blank slate open to God's word. I was filled to the brim with chaos and sin and anxiety and people who looked up to me.

The encroaching darkness gave me a safe covering to probe my inner darkness. Ken and Floy exuded peace, and I wanted that. But I did not want to give anything up to have it. Not yet.

———

Many years later, I started to reflect on the most divisive issue of today within Christianity: what the Bible means and what the Bible is. All the other debates are downstream from this one. And this makes sense, as the person and work of Jesus are manifestly intertwined with the word of God. Other questions that plague readers of the Bible include who the writers were, whether we can trust the text and translation, and the role played by the social location of the reader (our age, race, sex, socioeconomic status, and education, among other factors). Simply saying "The Bible says . . ." isn't going to solve many debates today.

We may believe that we are talking about something like homosexuality only to discover deep into the conversation that we have competing ideas of what the Bible is—what it actually *is*. Is it an ancient book suspect to problems of translation and textual authenticity? Is it a living double-edged sword: "The word of God is living and active, sharper than any two-edged sword, piercing to the division of soul and of spirit, of joints and of marrow, and discerning the thoughts and intentions of the heart" (Heb. 4:12)? Is the Bible a human-composed book whose moral vision requires the brilliance of man? Or does the Bible root out all such prideful self-aggrandizement? "And no creature is hidden from his sight, but all are naked and exposed to the eyes of him to whom we must give account" (Heb. 4:13).

THE BIBLE KNOWS ME BETTER THAN I KNOW MYSELF

In time the Holy Spirit opened my eyes to see that the Bible is an inerrant, infallible, inspired, sufficient, authoritative, and living book, inextricably coupled with our Lord and Savior, his kingship and loving sacrifice for all who believe. But what I have just written is rejected as foolish by many, many people—smart people—who call themselves Christian. We must know what is true, and we must also know how to confront what is false.[3]

Some people believe that the Bible is an outdated ancient book filled with hateful ideas about women. Some people believe that in order for women to be helped and not hurt by Scripture, we must import a feminist interpretation. This has become an effective attack on the integrity of the word of God.

After Ken presented to me his lecture on the Bible, I started to read it for my own sake. I abandoned the book project that had initiated my article on Promise Keepers and my first meeting with the Smiths. I realized that I needed to know for myself if the Bible is true and trustworthy. As I studied and reflected and prayed, I realized that my own feminist worldview was more than just a set of ideas. It was a religion. My question now was

---

3 I highly recommend Michael J. Kruger, *Surviving Religion 101: Letters to a Christian Student on Keeping the Faith in College* (Wheaton, IL: Crossway, 2021), 19. In it he tells of a personal crisis: "In the spring of my freshman year . . . I took a religion course titled Introduction to the New Testament. The professor was a young scholar who was bright, engaging, funny, and persuasive. It didn't take long to see that he lectured with an eye toward evangelicals, even sharing how he was once an evangelical himself not long ago. He used to believe what we believe, he told us. He used to think like we did. And then during his graduate studies, after deep engagement with the text, he realized he could no longer maintain his evangelical beliefs. The New Testament wasn't inspired after all but was full of mistakes. It wasn't reliable but was filled with made-up stories and fabrications. And its original form wasn't even accessible to us but had been badly corrupted by scribes over years of transmission. In short, argued my professor, the historical evangelical position on the Bible is intellectually untenable. It is a book not from God but from men. *You can believe it with your heart—after all, isn't that what religious people do?—but you cannot (or at least should not) believe it with your mind*"; emphasis added.

this: Could I reconcile my feminism with the Bible's teaching? *Reconcile* means "restoration" and seeks friendly relations between two opposing forces. Is feminism "in" the Bible? I wondered. I doubted it. And if it is not in the Bible, is it "biblical" to use it as an interpretive frame?

I came to the decision that the answer was no. But not everyone agrees.

Let's turn now to Lie #3, which says that feminism is good for the church and the world.

LIE #3

FEMINISM IS GOOD
FOR THE WORLD
AND THE CHURCH

7

Do You Know Yourself and
How Do You Know?

He said, "There was a man who had two sons. And
the younger of them said to his father, 'Father, give
me the share of property that is coming to me.' And
he divided his property between them. Not many
days later, the younger son gathered all he had
and took a journey into a far country, and there
he squandered his property in reckless living."

LUKE 15:11–13

IT IS A TERRIBLE FEELING to be pitted between your Lord and
your prodigal daughter. It is easy to confuse the line between loving your prodigal and participating in her indoctrination. No one
wants to be called "unkind." No one wants to lose a relationship
with a child for whom you have spent your life loving, praying, and
sacrificing. But what should you do if your child suddenly rejects
the church and adopts the thinking of the world? What if deep
down you know this is wrong? Dead wrong. Not (only) biblically
and morally wrong, but also out of character for your child. In this

chapter we will look at the way that feminism and the gay rights movement share an ideology that has been especially harmful to women even as it claims to offer rescue.

Standing in opposition to someone's identity is considered an act of abusive violence by gay and feminist Christians. It's a problem that has divided Christian families. But trying to appease the gay rights and feminist movement has not helped either. You know that when you appease your prodigal child, you are crumbling under her demands, and you are lying about what you know to be true. The Bible sees this as man-pleasing. You know you shouldn't fear your child's rejection, but you do. The fear of man is a trap that is hard to flee: "The fear of man brings a snare, but whoever trusts in the LORD shall be safe" (Prov. 29:25 NKJV). The fear of man—or the fear of our lesbian-identifying daughter's rejection—is a snare. A snare is a trap from which you cannot extricate yourself.

Following are four short anecdotes that reveal how this problem has intensified in the last two decades.

- In 2001 I was at the Thanksgiving dinner table of a retired pastor and pastor's wife who had a daughter who called herself a lesbian. They said to me, "When Beth was living with her boyfriend in college, that we could handle. But Beth's lesbian relationship is more than we can bear."

- In 2015 a family visited our church, brokenhearted about their daughter who had come out as a lesbian and was planning to marry a woman. The grieving Christian parents said, "If only Rachel would just live with her lesbian partner and not be so public as to get married, that we could handle. But this lesbian 'marriage' is more than we can bear."

- In 2019 a family visited our church, brokenhearted about their daughter who called herself a lesbian and was "married" to a woman but had also begun calling herself "non-binary," injecting testosterone, and believing herself to be a transgendered man. They said to me, "If only our daughter would just remain as a married lesbian, that we could handle. But the horror of transgenderism is more than we can bear. How can we support self-mutilation—a double mastectomy and a hysterectomy—and her growing facial hair and watching her masquerade as a man? The testosterone she is on has already made her suicidal and violent. And I named her Julie, not John!"

- In 2022 a Christian grandmother wrote to me, broken-hearted about her family. Her lesbian daughter is raising her three-year-old son to be a girl. The heartbroken grandmother said, "I could tolerate the gay rights movement when it was about consenting adults, but now I see it was always targeting the children!"

These are all heartbreaking and true anecdotes. And they all reveal the same problem: you cannot bypass repentance to get to grace. You must deal with sin at its root, and not shallowly, when it becomes a social embarrassment to you. In the first case, the parents had good reason to wish that their daughter was in a heterosexual relationship—it is the pattern that God designed—but ought to have been ashamed of her sin of cohabitating with a boyfriend. In the second case, the parents had good reason not to want the public spectacle of a sham wedding, as that gives a visible appearance of true evil. And in the third case, the parents had good reason to want to protect their daughter from the self-harm of genital mutilation. All three sets of parents are godly, faithful Christians, and in each case, they had a hard time dealing with an adult child's sin. But in each case, they got comfortable with a particular kind of sin. And once they got comfortable with that sin, two terrible problems came to light. First, they grew dull to the seriousness of the first sin; and, second, the job of mortifying the second sin showed itself a more formidable foe than the first sin would have ever been.

Hidden in these stories is a principle about dealing with sin. Sin should affect us so profoundly that the "nuanced" way that the world covers it up ought to feel repulsive. Puritan Thomas Watson puts it this way: "We are to find as much bitterness in weeping for sin as ever we found sweetness in committing it."[1] When our children are living in sin, at the first sight of it, we must be cut to the heart. We must deal with sin at its first occurrence, no matter how pragmatically our society domesticates that sin. And our own sin should bring us to our knees with a sense of shame and remorse that far outweighs the sin of others.

The First and Second Sin . . .

We must deal with sin at its first occurrence because the second will always be worse.

When I was in my late twenties, I took a feminist self-defense class called "Fight Back!" All of the women in my lesbian community took this self-defense class. It was a physically and emotionally

---

1 Thomas Watson, *The Doctrine of Repentance* (1668; repr., Carlisle, PA: Banner of Truth, 2012), 24.

rigorous class. Many of its lessons have stuck with me throughout all the decades since. One was the difference between what the instructor called "the first and second crime." Our instructor said, "If you are in the Walmart parking lot and a man puts a gun to your head and says, 'Get in the car and nothing bad will happen to you,' you need to have that fight right there in the Walmart parking lot. Because if you get shot in the Walmart parking lot, with people milling about, you have a much greater chance of surviving than you would if he puts you into his car. If he gets you in the car, he will take you to an isolated location, and you're a goner." Our self-defense instructor hit this point hard: "No one wants to get shot in the head. But getting shot in the head in a public place is the better option to being dragged off into the woods alone. At the scene of the second crime, you will have no backup."

This lesson has always stuck with me, and I think that it provides a good paradigm for dealing with sin. Face it now. Sin only grows uglier as it goes on.[2]

The Christian life is not about managing collateral damage but about an entire revolution of the heart and soul. If we no longer serve Satan but King Jesus, we need to take stock of which side we are rooting for. We can't split the difference, and we dare not root for Satan's team and call it grace. We can't serve the flesh and the

---

2   You can't domesticate sin, because sin is predatory. But if you normalize sin (parades, drag-queen story hour at the local library, and other oddities are meant to progress you in the normalization process), you grow insensitive to its real danger. This delusion can go on for a long time. It can even get so bad that at the gay Christian conference Revoice18, held at Memorial Presbyterian Church (PCA) in St. Louis, Missouri, someone will deliver teaching such as this: "Redeeming Queer Culture: An Adventure," addressing "What queer treasure, honor, and glory will be brought into the New Jerusalem at the end of time?" Unfortunately for the listeners, the talk was even more heretical than the title. See Owen Strachan, "Will There Be 'Queer Treasure' in the New Jerusalem? On Gay Christianity and Revoice," *Thought Life*, Patheos, July 5, 2018, https://www.patheos.com/.

Spirit simultaneously. Jesus told us so when he warned that the cost of our being disciples to the Lord Jesus Christ requires war with our flesh: "If anyone comes to me and does not hate his own father and mother and wife and children and brothers and sisters, yes, and even his own life, he cannot be my disciple" (Luke 14:26). Let's be clear on two crucial matters: (1) everyone who is a true disciple must be at war with the flesh of lust, the flesh of identity politics, and the flesh that tells you that you know how to love the people around you better than Jesus does, and (2) no one can do this without Spirit-wrought power.

The worldview of feminism, like that of homosexual rights, has powerfully persuaded Christians that those certain areas designated "women's rights" are off-limits to biblical scrutiny. The category sacred to feminism is women's equality with men in all things—to the point of denying the creation ordinance and basic biology. Under feminism, men and women are interchangeable. Under Scripture, such interchangeability is sin.

The Knowledge of God and That of Ourselves Are Connected

John Calvin writes: "It is certain that man never achieves a clear knowledge of himself unless he has first looked upon God's face and then descends from contemplating him to scrutinize himself."[3] Issuing a stern warning against our motives, our intentions, our desires, and our excuses as a fount of wisdom, Calvin writes: "Because all of us are inclined by nature to hypocrisy, a kind of empty image of righteousness in place of righteousness itself abundantly satisfies us."[4]

---

3   John Calvin, *Institutes of the Christian Religion*, ed. John T. McNeill, trans. Ford Lewis Battles (Philadelphia: Westminster Press, 1960), 1.1.2.

4   Calvin, *Institutes*, 1.1.2.

John Calvin's take on the invitation to know ourselves is especially instructive as I look back through the decades and try to make sense of my past lesbianism. Calvin is saying to me that I was abundantly satisfied with my lesbianism because by nature I am a hypocrite. I realize that this sounds harsh to our ears, but I am convinced it is spot on. We are much more comfortable with the idea that lesbianism is legitimate rather than hypocritical. We don't like to think of hypocrisy as foundational to homosexuality's nature. But hypocrisy is one of homosexuality's core attributes. Allow me to explain.

Everything fell with the fall, including our affection and our ability to create a just and moral society. But even though we did not choose our fallen nature, God says that we are responsible for it. Psalm 5:5 says that God hates all evildoers, and Romans 1:18 declares, "For the wrath of God is revealed from heaven against all ungodliness and unrighteousness of men, who by their unrighteousness suppress the truth." Given the seriousness of sin—even unchosen sin—one question stands: Will we be warriors against sin for Christ or hypocrites? That's John Calvin's question. Calvin goes on: "Because nothing appears within or around us that has not been contaminated by great immorality, what is a little less vile pleases us as a thing most pure—so long as we confine our minds within the limits of human corruption."[5]

The idea of something "a little less vile" against which to measure my life is helpful to me as I consider the loyalty to feminism that fettered my affection until my conversion to Jesus Christ at the age of thirty-six. Feminism was my religion before Christianity was, and it was the hardest thing to shake. Feminism and lesbianism fused

5 Calvin, *Institutes*, 1.1.2.

together in my worldview. Feminism was the blood that pumped my lesbianism into life. My feminism was my idol, and as a new believer I was tempted to build the gospel around it. And I am not alone in making feminism an idol or in trying to build the gospel around it. An almost-Christian feminist worldview championed by many Christian women runs rampant as I type these words. Its faithful members meet for worship on Twitter. Feminism is incompatible with biblical personhood because it contradicts the creation ordinance.

Early on in my Christian life as I was struggling with the relationship between feminism and the Bible, I found myself meditating on the pattern and design of creation. God used Psalm 72 to help me see it. One Lord's Day in church we sang, "Long as the sun and moon are known, they'll fear you through the ages all."[6] How do the sun and moon fear God? By fulfilling their creational design. The sun doesn't wonder if it is the moon. The moon doesn't think that perhaps it will wake up tomorrow as the sun. The design of the sun and moon is as plain as day and night. And for the sun and the moon to fulfill their design, they must do the work that matches their nature.

Yet we image bearers of a holy God are so hardened by sin that we don't see our rebellion. We call it *liberty, progress, feminism,* but God sees it as rejecting the brightness of glory, scorning our designated roles and places as kings and queens. We scoff at the glory God holds out for us when we deny the biblical gender roles he has reserved for his daughters.

God's design for women is as earth-shakingly excellent as God himself. His attributes inform his commands, his love for us and his law are inseparable, and he designs all of creation perfectly. God "is a Spirit, infinite, eternal, and unchangeable, in his being, wis-

---

6 *The Book of Psalms for Worship* (Pittsburgh, PA: Crown & Covenant, 2009), selection 72A, line 5.

dom, power, holiness, justice, goodness, and truth."[7] Every design crafted by our holy and good God has his thumbprint impressed upon it. Man and woman are his crowning glory. Zechariah 9:16 declares, "The LORD their God will save them, as the flock of his people; for like the jewels of a crown they shall shine on his land." Man and woman together are jewels of the same crown. The roles that women are blessed to embody cannot be replaced by a man. And likewise the roles that men are blessed to embody cannot be replaced by a woman. This is not a matter of competence, creativity, or modern medicine. God himself is holding the order and pattern of creation as a mandate for fruitful and good living.

What distinguishes men from women? Are these differences eternal or temporary, for this life only? The answer is yes. God designed women for both eternal and temporal displays of his glory. The temporal purposes sustain culture and civilization. The eternal purposes are mysterious (as everything relating to eternity is) but just as purposeful and glory-filled. God declares in Genesis 1:27, "So God created man in his own image, in the image of God he created him; male and female he created them." We see there that maleness and femaleness are connected to our image-bearing of God. This means our biological sex remains eternally true. We are born as men or women, and we will be men or women in heaven and the new Jerusalem.

Biblical patterns matter. About this, Kevin DeYoung writes, "The way in which [man and woman] was created suggests the special work they will do in the wider world—the man in the establishment of the external world of industry, and the woman in the nurture of the inner world of the family that will come from her

---

7 Westminster Shorter Catechism, Question and Answer 4.

as helpmate."[8] Pastor DeYoung's perspective is biblical: creational patterns are not merely suggestive; they are binding. The sun does the work of the sun. The moon does the work of the moon. And the sun and the moon aren't bickering about it.

A godly woman who is the wife of a godly man is receptive, teachable, and life-giving, her beauty increasing with her age because her Christian character is being more and more sanctified. God's design for a married woman is unlike any other designer's plan. In *Paradise Lost*, John Milton describes the mystery of the creation ordinance: "He for God only, she for God in him."[9] At its most basic distinction, God created men for strength, women for nurturance, and both for the other, her submission yielding to his headship creating the harmony of mutual work and worship of God. The simplicity, beauty, and perfection of the creation ordinance may be marred by sin but not by the designer's perfect plan.

One of my favorite literary expressions of what a godly wife looks like is found in another poem, one not as well-known as *Paradise Lost*. This one is tucked in the appendix of my favorite missionary book, *Pursuit of Glory: A Disciple's Journey with Jesus*. In this lovely book, coauthor Vince Ward records a poem written by two young women who served with the Wards in Sudan titled "Proverbs '32'":

An Excellent missionary wife who can find?
She is far more precious than cows.
The heart of her husband trusts in her,
For she said yes when he asked THE question.

---

8   Kevin DeYoung, *Men and Women in the Church: A Short, Biblical, Practical Introduction* (Wheaton, IL: Crossway, 2021), 29.

9   John Milton, *Paradise Lost*, vol. 4, ed. Rebekah Merkle (Moscow, ID: Logos Press, 2015), line 299.

She seeks angle iron and rebar
And works with willing hands.
She is like a cargo plane
She brings her food from Nairobi,
She is awake while it is still night
And soaks beans for her household
And a portion for her minions.
She considers and sketches her landscape plans
The work of her hands plants a garden.
She dresses herself in pants
And strengthens her arms to work.
She perceives that her wood and her metal are useful
And her mind does not go out at night.
She grasps the grinder with her hands
And with her hands she wields the welder.
She pours out chai for the thirsty
And is the community nurse for the needy.
She is not afraid of snow for her household
For in Sudan, there is none.
She hangs mosquito netting for the family beds
Her clothing used to be fine linen and purple.
Her husband is known in all the villages
When he sits among the chiefs of the clans.
Strength and discipline are her clothing
And she rejoices at the thought of heaven.
She teaches her children daily
And on her tongue is the law of patience.
She runs her household well
And does not taste the bread of idleness.
Her children rise up and call her "Amma"

While her husband praises her saying,
"Many women have done excellently,
But thou, my love, excel them all!"
Sweat is ever present and showers are in vain,
But the woman who perseveres shall be praised.
May she see the harvest of her labors
And may the work she has done praise her
In the heavenly gates. (Composed by Laura and Beth)[10]

What a delightful poem of praise! Julie, a godly wife, is represented here as strong, capable, skilled, persevering, and nurturing. She takes raw material (dry beans and metal) and makes them beautiful, useful, fruitful, and life-giving. She makes her husband look good, not because he is not good, but because he is better with her standing beside him. And she is busy—she is not fretful about what she cannot do or grumbling about what she must do. The work is hard, but the pursuit of glory is the mission that she shares with her missionary husband. And the fruit of her labors blesses everyone around her, with chai tea and a nurse's touch. Before being a missionary wife, did Julie have aspirations? Of course she did. But when she married, Vince's call to the mission field became Julie's to carry out. And God blessed the fruit of her hands in ways he would not if her calling was competing with her husband's.

The pastor's wife who discipled me, Floy Smith, had her own missionary story to tell (and boy, is it a doozy!). My favorite part isn't about how she and her eight-year-old son, Pete, became war refugees, although the war-refugee part of the story is filled with excitement and danger. Consider, for example, the time Floy went

---

10 Vince Ward and Samuel Ward, *Pursuit of Glory: A Disciple's Journey with Jesus* (Pittsburgh, PA: Crown & Covenant, 2018), Appendix B. Used with permission.

searching for a change of pants for her young son and instead found a suitcase filled not with clean clothes but instead packed to the gills with the G.I. Joe action figures that young Pete had packed. Nonplussed, Floy, a woman who pursued godly contentment, said that having toys to occupy an active boy might have been more useful than a change of pants.[11]

My favorite part of the story, however, is an interview with the foreign missions board before the Smith family departed for the field. Floy was asked to describe her calling to missions. She explained that she had no such calling. Her calling was to be Ken's helper and faithful wife. He was one who was called to the field. She was the one called to be by his side. With candor and honesty, Floy showed what submission looks like. A husband's call becomes his wife's to support. And God blessed Floy's submission to Ken richly.

The submitted, godly women who go before me—like Julie and Floy—are no doormats. They have taken the raw materials that God and their husbands have given them and made beautiful and useful and eternal things: children and food and laughter and innovation and a scrappy determination to give God all the glory. As "Proverbs '32'" puts it, "She is far more precious than cows." What an awesome line. And lest we forget, a cow in Sudan is gold.

Submission, too, is gold. The posture of submission explains how a godly wife uses sticks to make gold. A godly woman is not called to universal submission. She is called to submit to her husband, elders, and civil authorities. And her practice of submission to her husband and elders shapes her character and elevates her presence in the world.

---

11   Today, eight-year-old Pete is Pastor Peter Smith of Covenant Fellowship Reformed Presbyterian Church in Pittsburgh. He and his wife, Vicky, care for his father, Pastor Ken Smith, ninety-four years old at the time of this writing.

Importantly, her submission to her husband and elders never calls her to sin against God.

But what if her husband is an abuser? What if her pastor is an abuser?

Submission Is Biblical, but Is It Dangerous?

A godly woman's best defense against a potentially abusive husband is church membership in a biblically faithful church where she is a member in good standing. Especially if her husband is committing sin, a submitted wife has her best defense in church membership. Why? Because one crucial mark of submission is the godly woman who knows when it's time to call the police or the elders or bring the matter to higher church authorities, such as a presbytery or a general assembly. She needs to call the cops if the sin is also a crime—such as sexual abuse in the home or church. Not all sins are crimes, but when they are, the submitted wife needs to act.

Some issues are so bad that they require two phone calls—one to the elders and another to the police.

Men and women are called to submit to the government in nonchurch matters when the government is fulfilling its biblically prescribed duty. For example, we are called to obey traffic laws. But when the government overreaches the biblical frame and asks men and women to sin against God, we are not called to submit to that. God's law makes reference to civil government in Romans 13:1–7 and 1 Peter 2:13–17. That Christians need a healthy theology of civil disobedience might strike you as a peculiar notion, but I think it's one that will be gaining more and more traction.

My point about church membership bears repeating: a Christian's best defense against abuse of all authority is membership in a biblically faithful church. Submission doesn't imply brainless passivity.

Scottish Reformer Jenny Geddes was acting in submission when, one Lord's Day, July 23, 1637, she threw the stool on which she sat at the preacher's head after the unsuspecting preacher—James Hannay—opened the *Scottish Episcopal Book of Common Prayer*. Jenny hurled the chair at the state-sponsored pastor because the Bible had taught her that the state doesn't run the church, the state doesn't sponsor the pastor, and the state-sponsored prayer book contained serious theological errors. Jenny knew her doctrine well, and she showed herself to be quite a biblically submissive woman in her historic stool-hurling.[12]

How did Jenny know to throw the stool on that fateful day in 1637, and how can we know that throwing the stool revealed Jenny's submission to God rather than unmitigated rage and anger, or perhaps a preference, say, for a chair with a back? Because submission to church membership vows requires strength, courage, and the willingness to follow the martyrs for the cause of biblical doctrine. Calling a woman to submission is calling her to be like Jenny Geddes in times of war. Jenny threw that stool at great personal risk because she was obeying her church membership vows over a government policy, which could have resulted in great personal consequences according to the law of the day. In fact, Jenny Geddes's action launched the English Civil War.

When a godly woman submits to her church elders and her husband, she is safe, because no matter what happens as a result, she is walking the path of godliness. But that is not what feminism teaches. Feminism teaches that the church and the gospel need a feminist rescue. Let's turn to that quandary now.

---

12 George Grant, "Jenny Geddes," podcast, *Fight, Laugh, Feast*, May 18, 2021, https://flf network.com/.

8

Does the Gospel Need
a Feminist Rescue?

Search me, O God, and know my heart!
Try me and know my thoughts!
And see if there be any grievous way in me,
and lead me in the way everlasting!

PSALM 139:23–24

IT WAS ALL MY FAULT. I'm the one who caused my mother's explosion that morning in the kitchen, when she took out the blue china dinner dishes and hurled them like Frisbees against the wooden cabinets. My father's head was the original target of my mother's dish-hurling rage, but he took the first flying blue china dinner plate as his cue to exit stage left. My father was like Harry Houdini, the escape artist, always disappearing when it served him best and always leaving someone else to clean up the mess. My mother's countenance darkened and her rage detonated, and my dad was peace-out. My grandmother, Nani, was crying with her head in her hands. I stood transfixed, a familiar mix of rage and fear and a slowly pulsing migraine behind my right eye. My mother screamed obscenities as she trashed our kitchen. I could taste the ulcer in my stomach.

We were all terrified of my mother's rages, which rose, crested, and released like the tide. I kept a calendar of both my menstrual cycles and my mother's rages. I was a gymnast, so knowing the former was practical, while knowing the latter was a matter of life or death.

My mother loved me more than anything in her life. Her love was simultaneously life-giving and lethal. My mother tried unsuccessfully and for years to self-medicate for mental illness. It wasn't until she was seventy that she allowed herself the professional medical care she needed. It wasn't until she was eighty-five and on her deathbed that she received Christ. I still marvel at the Lord's mercy to me.

That morning in the kitchen of our 1960s split-level house, I answered my father's question about what Sister Mary Margaret was having us debate in our philosophy class. My answer sent dishes flying and my father running out the front door.

"Abortion," I said, gulping down a spoonful of oatmeal.

"Sister gave my team the pro-life side and Regina's the pro-choice side. Regina has a stronger team but I have an easier case."

"So, what do you think?" asked my open-minded dad. "Not about the debate per se but about the whole topic? Controversial, yes?"

My family was nominally Roman Catholic and religiously pro-choice. My parents believed that Planned Parenthood was a noble, magnanimous organization and that safe, legal, and free abortion was central to both a woman's humanity and a civilization's purpose. When my family talked about pregnancy, they used words like *strapped, enslaved, burdened,* and *oppressed.* I believed the pro-choice stance my family preached.

I should have known better before answering Dad's question honestly.

Part of me wonders if I was just edging for a fight.

"Well, if life begins at conception, abortion would have to be murder. If life begins with the ability to function purposefully in the world, anyone who is mentally disabled could be aborted at any age. Most toddlers would have to go. So I think the pro-life position makes the most sense and I think I have a good case."

My Nani turned pale. She was visibly shaken by my words. Nani was an old and kind woman, my caretaker throughout my whole childhood. She taught me to knit at the age of six, and her reminder to always move stitches off your needles every day has meant that for five decades I have knitted almost every day. My grandmother said her rosary daily and carried herself with gentleness. She was the last person in the world I would have wanted to hurt.

I lurched to a quick exit but made the tactical mistake of reaching across the table for my knitting, which I usually worked on during study hall and lunch. My mother grabbed my needles with the half-finished sock dangling and shoved them in my face. My mother's corporal punishment—at any age—was to shove an object or slap me in my face. So I think she was going for a face slap, but my half-finished sock cushioned the blow. My mouth was open and my wool yarn tasted earthy, like eating a carrot out of the ground.

"You piece of crap, you worthless piece of crap—"

I fled the kitchen without my knitting. Dish bombs and my mother's flow of hateful words exploding. Later at school, I wondered two things. First, what sent my mother into a rage this time? What did this have to do with pro-life or pro-choice? My mother was crazy but not stupid. She meant something by this rage, but I would have to ask my father later that night to get the answer. I knew better than to ask anyone at school what this meant. My mother's endless name-calling served as the humiliating drone in the background noise of my life. I wished that her rages wouldn't send my body into chaos, but I knew this was going to be another day when I wouldn't be able to hold down food. My heart escalated all day. My whole body was on alert, even though I knew that I was safe at school. Her rages had been steadily escalating, and as I went through my day—Latin, choir, algebra, lunch, church history, literature, debate, play practice, study hall—in each class I wondered when my mother would crash. Nani would escape into her rosary beads and soap operas. My mother likely would be in bed when I got home from school and would not talk to me for the next few days. I mentally went through the calendar on the wall and calculated that I wouldn't miss anything big while my mother was giving me the silent treatment. My mother drove me to my activities, but not if she was mad. But still I wondered, what was it that I had said?

I learned from my father that night that my Nani had used her knitting needles to give herself "home" abortions. My father told me this in a very matter-of-fact way, like he was reminding me to brush and floss. My understanding of anatomy did not allow me to even picture how this could be—or how Nani survived or why she would need to do this. The words *knitting needles*, *home*, and *abortion* did not match up in any logical way. (There was nothing even close to sex ed in my school.) After he finished speaking, he rubbed his soft hands together three times—his characteristic gesture to indicate he was finished. One. Two. Three. Done.

We never talked about it again.

As life marched forward and my mother's rages crested and fell, I searched for a worldview that would exonerate my mother's madness. My mother was a staunch feminist, and I found refuge in feminism too. In feminism, my mother could be a victim of her patriarchal circumstances. Feminism for me became a worldview of rescue. Mary Wollstonecraft (1759–1797), feminism's founder, was my hero. It's no wonder that a decade after this incident I wrote my PhD dissertation on her famous daughter, Mary Shelley (1797–1851), teenage author of *Frankenstein* (1818).

I completed high school and entered college and graduate school as a philosophical pragmatist, and with that, a staunch defender of abortion. It seemed to me that murder could not be helped. After my father died, I picked up his hand-rubbing gesture. One. Two. Three. Done. Murdering the vulnerable for the freedom of the woman was just inevitable.

In my growing-up years, what defined being a woman was the danger of getting pregnant and having this pregnancy ruin your aspirations. Being a woman always meant dodging your body. It seemed to me that she who is born woman got the short end of the stick.

But that's not what the Bible says.

God's Glory in Woman

Genesis 1 builds and progresses with an urgent sense of harmony and power. The prose is terse until you get to the crowning achievement of the magnificent creation of man and woman. That paragraph is long and liquid. Rather than tip the artistic balance, the glorious creation of man and woman is the great literary crescendo displaying the highpoint of creation. And man and woman are created for a purpose: to glorify God by reigning in his name and stewarding the earth. Adam and Eve's marriage points first to the God who made them and, after the fall, to the God who promises to redeem them. No more garden after the fall, so marriage reflects Christ and the church. Both in the Old Testament and the New, godly marriage is not self-referential—it never finds its meaning in itself. The institution of marriage is God's first government, and as such, marriage points to God's purpose in the world and the church.

Kevin DeYoung recounts five patterns that set us up for either grace or condemnation:

1. Male leadership (also known, from a biblical perspective, as patriarchy).
2. Godly women arrayed with heroic characteristics.
3. Godly women helping men.
4. Ungodly women influencing men for evil, while ungodly men abuse women.
5. Women finding meaning, grace, and suffering in bearing and caring for children.[1]

The power of these five patterns lies in not only what they communicate but also what they *are*. A pattern provides edges and direction. It tells us how to live and warns of the dangers of falling away. A pattern is to be followed, to be represented with accuracy, precision, and care. So we are to obey the Lord by copying his pattern in commands. If that seems oppressive, please read on, and we will perhaps uncover why you may respond in this way.

---

1   Kevin DeYoung, "Patterns That Preach," in *Men and Women in the Church: A Short, Biblical, Practical Introduction* (Wheaton, IL: Crossway, 2021), 36–42.

Remember back in Ken Smith's lecture to me, he talked about the tree of the knowledge of good and evil that was in the garden of Eden. That tree was off-limits, not because the fruit was bad, but because it served as a sign of God's love. God's love and law go together, and the temptation that Adam and Eve had was to worship the tree rather than God. How did Adam misread the meaning of the forbidden tree? By failing in his exercise of headship. Genesis 3:4–6 records the tragedy:

> The serpent said to the woman, "You will not surely die. For God knows that when you eat of it your eyes will be opened, and you will be like God, knowing good and evil." So when the woman saw that the tree was good for food, and that it was a delight to the eyes, and that the tree was to be desired to make one wise, she took of its fruit and ate, and she also gave some to her husband who was with her, and he ate.

Significantly, the woman was deceived. To be deceived is to be fully convinced of something that is simply not true. To be deceived means to be taken captive by falsehood. What did the serpent take captive? The serpent's strike took captive the creational order.

The creational order of biblical headship describes the biblical practice of responsible, caring, and sacrificial male leadership in the home and church. As a complement to the husband's leadership role, his wife, under her husband's leadership, helps steward God's creation and fulfill the creation mandate. Biblical headship is not an evil to be erased but rather God's design to run the wolves out of town. But Adam failed in his biblical headship; he failed to check the garden for the danger of an intruder, and he failed by obeying Eve's command to eat the forbidden fruit. The consequences of the fall are far-reaching and deadly: "Just as sin came into the world through one man, and death through sin, and so death spread to all men because all sinned" (Rom. 5:12).

Genesis 1–3 makes clear that God's design for a wife's submission is good, glorious, and life-giving and, simultaneously, that any rejection of God's created order—for whatever reason—is a rejection of God's design. It takes hubris and a darkened mind to believe that you can rewrite God's plan with impunity.

These opening chapters of the Bible create a frame through which to examine the rest of the biblical story. Biblical headship in marriage is the frame for how a wife serves as a helpmate. A helpmate is not a doormat. She is smart and strong and knows how to think and advise her husband when called upon. While she may also have a job or career that contributes to the household, being a helpmate means that the husband's vocation comes first. But we live in a sinful world where men and women have abused the roles to which they have been assigned. For many Christian women, God's pattern feels burdensome and unwelcome and may even seem dangerous, outdated, and unfair. God's pattern is not the problem. God's commands are never burdensome (1 John 5:3–4). God's commandments express God's love. If the problem is not God's commandments, what is it? The problem is our sinful response to it.

This leads us to how marriage reflects God's creational design:

Wives, submit to your own husbands, as to the Lord. For the husband is the head of the wife even as Christ is the head of the church, his body, and is himself its Savior. Now as the church submits to Christ, so also wives should submit in everything to their husbands. . . . "Therefore a man shall leave his father and mother and hold fast to his wife, and the two shall become one flesh." This mystery is profound, and I am saying that it refers to Christ and the church. However, let each one of you love his wife as himself, and let the wife see that she respects her husband. (Eph. 5:22–24, 31–33)

In this powerful epistle, Ephesians, Paul links together three features that show how a wife's submission to her husband is not some kind of humiliating servitude. First, a wife's submission to a godly husband is done "to the Lord" and never against the clear teaching of Scripture. This means that if a husband asks a wife to sin against God's word, she is bound by these verses not to submit to that. Second, a wife's submission to her husband is a reflection and expression of her submission to Christ. Paul writes that the husband is to the wife as Christ is to the church. Third, a wife's submission to her husband reflects her respect both of him as a man and of his role as a husband. Wives are to respect their husbands even when their husbands fail—especially when they fail. God will work through a husband to bless the wife and the rest of the family, so any act of disrespect or refusal to submit denies God's avenue of blessing. By receiving a husband's love, direction, and guidance, and then building on these things to create a home that honors the Lord in all aspects, we see that submission is not an endpoint but a launching pad.

The creation order—not culture—sets a pattern for godly living:

Now I commend you because you remember me in everything and maintain the traditions even as I delivered them to you. But I want you to understand that the head of every man is Christ, the head of a wife is her husband, and the head of Christ is

God. . . . For man was not made from woman, but woman from man. . . . Nevertheless, in the Lord woman is not independent of man nor man of woman; for as woman was made from man, so man is now born of woman. (1 Cor. 11:2–3, 8, 11–12)

This passage moves our discussion of submission and headship into the assembly of public worship, with Paul reminding the Corinthians that the pattern God established in the garden is a morally binding blessing. A pattern is a blueprint for right living. And therefore, in the worship assembly, men and women and children are to conduct themselves in accordance with that pattern. A woman's personal gifts do not take priority over the design pattern that God established in the garden.

Being made by God's design according to the pattern of creation is therefore a statement about both what it means to be human and what it means to interpret a text with accuracy. Every person lives under the authority, influence, or manipulation of someone or something. Everyone lives under sovereignty, whether the sovereign is God or personal feelings or some evil tyrant.

Being made according to a pattern does not imply tyranny to an outmoded cookie-cutter model. Biblical patterns created by a loving God for his children aren't rigid. They are revealing. What we do with God's patterns reveals much about who we are.

9

The Power of a Woman's Voice

I hate the double-minded,
but I love your law.
You are my hiding place and my shield;
I hope in your word.

PSALM 119:113

I RECALL A TIME when my youngest children were babies—
Mary was a newborn, and Knox was almost three. Mary was
softly cooing in my arms, and Knox gently put his head next
to her heart.

"Mama! Hear that? Baby Mary wants to play cars and trucks with
me!" Knox exclaimed. Now, there is no way that a newborn baby
can play cars and trucks. And there is also no way that Knox could
read Mary's intentions. But none of this quenched his enthusiasm.
Knox was confident that Mary's deepest desire at forty-eight hours
old was to play cars and trucks with him.

When siblings do that, we call it cute.

When readers of the Bible do it, we call it sin: "You shall not add
to the word that I command you, nor take from it, that you may

keep the commandments of the LORD your God that I command you," declares Moses, the lawgiver (Deut. 4:2).

It was funny when my almost three-year-old son started to "talk" for my newborn daughter, but this is not a method of Bible interpretation that holds water.

Today there is an entire worldview that stands in opposition to faithfully reading the Bible you hold in your hands. A faithful Christian is called to read the Bible and to submit to *what is there in the Bible,* not to seek a universal woman's voice—a "gynocentric interruption"[1]—or to read what you imagine should be written on the page. Biblical feminists reject the plain reading of the text. They also reject the pattern of the creation ordinance as something we must follow today in careful obedience to God's word.

Author Carolyn Custis James writes that the problem Christian women must overcome as they read the Bible is patriarchy. She writes:

> The story of Ruth takes place within a full-fledged patriarchal culture. Patriarchy is a social system that privileges men over women, where the actions of men command the focus, and women (with few exceptions) recede into the background. Under patriarchy, a woman derives her value from men—her father, husband, and especially her sons.[2]

To James, patriarchy is "the cultural backdrop against which the gospel message of Jesus stands out in the sharpest relief."[3] She

---

1 To go deeper into this contemporary unbiblical view, see Richard Bauckham, in *Gospel Women: Studies of the Named Women in the Gospels* (Grand Rapids, MI: Eerdmans, 2002).

2 Carolyn Custis James, *Finding God in the Margins: The Books of Ruth* (Bellingham, WA: Lexham Press, 2018), 9.

3 James, *Finding God in the Margins,* 10.

continues, "The Book of Ruth is . . . a critique of patriarchy."[4] Jesus is featured here as the savior of both our individual sins and the sin of patriarchy. However, because women do not derive their value from men but from God alone, this is a false understanding of biblical patriarchy.

Things have an uncanny way of becoming what they were designed to be. If you are reading this and need to regroup on the interpretative approach you are using during your Bible study time, then course correct. But, also, please hear this as well: the belief that biblical headship or biblical patriarchy is sin is simply not biblically true. This position is an inaccurate reading of the Bible. Biblical patriarchy is a blessing, not a crime, and women who support biblical inerrancy and the fulfillment of biblical gender roles willingly and joyfully support and build up biblical patriarchy.

If you have put any stock in the idea that you need to read the Bible to find special moments when a woman's voice breaks through to speak to your heart, as many feminist scholars are doing these days, you need to examine your heart before the Lord. Feminist biblical interpretation is bondage, not freedom. Every word in the Bible is yours for your edification, comfort, and direction: "Every word of God proves true; he is a shield to those who take refuge in him" (Prov. 30:5).

When feminism is the interpretative tool for reading Scripture, the powerful, supernatural word of God shrinks into an easily manipulated tool of sociology, revealing power plays and oppressors and offering no hope beyond its creation of new possibilities and new words to express one's never-ending hurt. If repentance is the threshold to God—not new words or new hashtags for expressing

---

4 James, *Finding God in the Margins*, 10.

your hurts—this unbiblical approach can be at very least a distraction if not a danger to your soul. How we read the Bible reveals what we think the Bible actually *is*. The problem with interpreting the Bible through a feminist lens is not only that it misreads what the Bible says about creation and the created order but also that it misreads what the Bible actually *is*.

Jesus and John Wayne and Other Bad Ideas

Kristin Kobes Du Mez's *Jesus and John Wayne: How White Evangelicals Corrupted a Faith and Fractured a Nation* illustrates my point that feminism misreads not only what the Bible says but also what the Bible *is*.[5] Her book seeks to expose how male dominance has both weaponized and corrupted the true Christian faith. Du Mez's book is readable and fascinating, describing the rise and fall of men who have been associated with evangelicalism. I have no reason to doubt Du Mez's credentials or integrity, but her case depends on pitting the stereotype of the virtuous woman against the dangerous man, attributing authentic, uncorrupted Christianity to the women and corrupt, political motivations to the men. Let's see what Du Mez believes about inerrancy:

> The issue of inerrancy did rally conservatives, but when it turned out that large numbers of Southern Baptists—even denominational officials—lacked any real theological prowess and were in fact functionally atheological, concerns over inerrancy gave way to a newly politicized commitment to female submission and to related culture war issues. . . . Al Mohler, who oversaw the purging of moderates from Southern Baptist Theological

5 Kristin Kobes Du Mez, *Jesus and John Wayne: How White Evangelicals Corrupted a Faith and Fractured a Nation* (New York: Liveright, 2020).

Seminary, offered a revealing glimpse into this process: "Mr. and Mrs. Baptist may not be able to understand or adjudicate the issue of biblical inerrancy when it comes down to nuances, and languages, and terminology," he acknowledged. "But if you believe abortion should be legal, that's all they need to know. . . ." The same went for "homosexual marriage." *Inerrancy mattered because of its connection to cultural and political issues.* It was in their efforts to bolster patriarchal authority that Southern Baptists united with evangelicals across the nation, and the alliances drew them into the larger evangelical world. Within a generation, Southern Baptists began to place their "evangelical" identity over their identity as Southern Baptists. Patriarchy was at the heart of this new sense of themselves.[6]

Du Mez wants you to believe that politics is the primary reason that conservatives embrace biblical inerrancy. She apparently thinks that we interpret the Bible as inerrant not because we believe that this honors God or because the Bible reveals itself as inerrant and God-breathed. No, it is out of politics and power that our inerrancy is embraced.

I am not Southern Baptist, and I cannot speak to the inner workings of the Southern Baptist Convention. But to suggest that Al Mohler's commitment to inerrancy is only rooted in politics imputes false motive and misunderstands the connection between inerrancy and obedience to God's law.

What does Du Mez believe? Does she believe that abortion is a nonissue, or acceptable to God, or only a sin in the eyes of the beholder, or safe, legal, and rare? Mohler chose the example of abortion,

6 Du Mez, *Jesus and John Wayne*, 109; emphasis added.

which violates the sixth commandment: "You shall not murder" (Exod. 20:13). The issue is not patriarchy. But to a feminist, every problem comes down to patriarchy. This reveals an important distinction in how people interpret the Bible. Inerrantists—and those who believe every word is inspired by God—read what the Bible says and interpret a text by allowing Scripture to interpret Scripture. Feminists read the Bible for what it might say or could say given its trajectory or vision in a world that believes "the future is female."[7]

I took a vow to uphold Scripture's infallibility when I joined the Syracuse Reformed Presbyterian Church in 1999. The first of seven vows says, "Do you believe the Scriptures of the Old and New Testaments to be the Word of God, the only infallible rule for faith and life?"[8] My assent condemned everything I had believed, which included the belief that the reader, not the author, gives the text its meaning. Why do you think the Reformed Presbyterian

7   This is a 1970s lesbian separatist slogan repurposed by presidential candidate Hillary Clinton in 2016.

8   *The Constitution of the Reformed Presbyterian Church of North America* (Pittsburgh, PA: Crown & Covenant, 2005), G-1. The remaining membership vows include the following: (2) Do you believe in the one living and true God—Father, Son, and Holy Spirit, as revealed in the Scriptures? (3) Do you repent of your sin; confess your guilt and helplessness as a sinner against God; profess Jesus Christ, Son of God, as your Savior and Lord; and dedicate yourself to His service: Do you promise that you will endeavor to forsake all sin, and to conform your life to His teaching and example? (4) Do you promise to submit in the Lord to the teaching and government of this church as being based upon the Scriptures and described in substance in the *Constitution of the Reformed Presbyterian Church of North America*? Do you recognize your responsibility to work with others in the church and do you promise to support and encourage them in their service to the Lord? In case you should need correction in doctrine or life, do you promise to respect the authority and discipline of the church? (5) To the end that you may grow in the Christian life, do you promise that you will diligently read the Bible, engage in private prayer, keep the Lord's Day, regularly attend the worship services, observe the appointed sacraments, and give to the Lord's work as He shall prosper you? (6) Do you seek first the kingdom of God and His righteousness in all the relationships of life, faithfully to perform your whole duty as a true servant of Jesus Christ, and seek to win others to Him? (7) Do you make this profession of faith and purpose in the presence of God, in humble reliance upon His grace, as you desire to give your account with joy at the Last Great Day?

Church lists as its first vow of membership a statement of biblical infallibility? Our first membership vow provokes the vow taker to ask herself some vital questions: What do I think about the Bible? Is it true? Do I seek to submit to it or subvert it? Am I willing to submit to the Bible, or is there another authority to which I appeal? As a new believer, I realized that the main thing is not the gospel alone because the gospel is never alone. The inerrant word undergirds the gospel.

My life was a jumble of contradiction when I took this vow. I had, a few weeks before taking this vow, broken my relationship with my lesbian partner. I packed my bags and moved out of the house we owned together. But my ex-partner was still covered under my health insurance. (I cowrote the university's same-sex family plan, a forerunner to gay marriage.) Both of our names were still on the mortgage. This membership vow—and the inerrant Bible itself—crossed me on every point. And my faithful pastor and elders helped me bear up under its condemnation. I had to change. I had to change everything. But I couldn't change everything at once. The Bible showed me how to change, the church held me tenderly, and the Lord provided for me at every juncture.

For almost all of church history, a Christian was defined as someone who upheld the truth of Scripture—both the truth of the meaning of the words themselves and the living power of the book itself. For almost all of church history, we did not quibble over the meaning of every word that crossed us. A word stood for its plain meaning as it would have been understood at the time the Bible was written. In today's modern evangelical culture, a Christian is a Christian if she says she is. This "self-ID" approach to truth is both dangerous and foolish. The Christian faith is about lived obedience to the word of God, not verbal affirmation.

Attributing a false and narrow motive to a historic approach to Christian interpretation is just one major flaw with Du Mez's book. The other is her tendency to attribute new meaning into old words and then demand that it bear historical weight. Take, for example, Du Mez's discussion of 2016 presidential candidate Hillary Clinton, whom she describes as a "devout Christian." Let me quote Du Mez in full here, so you hear her in her own words:

> Clinton was a devout Christian, but the wrong kind. She spoke about her Methodist faith frequently during the 2016 campaign, reciting favorite passages of Scripture with ease. Tapping into a tradition of American Civil Religion, she reminded Americans that they were great because they were good, and she urged them to summon the better angels of their nature. On the campaign trail, she seemed especially at home among black Protestants, whose prophetic faith tradition bore many similarities to her own progressive Methodism. But for white evangelicals, Clinton was on the wrong side of nearly every issue. A feminist and a career woman, she thought it took a village to raise a child. She promoted global human rights and women's rights at the expense of US sovereignty, at least in the eyes of her critics. And she was pro-choice. The fact that she read the same Bible didn't register for most evangelicals, and her faith testimony came across as political pandering, or just plain lying.[9]

Let's unpack a few lines there. Du Mez writes, "Clinton was a devout Christian." Devoted to what? A devout person is someone "devoted to divine worship or service, earnestly religious, pious,

9 Du Mez, *Jesus and John Wayne*, 250.

showing religious devotion, reverential."[10] A devout Christian has historically referred to someone who upholds the moral law of God as found in the Bible through the power of the Holy Spirit, knowing that she is saved by faith alone through Christ alone. We usually speak of "devout Christians" as those who have undergone hardship with faith strengthened by suffering, such as Elisabeth Elliot.[11] But only in a feminist sense is it logical that both Hillary Clinton and Elisabeth Elliot can be seen as devout Christians. These women are far, far apart in their upholding of biblical truth. What legitimates a Christian to Du Mez and other feminists is a claim on an identity, not an objective standard by which such a claim can be measured or judged.

Du Mez also says, Clinton was "the wrong kind" of Christian. The Bible does not talk about wrong kinds of Christians. The Bible just talks about Christians—people who claim Christ as King, dedicate their life to him, recognize that he is the Word made flesh, and put their hope and faith in Christ's atoning work. A Christian is someone who believes the gospel. We'd all do well to memorize some key Bible passages that explain the gospel, such as:

Unless you repent, you will all likewise perish. (Luke 13:3)

Jesus said to him, "I am the way, and the truth, and the life. No one comes to the Father except through me." (John 14:6)

---

10 *The New Shorter Oxford English Dictionary on Historical Principles*, vol. 1, ed. Lesley Brown (Oxford, UK: Clarendon Press, 1973), s.v. "devout."

11 Elisabeth Elliot (1926–2015) was a famed and devout Christian author and missionary whose first husband, Jim, was killed in 1956 when he made contact with the Auca people in Ecuador. As a widow and mother of a baby, Elisabeth returned to the tribe members who killed her husband and was used of the Lord to bring many of them to faith in Jesus Christ.

For all have sinned and fall short of the glory of God. (Rom. 3:23)

For by grace you have been saved through faith. And this is not your own doing; it is the gift of God. (Eph. 2:8)

The Lord knows how to rescue the godly from trials, and to keep the unrighteous under punishment until the day of judgment. (2 Pet. 2:9)

This is the love of God, that we keep his commandments. And his commandments are not burdensome. (1 John 5:3)

Christians do disagree on matters of doctrine, and we disagree because we see through a glass darkly, not because we abandon the inerrancy of Scripture. Disagreeing about infant baptism is not the same thing as disagreeing about whether murder or adultery or fornication is a sin. When someone's profession of personal faith defies Jesus, God's word says:

"Not everyone who says to me, 'Lord, Lord,' will enter the king-dom of heaven, but the one who does the will of my Father who is in heaven. On that day many will say to me, 'Lord, Lord, did we not prophesy in your name, and cast out demons in your name, and do many mighty works in your name?' And then will I declare to them, 'I never knew you; depart from me, you workers of lawlessness.'" (Matt. 7:21–23)

And the word of God is a complete biblical revelation. A feminist rescue of Scripture is its corruption:

Long ago, at many times and in many ways, God spoke to our fathers by the prophets, but in these last days he has spoken to us by his Son, whom he appointed the heir of all things, through whom also he created the world. He is the radiance of the glory of God and the exact imprint of his nature, and he upholds the universe by the word of his power. (Heb. 1:1–3)

Jesus and his word cannot be broken, separated, or in conflict.

Thus, the only wrong kind of Christian recorded in the Bible is the one who thinks wrongly that she is one.

Let's look at more of Du Mez's observations about Hillary Clinton. Du Mez writes, "She spoke about her Methodist faith. . . . Tapping into a tradition of American Civil Religion . . ." American civil religion is a sociological theory that the United States holds broad deistic beliefs that Democrats and Republicans can mostly agree upon.[12] The organizing idea behind civil religion is the rejection of the biblical account of the fall and the sin nature we inherit in Adam. American civil religion cannot save your soul, but if you anchor your Methodist faith to it, it could damn you to hell. At least, that is how a plain reading of the Bible understands this.

Du Mez writes of Clinton, "She reminded Americans that they were great because they were good." The Bible records that we are not good: "All have sinned and fall short of the glory of God" (Rom. 3:23). Declaring our own greatness apart from Christ's righteousness is sin, and those who sin and do not repent incur God's wrath, not his favor: "God opposes the proud but gives grace to the humble" (1 Pet. 5:5). Reminding Americans that

---

12 The term *American civil religion* was developed by sociologist Robert Bellah in an article entitled, "Civil Religion in America" (1967).

they are great because they are good is a twisted misuse of the gospel witness.

Concerning Clinton, Du Mez writes, "She was pro-choice." Because murder attacks the image of God, you cannot advocate for abortion and for the moral law of God at the same time. If you advocate for murder, you incur the wrath of God. To a progressive feminist, however, the Bible cannot be so binding on matters of moral law.

Du Mez adds, "The fact that she read the same Bible didn't register." It isn't the reading of the Bible only, but also the application of it. God gave us the full story of Judas Iscariot so that we can understand how people can read the same Bible, or in Judas's case, be a disciple of Jesus and live with him and other disciples and reject the real Jesus for one you make in your imagination. Judas could live with the Lord and betray him fully. And so can anyone else. The fact that we read the same Bible means nothing except that sin deceives us.

Upon what do we break our will if not the inerrant word of God? To an inerrantist the idea that reading the same Bible sends some to Christ and others to Satan makes perfect sense. It registers quite resoundingly. Anyone who reads the Bible and re-creates it on their own terms is guilty of this pronouncement of judgment:

> Woe to those who call evil good
>   and good evil,
> who put darkness for light
>   and light for darkness,
> who put bitter for sweet
>   and sweet for bitter!
> Woe to those who are wise in their own eyes,
>   and shrewd in their own sight! (Isa. 5:20–21)

The options are clear: you can either be wise in the word of God or wise in your own eyes. We biblical inerrantists do not trust earthly or worldly wisdom, because we know that we have a sin nature—even as redeemed people. We sin terribly. We seek forgiveness from the Lord and from one another—daily.

Du Mez's book makes the case that Christianity is a mere world-view—a lens through which to look at the world. Some call abortion a sin; others call it a grace. Who can judge? When Christianity becomes sociology, the resurrected Jesus is reduced to a good and gentle man who understands that sin is an issue that must be interpreted according to the good intentions of all these good people out there. This heresy is not how the Bible records the plight of humanity. To reject biblical inerrancy is to reject the reality of the fall of Adam, the sin nature that it produced in all of us, the death that Adam's sin introduced into the world, the sacrifice and love of the Lord Jesus Christ in taking a human body and paying for our debts with his life and blood, the power of the resurrected Christ as he gives his power and glory to all believers, and the new life in Christ that establishes an everlasting peace. A sociological approach to the Christian faith, like the one offered by feminism, is mere talk. But the gospel is power. Jesus acted, and the gospel unleashed into the world changes everything. Talk is cheap, but the blood of Christ is priceless: "The kingdom of God does not consist in talk but in power" (1 Cor. 4:20). Books like Du Mez's have a veneer of Christianity, but woe to the foolish reader who thinks there is genuine, saving faith to be found in their pages.

When feminism meets Scripture, it leads to any number of false interpretations that have given way to fracturing movements: the ordination of women to the office of elder and pastor and the birth of gay Christianity, to name two. The cause of the fracture is not inerrancy. It's not faithful and sacrificial faith. The cause is the proclamation of a false gospel.

So which is it? Is biblical headship a form of violence against women, something that must be corrected by feminism? Is Jesus the hero that saves women from patriarchy? Or is he the Savior King who saves us from our own sin and rules the world? Is feminism a frame that can be marshaled to serve the gospel? We need to ask the question, If the biblical account of creation cannot be trusted to teach us about what makes women distinct, where ought we to go for this insight? This is where the usefulness of feminism as a gospel frame crumbles in the foolishness that it is. It wants an essential and distinct women's voice at the same time that it rejects a biblical origin for what makes a woman distinct. Without a biblical basis for sexual difference, any feminist enterprise crumbles. Let me explain.

If there is no biblical creation account that explains what makes women distinct but there is a narrative that gives women a voice in Scripture with the power to overturn God's commands, then what makes women distinct is our grievances, not our creational design or purpose. Let that level of foolishness sink in for a moment.

Feminism lies. It believes that grievances from patriarchy and not God's design from creation make women distinct from men. Women are thus taught to believe that our bodies are vulnerable to abuse because patriarchy is dangerous. That's a deceptive half-truth. Biblical patriarchy protects women by giving a wife a godly man as "head" to love and protect her; a daughter, a godly father; and a single woman, a church to protect her. In contrast, the world produces many "heads," some of them tyrannical. A woman's body is a life-giving one, and the Bible celebrates and protects that. The Bible declares that woman is distinct because she is made in the image of God (Gen. 1:27) and "the glory of man" (1 Cor. 11:7). The distinction of woman is a mark of power and grace and celebrates her unique calling to give life and serve as mother and wife, sister and daughter, grandmother and friend.

Feminism's war against patriarchy isn't its only problem. By denying the centrality of the creation ordinance in defining woman and her glory, feminism insults women. Worse still, feminism can't offer the protections against violence that it promises. In fact, feminism has become a place of such confusion that it cannot define what a woman is without offending the LGBTQ+ movement—especially the *T* part (transgenderism).

The year 2022 revealed the Achilles' heel of feminism: transgenderism. Let's turn now to transgenderism, Lie #4.

LIE #4

————

TRANSGENDERISM
IS NORMAL

10

The Sin of Envy

Thus says the LORD:

"Cursed is the man who trusts in man
and makes flesh his strength,
whose heart turns away from the LORD."

JEREMIAH 17:5

TRANSGENDERISM IS TAKING our world by storm. The idea that men can transition into women or women into men defies logic, sanity, and history. It creates a world where defining *woman* has become the domain of biologists instead of kindergartners. Transgenderism has erased parental authority in government schools. And transgenderism will be the final nail in the coffin of feminism. Why? Because you cannot defend the civil rights of a woman if you don't know what she is. Transgenderism is the mark of a world that has swapped Christian morality for postmodern angst.

A Christian needs to think about this. Is transgenderism something a person "navigates" or repents of and heals from? Is transgenderism a sign of mental illness or sin?

I have known many people who called themselves transgendered. Let me introduce you to a couple of them.

Macy

In 1996, one of the women on my running team started to take testosterone. Macy was my size (small), but unlike me, she was fast. After she began the testosterone, Macy's voice got deep, and for about six months, she croaked like a teenage boy. She retained her great sense of humor and said that she never thought she would have to go through puberty again. She asked that we call her Ty. Her lesbian partner, Violet, broke up with her. Violet said that she didn't want to be in a relationship with a man. Macy/Ty continued to run with the team, and we stumbled over pronouns, broken friendships, rejection from the lesbian community, and Gothic medical intrusions that sidelined her for the best fall races. Things got worse and worse. Ty came over for dinner once a week, so I had a front-row seat to the horror. She dropped out of graduate school and got a desk job at which problems with bathrooms and pronouns mounted. After a painful and somewhat botched sex-change operation (now called "gender affirmation surgery"), Ty got a letter from her insurance company with a past bill for previous pap smears. Talk about adding insult to injury. This letter was an ever-present reminder that no matter how hard she tried, she never truly arrived at manhood. Macy/Ty was never in a relationship after surgery and often spoke of loneliness and depression during our long-distance runs on gray Syracuse afternoons. She told me that she regretted the surgery part and wished that she had just remained a person who lived between two genders. She did not participate in gay Pride marches or in any political activism. She wanted to be left alone but wished that something could help with the depression and pain.

I think of her often. Every spring, I pull out a recipe card she had written for me: "Macy's Strawberry Cobbler." The recipe card has "Macy" scratched out and "Ty" written over it.

There is no doubt that something was wrong and that Macy was in a great deal of turmoil and agony. But mutilating her body did not make things better. It made things worse. One of the many things Macy lost was the lesbian community, which rejected her as a traitor.

Jill

In 1997 my transgender friend Jill told me about Jesus. Jill was a biological man who lived as a woman. I did not know that Jill's real name was Matthew until I saw it penned inside the book cover of Calvin's *Institutes*. At one of the open Thursday night dinner parties my lesbian partner and I hosted in the gay community,[1] Jill told me about having once been a born-again Christian and pastor. At about the same time that Jill and I became friends, I started meeting with Pastor Ken Smith and his wife, Floy, and began to read the Bible. But my Jesus and Jill's Jesus were not the same. One Thursday night, I told Jill that I was starting to believe that Jesus is alive and that we were all in trouble. We spent many an evening afterward discussing the roles of pastor, husband, and father that Jill had left behind for full makeup and drag. That Jill's past included a betrayed wife and confused children made me sad. Jill was not a political activist and did not want attention. Jill wanted to be left alone. I only knew Jill as a pretend woman.

Macy/Ty and Matthew/Jill didn't want to draw attention to themselves. They were driven by pain into solutions that caused

---

1   That kind of camaraderie was typical of the gay community during the confusing days of the AIDS pandemic: the community gathered over meals to make sense of pervasive death.

more pain. I watched Macy/Ty's medical transition—including "top" surgery (double mastectomy and hysterectomy) and phalloplasty (the construction of a plastic penis). I've always been a little put off by invasive medical procedures, and this confirmed my squeamishness. Transgender surgery is Gothic. Frankensteinian.

I met Matthew/Jill decades after he had made the fateful decision to take enough estrogen to be chemically castrated for life. That's where Jill stopped, living in between stable categories of man and woman and never fitting in anywhere. For years I honored my transgendered friend's preferred names and pronouns because I saw this as an act of hospitality, of meeting people where they are. Everything about Matthew/Jill was fragile, and I never want to push people over the edge.

What Matthew did to himself in the name of self-actualization was more harmful than anything else imaginable.

Pronouns, Battlefields, and Government Schools

I have been homeschooling for twenty years now, but it was only this year, with high school–aged children, that we really started to study bloody battlefields from the boots-on-the-ground point of view. I realized that if the battle changes when soldiers have their boots on the ground, some of the soldiers go into shock and refuse to believe the truth. And then those soldiers die on the battlefield or are captured by the enemy.

Spiritual battlefields also change. And since we do not want to die or be captured by the enemy, we better wake up.

When it comes to spiritual battlefields, the good news is that while you cannot trust what you see with your own eyes (or your best intentions), you can always trust God's word. As challenging as this is to remember, the word of God knows us better than we know ourselves. As we seek to help those around us who call themselves transgendered, we would do well to start with thinking about what transgenderism means from the Bible's perspective.

Remember that our mission is set for us by God and found in Genesis 1:27–28:

> So God created man in his own image,
>   in the image of God he created him;
>   male and female he created them.

> And God blessed them. And God said to them, "Be fruitful and multiply and fill the earth and subdue it, and have dominion over the fish of the sea and over the birds of the heavens and over every living thing that moves on the earth."

Because we have denigrated God's design by believing the lies of homosexuality, feminism, and transgenderism and have allowed false and true teaching to coexist by rejecting biblical inerrancy, the battlefield now rages dangerously for children. One case in point is what is happening in government schools, specifically bathrooms.

Bathrooms in government schools are coed by law so as not to infringe upon the civil rights of transgendered students. A crisis regarding this policy erupted in May 2021, in Loudoun County, Virginia,[2] when this foolish practice of federally enforced coed

---

2 Scott Zeigler, Loudoun County Public Schools superintendent, lied about his knowledge of a male high school student who date-raped/sodomized a ninth-grade girl in the girl's restroom while wearing a skirt on May 28, 2021. Zeigler failed to call the police and report the crime. He solved the problem by moving the male student who identifies as transgendered to Broad Run High School, a neighboring Loudoun Country high school, where he molested another female student in the girls' bathroom a month later. The situation came to an explosive head in October 2021 when the enraged father was arrested for using salty language at a school

bathrooms became the setting where a ninth-grade girl was sodomized by a boy in a skirt. It turns out the boy was her boyfriend, who called himself "nonbinary." (Nonbinary also goes by the term *genderqueer* and refers to people who believe that they are neither male nor female.) All that we know is that the boyfriend used female pronouns and had a penchant for ruffles and that he brutally sodomized a girl when she rebuffed him. The understandably outraged girl's father was arrested at a school board meeting, and emails emerged that proved the superintendent knowingly covered up the crime. Perhaps not wanting to buck the LGBTQ+ mafia, the superintendent moved the perpetrator to a neighboring school, where he molested another girl in a classroom. In public schools, apparently bathrooms are the new brothels where all it takes to bamboozle school administrators is a boy in a skirt. Apparently, not even the #MeToo movement holds up against LGBTQ+ demands.

Three cultural forces coalesced to change the battlefield, as we discussed in the introduction. In 2015 gay marriage became legal in all fifty states; the LGBTQ+ movement started to promote transgender identity, a departure from its previous rejection, and formed a coalition for "sexual orientation and gender identity" (SOGI) laws. Transgender identity strengthened this political coalition. *T* became the cool and cutting-edge expression of individuality. Transgenderism had come to refer both to someone with a medi-

---

board meeting, the transgender student was found guilty in a Virginia juvenile court, and the superintendent's coverup of the crime came to light. That the perpetrator was the girl's on-and-off boyfriend points to one thing only: even the #MeToo movement must bow to transgender rights. Loudoun County Public Schools is one of the wealthiest school districts in the nation. See Caroline Downey, "Loudoun County Students Stage Walk-Outs to Protest Sexual Assault in Schools," *National Review*, October 26, 2021, https://www.nationalreview.com/.

cal manifestation of gender dysphoria or intersex condition and someone who just self-identifies as gender nonconformist.

When transgenderism became a political achievement, this unleashed a social contagion. Public schools became the place where children could not dodge the indoctrination, because the LGBTQ+ advocacy was removed from elective programs of sex education and placed within the required programs of antibullying curriculum. Parents cannot exempt children from antibullying programs for any reason, and this is how transgender activists have made children in government schools a captive audience. With this innocent audience, the new face of transgenderism was launched. No longer men in dresses with bad wigs and drippy eyeliner, the new face of transgenderism is a fourteen-year-old girl with bound breasts and a butch haircut who flies under the banner of genderqueer. Such girls find "freedom" by following the advice of YouTube influencers, school counselors, and supportive peers to lance off breasts and purge ovaries in the name of emancipation. If you think I'm exaggerating, consider the fact that in 2007 there was one pediatric gender clinic in America. Today there are nearly one hundred.[3]

There's a significant difference between an adult suffering from a mental or medical illness leading her into sinful envy, and a manipulated teenager or child under the influence of a social contagion that has snowballed into mass hysteria. Christians bear a responsibility to minister to both, as both are hurting people, but to help, we need to distinguish between the two and diagnose the problem accurately. The former, adults suffering from an illness, requires biblical counseling and Christian medical care. The latter, manipulated kids, requires that we protect them (and ourselves)

3 Abigail Shrier, "Gender Ideology Run Amok," *Imprimis*, Hillsdale College, June/July 2021, https://imprimis.hillsdale.edu/.

from false teachers and remove them from government schools whenever possible.

The alternative to swift action is the acceptance of transgender normalization. And personal pronouns as a battlefield of personhood and freedom are compulsory in the normalization of transgenderism. Who could have seen this one coming?[4]

Denying the right to use accurate personal pronouns makes it possible to manipulate anyone for any reason.

Transgenderism denies the eternal and essential difference between men and women, designed by God for a purpose. Transgenderism hates women, destroying women's opportunities for advancement and achievement, and renders school locker rooms and bathrooms danger zones. But this is not the only problem with transgenderism. The root problem is that transgenderism is a sin. It is a sin that tears apart truth and tears down families. Transgenderism is the sin of envy.

The Sin of Envy

Christian tradition records envy as one of the seven deadly sins, along with lust, gluttony, greed, sloth, wrath, and pride. Classical literature boasts exciting plots that twist and turn on the driving force of a tragic hero's envy. From Homer to Milton to Shakespeare,

---

4 One who saw this coming was Ayn Rand, a Russian writer and philosopher. Having lived through the Bolshevik takeover of Russia in 1917, Rand—whose given name was Alissa Rosenbaum—understood the type of society that wants to reclaim personhood on its own terms. The protagonist of Rand's 1937 dystopian novella, *Anthem*, goes by the name Equality 7-2521 and must use the pronoun *we* to refer to himself. The story's climax occurs when Equality 7-2521 discovers the pronoun *I*. It should give us more than a little pause to realize that the only historical literary example of a pronoun war occurred in a novella written by a woman who fled the Russian Revolution and knew that the dangers—and the stages—of totalitarianism included rewriting the very rules of language—with pronouns at the center.

tragic plots climax on the passion of envy and normalize it as part of what makes human nature complex and interesting.

Envy is defined as "hostility, malice, enmity, a feeling of resentful or discontented longing aroused by another person's better fortune."[5] Even though the Bible has a lot to say about envy, it is hard to pin down. Envy is often one of those behind-the-scenes instigators. We see how the sin of envy pulses through the concept of transgenderism. People obsessed with having a sex and gender not rightly theirs, and people who are willing to mutilate themselves and manipulate others to get this, are under the control of the sin of envy.

Proverbs 27:3–4 paints an ugly picture of envy: "A stone is heavy, and the sand weighty; but a fool's wrath is heavier than them both. Wrath is cruel, and anger is outrageous; but who is able to stand before envy?" (KJV). Envy, biblically speaking, is a self-destructive passion that insatiably drives a person to desire another's gifts, possessions, or achievements. Envy is sinful jealousy—it's the false entitlement that says you may possess that which justly belongs to another and fuels the blind arrogance to pursue it. About these verses, Matthew Henry says, "Those who have no command of their passions sink under the load."[6] Proverbs 14:30 says it bluntly: "Envy makes the bones rot." In other words, if you do not deal with the sin of envy in its infantile stage, it will devour you. Envy will eat you from the inside out. Envy transforms a person into a monster.

Envy is the result of human sin. When Paul wrote his letter to the Galatians, he was writing to a church pressed under the weight of false teachers who had troubled (1:7) and unsettled (5:12) the

---

5 *The New Shorter Oxford English Dictionary on Historical Principles*, vol. 1, ed. Lesley Brown (Oxford, UK: Clarendon Press, 1973), s.v. "envy."

6 Matthew Henry, *Matthew Henry's Concise Commentary on the Whole Bible* (Nashville, TN: Thomas Nelson, 1997), 604.

believers. These teachers had introduced a new gospel, one in which believers are saved by works as well as by grace. To be clear: all believers are to have fruit, good works that flow out of God's election, the Lord Jesus Christ's redemption, and the Holy Spirit's conviction of sin. Our works reveal that we belong to Christ. Our works do not indebt God to us in any way. Because the battle between the flesh and the Spirit continues in the life of the believer, we must be on guard against the sin of envy. Galatians 5:16–21 records the danger of this sin:

> I say, walk by the Spirit, and you will not gratify the desires of the flesh. For the desires of the flesh are against the Spirit, and the desires of the Spirit are against the flesh, for these are opposed to each other, to keep you from doing the things you want to do. But if you are led by the Spirit, you are not under the law. Now the works of the flesh are evident: sexual immorality, impurity, sensuality, idolatry, sorcery, enmity, strife, jealousy, fits of anger, rivalries, dissensions, divisions, envy, drunkenness, orgies, and things like these. I warn you, as I warned you before, that those who do such things will not inherit the kingdom of God.

The apostle Paul places envy in a dire light. It ranks right up there with other lethal sins, and its consequence is deadly: no peace with God, no redemption, no salvation. In other words, those who die in an unrepentant state of envy are hell-bound. Envy is delusional entitlement masked in a package of victimhood and unbearable pain. If transgenderism is envy's modern face, then there is truly no such thing as a "transgendered Christian," if by this term we mean something celebrating a transgendered identity as somehow honoring to Christ or the church.

Paul indicates that the sin of envy is a consequence of turning away from God. Those given up to a "debased mind" (Rom. 1:28) suffer consequences. They are "filled with all manner of unrighteousness, evil, covetousness, malice. They are full of envy, murder, strife, deceit, maliciousness" (Rom. 1:29). To be full of envy is to be blinded by the predatory desire to have what belongs to someone else.

We can all think of examples in a sinful and broken world where people desire what belongs to someone else. But this is where we need to be watchful of the analogies we draw. It is not an act of envy for a person with a disease to desire a medical cure. Using modern medicine or God's intervention to heal broken bones does not steal God's glory from another person. But the thinking Christian cannot simply nod and smile to everything we read in the DSM-5.[7] A physical diagnosis of gender dysphoria shows significant clinical distress arising from genetic, biological, environmental, or cultural factors. From a biblical perspective, gender dysphoria is a psychological health problem, not only a mental health problem. And a Christian response to people with problems is to help. Godly help for the gender dysphoric is genuine love, godly compassion, biblical counseling, and potentially hormonal treatments that restore normal hormonal balance. Godly help for the gender dysphoric understands medical and psychiatric problems as serious and does not believe that a gay Pride parade, a *Blue's Clues* sing-along, or an opportunity to appear in drag and read to children at a public library offers an adequate solution. Rather, these "solutions" show a world given over to sin; a world where scandal barely rouses us from our stupor.

7   The DSM-5 is the fifth edition of the *Diagnostic and Statistical Manual of Mental Disorders* published by the American Psychiatric Association.

What these verses point out is that even Spirit-wrought Christians must fight against the flesh. Reframing sinful deeds and desires of the flesh in worldly or therapeutic terms is sinful. It tells lies and betrays the power of God's election, Christ's redemption, and the Spirit's comfort. It rewrites the gospel, entangles the church into foolish debates, and confuses our young people. This is the appalling situation in which we find the evangelical church today. We who love the Lord have failed to love people deluded by sin in a biblical, godly, and courageous way. We who love the Lord have failed to drive the wolves out of our churches.

In Paul's first letter to Timothy, he advises his young colleague about dangerous issues arising in the church in Ephesus. Specifically, Paul introduces a paradigm to discern false teaching and false teachers who are already in the church. Hear these loving words from the apostle Paul:

> If anyone teaches a different doctrine and does not agree with the sound words of our Lord Jesus Christ and the teaching that accords with godliness, he is puffed up with conceit and understands nothing. He has an unhealthy craving for controversy and for quarrels about words, which produce envy, dissension, slander, evil suspicions, and constant friction among people who are depraved in mind and deprived of the truth. (1 Tim. 6:3–5)

Love holds people to the impartial, objective, and safe standard of God's truth, not the malleability of sinful desires and the posturing of sinful people. When the apostle Paul talks about "teaching that accords with godliness," he has in view the Bible as a unified revelation, one where patterns of God's design lead logically to patterns of gender roles and responsibilities. We also see here what produces and multiplies envy: false teaching. We see a plethora of false teaching embraced by the evangelical church today about caring well for supposed sexual minorities.

Scripture gives us clear and unwavering commands about what to do with envy. The apostle Peter in his first letter tells us to "put away all malice and all deceit and hypocrisy and envy and all slander" (1 Pet. 2:1). In other words, do not give it a moment's attention. Do not heed its bidding. Do not satisfy its demands. Do not be taken hostage by your envy or by the envy of someone else. This is easier said than done because envy tells the story of victimhood, working through an appeal to pity. If someone driven by envy wants to become the opposite sex, we are told that to discourage her in any way results in suicide. Envy tells us not to look at the truth of her biological sex or the truth of God's word, although biological sex and the application of gender roles and responsibilities are intertwined. Envy tells us that believing God's word hurts her feelings and causes her suicide. This logical fallacy holds the truth hostage. But we are all vulnerable in this regard, as the apostle Paul tells Titus: "We ourselves were once foolish, disobedient, led astray, slaves to various passions and pleasures, passing our days in malice and envy, hated by others and hating one another" (Titus 3:3). In other words, our own experience with sin should make us wise and skeptical when envy tells its sad story. Real love confronts the lie that suffering people can't help but envy others. Real love does not envy (1 Cor. 13:4).

People driven by the sin of envy gather enablers. A powerful Bible book, 1 Kings, records the spiraling descent of a person whose envy is enabled instead of confronted. Largely composed between 586 and 561 BC, it marks the destruction of Jerusalem, the death of the Babylonian King Nebuchadnezzar, and the decline and dispersion of the kingdom of God through the sons of David.

First Kings makes clear that apostasy leads to God's judgment even as God remains faithful to his covenant.

In 1 Kings 21 we meet the brooding and envious Ahab. King Ahab had all he needed, but he was envious of Naboth's vegetable garden and wanted to seize it and make it a vineyard. But Naboth could not possibly sell it because it was the inheritance of his fathers. In other words, it was the Lord's. King Ahab became enraged. He was envious of Naboth and his vegetable garden, not because he needed the garden or because God had promised it to him, but merely because he was discontented and envious. Envy rendered him "vexed and sullen" (1 Kings 21:4).

His evil wife Jezebel concocted a plan to use Ahab's governing power for personal gain. She told King Ahab to call a national fast and set Naboth in charge. She then guided Ahab to hire two hit men to falsely accuse Naboth of violating God's law, which would result in Naboth's execution, thus freeing up his vegetable garden for Ahab's personal use. Jezebel and Ahab were pleased with the plan, and they executed it swiftly. But the Lord in his mercy sent Elijah the Tishbite to confront Ahab: "In the place where dogs licked up the blood of Naboth shall dogs lick your own blood" (1 Kings 21:19).

It ended well for Ahab, who repented, but not for Jezebel, who never repented. This is how the Bible records Ahab's sinful envy and Jezebel's sinful enabling of it:

(There was none who sold himself to do what was evil in the sight of the LORD like Ahab, *whom Jezebel his wife incited*. He acted very abominably in going after idols, as the Amorites had done, whom the LORD cast out before the people of Israel.) And when Ahab heard those words, he tore his clothes and put sackcloth on his flesh and fasted and lay in sackcloth and went about dejectedly. And the word of the LORD came to Elijah the Tishbite, saying, "Have you seen how Ahab has humbled himself before me? Because he has humbled himself before me, I will not bring the disaster in his days; but in his son's days I will bring the disaster upon his house." (1 Kings 21:25–29)

Envy is a predatory longing for that which is not rightfully mine, often enlisting enablers to slander, lie, steal, and murder. When the sin of envy is bolstered by the additional sin of enablers, envy becomes a social sin of monstrous proportion. In plain speech, transgenderism is the sin of envy with a host of enablers, some of them calling themselves Christian. In transgenderism, God's design for human beings, to reflect his image, is maimed and surgically destroyed. But not eternally. Man may maim the body but cannot destroy what God has created. That is in part why people who repent of the sin of transgenderism long for heaven and the new Jerusalem in perhaps the deepest way, because God promises that our glorified souls and bodies have no remnant of the sin of our lives on earth, thus no genital mutilation. A person who has been enabled to pursue the mutilation of her body through hormones or surgery or has been encouraged to keep alive the false identity of transgenderism has been enabled to cultivate the dangerous sin of envy. Those who enable transgender identity as somehow compatible with the Christian life are false witnesses to what the Bible plainly proclaims. Biblically speaking, witnesses who invent their own messages are called ravenous wolves.

The Bible has a name for those who support and enable the sin of envy: Jezebel.[8] That envy is the result of human sin, replete

---

8 My thanks to my dear brother Christopher Yuan for bringing to my attention this bold observation.

throughout Scripture in many examples. Cain envies Abel, and it leads to murder (Gen. 4:3–5). Esau envies Jacob, and it leads to strife (Gen. 27:45). Rachel envies Leah, and it ends in sexual sin and family division (Gen. 30:1). Joseph's brothers envy Joseph, and it leads to slander, prison, and division (Gen. 37:4). And Jesus was crucified because of envy (Matt. 27:18). No matter the intention, envy results in further pain and chaos. Even though God uses the sin of man in a sinless way,[9] that never excuses envy.

The results of envy are disastrous. James 3:14–16 records, "If you have bitter jealousy [envy] and selfish ambition in your hearts, do not boast and be false to the truth. This is not the wisdom that comes down from above, but is earthly, unspiritual, demonic. For where jealousy [envy] and selfish ambition exist, there will be disorder and every vile practice." The barbaric celebration of transgenderism's medical mutilation puts us in the same company as those who sacrificed their children to the Canaanite deity Molech (Lev. 18:21). Lest you think I exaggerate, think about the consequences. Breast binding (resulting in fractured ribs, collapsed lungs, and deformed tissue unable to breastfeed),[10] testosterone treatments for teenage girls (leading to future sterility of adolescents), and sex-change mutilation (enough said).

The Bible records how God's people become deceived. They follow false teaching, and they sincerely believe that they are in God's grace. Like a hiker who falls off a cliff into a snowdrift and doesn't know which way is up, God's people, perhaps with the best

---

9 Drew Poplin, associate pastor of the First Reformed Presbyterian Church of Durham, pointed out to me "God's sinless use of sin."

10 Abigail Shrier, *Irreversible Damage: The Transgender Craze Seducing Our Daughters* (Washington, DC: Regnery Press, 2020), 47.

of intentions, follow their sinful hearts and refuse to receive God's correction. The root of this is the fear of man. Obeying God elicits the hatred of culture—including fallen evangelical culture. People will hate you for following the God of the Bible.

> Behold, you trust in deceptive words to no avail. Will you steal, murder, commit adultery, swear falsely, make offerings to Baal, and go after other gods that you have not known, and then come and stand before me in this house, which is called by my name, and say, "We are delivered!"—only to go on doing all these abominations? Has this house, which is called by my name, become a den of robbers in your eyes? (Jer. 7:8–11)

This passage in Jeremiah has special weight because Jesus uses it when he rebukes the Pharisees, the religious leaders of the day: "It is written, 'My house shall be called a house of prayer,' but you make it a den of robbers" (Matt. 21:13). This problem of assuming that we are in God's favor because all the other "Christians" around us are equally embracing heresy does not make it safe.

After setting up the problem, Jeremiah writes what is most relevant for Christians who think transgenderism is normal for some people, that "transitioning" is ever an act of compassion, or that there is such a thing as a male brain in a female body:

> The sons of Judah have done evil in my sight, declares the LORD. They have set their detestable things in the house that is called by my name, to defile it. And they have built the high places of Topheth, which is in the Valley of the Son of Hinnom, to burn their sons and their daughters in the fire, *which I did not command, nor did it come into my mind.* (Jer. 7:30–31)

Child sacrifice became the ultimate expression of their barbarity, but take note here the terms of God's condemnation of it. God could have appealed to their reason or compassion, pointing out that mutilating and murdering one's children violates the sixth commandment, and destroying one's progeny violates all standards of reason and kindness. And all of that would be true. But God doesn't argue the case this way. God's people need to resist the prideful thinking that says God wants us to be innovative, to keep in step with the culture, to be loved by the world and by the world's standards, and to honor and worship those things that stand in violation of the creation ordinance. God's people need to care more about what is in the mind of God than what is in the heart of culture. I am convinced that should Jesus tarry and historians look back on the days of the transgender revolution, the people who advocated for transgender mutilation and the weak Christians who did not oppose it will stand in the infamy of Molech.

In addition to biblical mandates that prohibit any Christian from supporting transgender rights or bodily harm, the idea that transgenderism is normal for some people is against reason and logic. Sound logic, biblical creation, and God's law all weigh into the equation, helping us see through the sin of envy. God forbids envy: "Fret not yourself because of evildoers; be not envious of wrongdoers!" (Ps. 37:1). It is sinful to mutilate your body or to reject the goodness of God in your sex and gender. "Let us not become conceited, provoking one another, envying one another" (Gal. 5:26). When we envy something that someone else has, we are showing how conceited (proud) we are. We express sinful entitlement. And when we encourage people to be filled with pride and entitlement, we ourselves are in sin.

Envy is a pervasive and ubiquitous sin, but it is also a deadly one. Victimhood and pain conceal it in robes of social-justice righteousness. And because of its intimate link with victimization, envy (like all sin) infantilizes a person. Instead of acting with maturity, the slave to envy acts like a spoiled toddler.

Envy and voyeurism fester in transgenderism—and in social media that creates a false community—and fuel its predatory envy. Transgenderism is reckless exhibitionism, taking captive image bearers of a holy God for harm and danger. Why would the church look on and smile? Why would anyone?

11

The War of Words

Come to me, all who labor and are heavy laden, and I will give you rest. Take my yoke upon you, and learn from me, for I am gentle and lowly in heart, and you will find rest for your souls. For my yoke is easy, and my burden is light.

MATTHEW 11:28–30

TRANSGENDERISM IS SUCH a new concept that the 1973 *Oxford English Dictionary* that sits open on my desk has no entry for it. The word came into existence in 1974 as an adjective referring to "persons whose sense of personal identity does not correspond with their anatomical sex."[1] This term combines two older words. The first is *trans*, which means "to bring across or over, to transfer, to cause to cross, to extend across, to convert." The second word is *gender*. Until the twentieth century, gender meant being male, female, or neuter. It wasn't until 1963 that gender began to refer to social attributes that differ from biological sex. This new definition was used by feminists Betty Friedan, Kate Millett, Gloria Steinem,

---

1 "Transgender," *Online Etymology Dictionary*, accessed September 8, 2022, https://www .etymonline.com.

Germaine Greer, and Simone de Beauvoir to suggest that gender is the cultural manifestation of biology. To these feminists, culture is male-dominated and misogynist (woman-hating), and women's gender roles are cultural constructs that needed to be destroyed. How quickly, even manically, we have gone from *gender* and *biological sex* as synonyms to seventy-two genders or more. Having more genders than letters is a big deal if your movement is represented by an acronym that depends on the alphabet.

As the short history of the word *transgender* implies, there is a great deal of variety in what people mean when they use it. There is also an important variety in the subtle but meaningful changes in how the word is used. Let's look at two of these ways.

Transgendered. When I type this word, my grammar check tells me that *transgendered* is an outmoded term and might offend someone and suggests that I use the word *transgender* or *trans*.*[2] Why? Because transgendered (with the suffix *-ed*) describes a person changed because of something acting upon him.

Transgender (no suffix) or trans*. The reason that LGBTQ+-rights activists seek to replace *transgendered* with *transgender* and now *trans** is to define who a person eternally and originally is. *Trans** implies that original biological sex has no design pattern or purpose and therefore can be easily replaced by anything else if your feelings so dictate. And if your feelings are strong enough, this rewrites history and "proves" that how you feel is who you have always been. It makes the false claim that who you are originally, deeply,

---

2 *-ed* is a suffix that implies an outside force acting upon the noun. So *transgendered* implies that some outside force is troubling this person, while *transgender* implies that this is simply who this person naturally is. *Trans**, with the asterisk, means that the person is not "constrained" by his gender identity today (which he has the liberty to change tomorrow). *Trans** also combines people who seek genital mutilation and those who don't together in the same category.

really, is your psychological choice. We are told that we need to show empathy, but empathy is a cheap substitute for God's grace.

Understanding Today's Lingo

Gender Dysphoria and Transgenderism

There are two camps of transgenderism, one medical and the other experiential. The first camp refers to people with a medical diagnosis of gender dysphoria. Although very rare, gender dysphoria can be understood as a medical problem with significant emotional consequences. Christians can and should be compassionate and sympathetic to people who are burdened by gender dysphoria and help them seek the care that realigns their confused feelings with the reality of their bodily sex. Christians who have a medical diagnosis of gender dysphoria have the hope of the gospel, progressive sanctification, the community of the church, the means of God's grace, and biblical counseling from church elders and other health professionals. There is hope in the gospel.

Transgenderism is not the same thing as gender dysphoria. According to Toronto psychologist Ken Zucker, transgenderism is an "overarching ideology"—this means it is filled to the brim with politicized gender theory. Zucker, who focuses his work on children, writes, "The term 'transgender identity' is hardly an objective label for a child's gendered subjectivity."[3] Zucker prefers instead "gender-anxiety" to refer to children who experience emotional incongruity with their sex. Gender dysphoria in children is a highly charged issue. At its center is a question about persistence of gender anxiety

3 Kenneth J. Zucker, "The Myth of Persistence: Response to 'A Critical Commentary on Follow-Up Studies and "Desistance" Theories about Transgender and Gender Nonconforming Children' by Temple Newhook et al." *International Journal of Transgenderism* 19.2, May 29, 2018, http://doi.org/10.1080/15532739.2018.1468293.

or desistance. *Desistance* means that gender anxiety stops on its own with adolescence and the natural passing of time. The majority of children who experience gender anxiety will experience desistance through the normal process of growing up—85 percent by puberty and almost everyone else by adulthood. But hormone blockers will indeed block the normal way that the body will right itself.[4] This is a very serious matter.

But what about those adults who continue to experience same-sex attraction and gender dysphoria? Even if the percentage is minuscule, Christians care about each and every human being. From a Christian perspective, all death and illness are a consequence of the fall of Adam. Adam's sin resulted in our sin nature, our fallen bodies, our broken world, and our need for a savior. Gender dysphoria is a consequence of the fall of Adam. It is a manifestation of our sin nature that may be exacerbated by the sin of childhood trauma or neglect. Christians who struggle with gender dysphoria need to be reminded that a Christian's new nature is in Christ, not Adam. And as they struggle, they need to do so with the light and love of the church. *The New Reformation Catechism on Human Sexuality* asks this question: "What about believers who fight against same-sex attraction but continue to experience shame and guilt for their desires?" This question could be expanded to include gender dysphoria. Pastor Christopher J. Gordon provides this biblical and pastoral answer:

> God, in the gospel of his Son, has announced that there is no condemnation for those who are in Christ Jesus (Rom. 8:1). Any unholy desire, even if unchosen, such as same-sex attraction [or

4 Zucker, "Myth of Persistence."

transgenderism], is covered by the blood of Christ (Col. 2:13). Believers who continue to struggle against same-sex attraction should trust in God's forgiving mercies (1 John 1:9), and with earnest purpose, by the strength of the Holy Spirit, strive to live in the newness of life (Rom. 6:4; Col. 3:1–5). Further, the body of Christ should not avoid or shun those who struggle against any sexual sin (2 Sam. 12:1–13; Luke 15:1–2). Instead, believers, with a spirit of compassion (Jude 22; 1 Pet. 3:8), should "bear each other's burdens, and so fulfill the law of Christ" (Gal. 6:2).[5]

In this context, "those who struggle" refers to people who are going to war against sin, not those who believe they are gay Christians or transgendered Christians and seek "minority" status and victims' rights from within the church. Christians battle with sin as a new creation with a new nature: "If anyone is in Christ, he is a new creation. The old has passed away; behold, the new has come" (2 Cor. 5:17).

Self-Identification

Another group within the transgendered label refers to those who subscribe to what is called the "self-ID" perspective. If you say you are transgendered, then you are. If you believe that you have a male brain in a female body, then that is true. We live in a culture that ascribes truth to feelings and perceptions, and it fears hurting people's feelings more than encouraging them to permanently mutilate their bodies. Christians must stand in a discerning place. Our culture says things like not being believed is more traumatic than abuse. But believing things that aren't true is a sin and leads people into further sin. Eve's sin in the garden was believing a lie. Obviously, anyone identifying

5   Christopher J. Gordon, *The New Reformation Catechism on Human Sexuality* (Grand Rapids, MI: Reformation Heritage, 2022), 23–24.

as transgendered is living in some state of confusion and pain. But asking people in pain to define their own problem without stable, objective standards is the height of irresponsibility and cruelty. This has wrecked the lives of countless teenage girls, families, workplaces, and schools (just to name a few of the casualties).

Transgenderism's War against Children

California was the first state to guarantee "gender-affirming" health care for transgender foster youth. California's AB2119 was signed into law by Governor Jerry Brown on September 14, 2018, and lauded by Lambda Legal Defense as wonderful news.[6] But is it? What is gender dysphoria? How is it different from transgenderism? The LGBTQ+-rights movement wants you to believe that gender dysphoria in children is persistent, and unless hormone blockers are administered, that child will commit suicide. (Hormone blockers, such as leuprolide acetate or degarelix, also used to chemically castrate pedophiles, are dangerous drugs with devastating consequences when administered to children.[7]) According to Christian family physician Andrè Van Mol, "gender dysphoria is a serious mental health issue. By contrast, transgenderism is a belief system that increasingly looks like a cultish religion."[8]

What does Van Mol mean? In 85 percent of all children who experience clinical gender dysphoria, the illness corrects itself through the normal process of puberty unless hormone blockers

---

6   Amanda Remus, "Lambda Legal Applauds as California Becomes First State to Guarantee Gender-Affirming Health Care for Transgender Foster Youth," Lambda Legal, September 21, 2018, https://www.lambdalegal.org/.

7   "Drug Reduces Risk of Pedophiles Re-Offending," NeuroscienceNews.com, April 29, 2020, https://neurosciencenews.com/.

8   Andrè Van Mol, "Transgenderism: A State-Sponsored Religion?," *Public Discourse*, journal of the Witherspoon Institute, January 24, 2018, https://www.thepublicdiscourse.com/.

are administered and prevent the body's normal healing process.[9] So which is it? Do hormone blockers save a child from suicide? Or do they set children on a lifelong Frankensteinian journey where they become a medical patient for the rest of their lives? Even the LGBTQ+-affirming American Psychological Association reports that gender dysphoria does not persist into adolescence or adulthood in most cases. So why would the state of California place its most vulnerable children—orphans—in a position to be harmed like this? What kind of mass delusion have we fallen under?

Rapid-Onset Gender Dysphoria (ROGD)

Under the umbrella of the "self-ID" rubric for transgenderism, we find ROGD (rapid-onset gender dysphoria), a social contagion experienced by teenage girls as described by Abigail Shrier in her powerful book *Irreversible Damage: The Transgender Craze Seducing Our Daughters* (a book I highly recommend).[10] ROGD operates like anorexia did in the 1980s and in the false memory syndrome of the 1990s. In the 1980s it was common to find entire gymnastics teams suffering from anorexia and bulimia. In the 1990s a contagion of false reports of incest, resulting in prison time for innocent men and broken families from the weight of accusation, ran like fire through the United States. All three of these social contagions— anorexia among competitive teenage athletes, false reporting of

9   "In no more than about one in four children does gender dysphoria persist from childhood to adolescence or adulthood. . . . Rates of persistence translate to rates of desistance in natal males from 70 to 97.8% and natal females from 50 to 88%." *Diagnostic and Statistical Manual of Mental Disorders*, 5th ed. (Arlington, VA: American Psychiatric Association, 2013), 455. University of Toronto psychologist Kenneth Zucker summarizes numerous studies showing desistance is common, meaning that gender dysphoria does not persist in children in 85 percent of cases. See Zucker, "Myth of Persistence."

10   Abigail Shrier, *Irreversible Damage: The Transgender Craze Seducing Our Daughters* (Washington, DC: Regnery, 2020).

incest, and self-identification of transgenderism—reveal that even when the disease isn't real or objectively discernable or even true, the consequences of trying to fix it are devastating. The False Memory Syndrome Foundation came to a crash when children who once believed that they were the victims of incest (and who were encouraged to think they were, through empathetic counselors) sued the counselors who used their vulnerabilities to destroy their families. People like Abigail Shrier and others anticipate the transgender craze might crash to the ground when today's children, manipulated into hormone blockers and "gender affirmation surgery," grow into adulthood and sue their parents, therapists, and surgeons.

In interviews with Amanda Rose and Lisa Littman, two clinical psychologists who express concerns for girls manipulated by the transgender indoctrination who now "have" ROGD, Abigail Shrier assembles a list explaining why girls are so vulnerable to this social contagion. The tendency among teenage girls is to engage in *corumination*, the excessive sharing of hardships and negative feedback–enseeking. Shrier summarizes:

> Teenage girls spread psychic illness because of features natural to their modes of friendship: co-rumination, excessive reassurance-seeking, and negative feedback-seeking, in which someone maintains a feeling of control by angling for confirmation of her low-concept from others. It isn't hard to see why the 24/7 forum of social media intensifies and increases the incidence of each.[11]

While my heart breaks for the girls who spend their time in the negative feedback loop of social media, corumination, and nega-

---

11 Shrier, *Irreversible Damage*, 36.

tive feedback–seeking, I can't help but wonder how Christian girls have ended up in this place. Shrier fingers government schools. The public-school system's antibullying program, a program from which no parent who enrolls their child in a government school can exempt them, are the breeding ground for this mass hysteria.

But the issue isn't just about mass hysteria. While not popular to discuss, legitimate mental health issues abound in the transgender community, making people who identify as transgender vulnerable to manipulation and bullying—including the manipulation and bullying from the DSM-5 and the supposed health practitioners or public-school teachers who rush them headlong into mutilating surgeries.

The DSM-5 is not a credible source for sound biblical counseling. Nonetheless, even the DSM-5 sees a role for parents in assessing the potential gender dysphoria of a child because parents are the primary caregivers of children and spend the most time with them. According to the DSM-5, a child's diagnosis of gender dysphoria must include six of the following symptoms:

1. A strong desire to be of the other gender or an insistence that one is the other gender.
2. A strong preference for cross-dressing.
3. A strong preference for cross-gender roles in make-believe play or fantasy play.
4. A strong preference for the toys, games, or activities stereotypically used or engaged in by the other gender.
5. A strong preference for playmates of the other gender.
6. A strong rejection of toys, games, and activities typically associated with birth sex.
7. A strong dislike of one's sexual anatomy.

8. A strong desire for the primary and secondary sex characteristics that match one's experienced gender.[12]

Citing Littman, Shrier notes that many of these symptoms are readily visible. And any diagnosis based on visible symptoms means that if the symptoms aren't visible, there is no diagnosis. By definition, a child cannot "self-ID" his gender anxiety. An observing adult must see the above presentations. And yet the parents of the girls who supposedly have ROGD reported to Littman that they did not see any of this because their children did not present these behaviors. Littman believes that girls misdiagnosed with gender dysphoria are actually suffering from a "maladaptive coping mechanism." They are dealing with real concerns and problems in dangerous ways. Specifically, they are dealing with normal body-image problems by adapting the mass hysteria of the LGBTQ+ movement and applying it to their suffering. Shrier writes, quoting Littman's research, "Never before had gender dysphoria sufferers 'come out' as trans based on the encouragement of friends or following self-saturation in social media. Never before had identification as 'transgender' preceded the experience of gender dysphoria itself."[13]

The LGBTQ+-activist outcry against Littman was fierce. And although an outside research group conducted a postpublication review that revealed not one of Littman's results was false, she nonetheless was removed from her post at Brown University. (Littman was not tenured, which made her vulnerable to termination.) Because Littman relied on parents to report about the early sign of gender dysphoria, she was accused of "recruiting from Klan or alt-

---

12 American Psychiatric Association. 2013. *Desk Reference to the Diagnostic Criteria from DSM-5 (R)*. Arlington, TX: American Psychiatric Association Publishing.

13 Shrier, *Irreversible Damage*, 39.

right sites to demonstrate that blacks really were an inferior race."[14] As Shrier points out, "The 'Klan' in this case was the parents who had simply been asked questions about their own children."[15] Ironically, 85 percent of the parents interviewed identified as supporters of LGBTQ+ rights. Because Littman believed that parents—even LGBTQ+-affirming parents—are the most reliable witnesses of their children, her research was debunked as dangerous. Remember: Brown University removed Littman from her post, not because the science was wrong; no, Littman was removed because she was considered dangerous to the self-esteem of "trans people."[16]

Those who find Littman dangerous to transgendered people believe a common mantra of our day. Not believing someone's interpretation of abuse or identity is more harmful than whatever the truth is, perhaps even more harmful than the original trauma.[17] It is based on this paradigm that Littman could be so despised. This is the Gothic haunted house that empathy builds.

Intersex

Intersex condition—being born with both male and female sex characteristics, chromosomes, and hormones—sometimes falls under the transgender umbrella, but this is more political nonsense. Intersex condition is a Disorder of Sex Development (DSD), which is a definable medical problem, not an identity. A DSD reflects "a

---

14 Shrier, *Irreversible Damage*, 28–29.

15 Shrier, *Irreversible Damage*, 29.

16 The peer-reviewed scientific journal of the Public Library of Science that published and then repeated Littman's study tested and affirmed its validity.

17 "There are . . . powerful things you can do as a ministry leader. First, you can *believe the victim*. 'Innocent until proven guilty' is the appropriate legal standard, but you are a ministry leader, not a judge or investigator. We take the posture of 1 Corinthians 13:7, 'love believes all things.'" Brad Hambrick, ed., *Becoming a Church That Cares Well for the Abused* (Nashville, TN: B&H, 2019), 87; emphasis original.

diverse group of congenital conditions where the development of the reproductive system is different from what is usually expected."[18] People with intersexuality make up 0.02 percent of the population. While intersex condition involves chromosomal abnormalities, there is no such thing as a singular intersex condition. Down syndrome is a well-known condition caused by chromosomal abnormalities. While intersex condition is often used to defy the gender binary (male or female), this is not a feasible argument since most people diagnosed with intersex condition appear clearly male or female. Like other medical illnesses, intersex condition comes with a hefty load of psychological stress and should be met with Christian compassion, sound biblical counseling, and wise Christian medical care.

But let's be clear: what is helpful here is sympathy and care, not political activism. To think that the pain of illness, disability, or moral corruption can be made better by a parade and a sticker and a slogan is vile, and Christians should hang their heads in shame if they endorse this. When a Christian responds to the natural effects of Adam's sin with faith, obedience, and good works, this brings glory to God and peace with God to the believer. When anyone responds to the natural effects of Adam's sin with envy and self-harm, this elicits God's anger.

We know that there was no physical illness, disability, mental illness, or sin before the fall in the garden. Therefore, we can state that an intersex condition (a physical deformity) also comes from the fall. We know this is true because the Bible is the word of Christ,

---

18 Jennifer M. Beale and Sarah M. Creighton, "Long-Term Health Issues Related to Disorders or Differences in Sex Development/Intersex," in Andrè Van Mol, "Gender Dysphoria, the Transgender Tsunami, and Our Response," lecture, April 2022. Used by permission of author.

inerrant, sufficient, inspired, eternal. Christians will be called to suffer, and as we suffer in faith and obedience, God promises to be with us, to sanctify us for our good and for his glory. Claiming that intersex condition is an effect of the fall should not be controversial, as all illness is an effect of the fall, but apparently among some self-described Christians today, it is.

Not surprisingly, people who believe that you can be a transgendered Christian often promote false teaching that relies on other theological lapses. Understanding the basics of Christian theology and ethics—what the writer of Hebrews calls "the elementary doctrine" (Heb. 6:1)—is often rejected flat out. Did God really say that hell is eternal? Did God really say that Adam's sin passes down to every human being since? Is the Bible anything more than a bunch of paper and glue?

One influential Christian writer wants you to know that, in his self-promoted humility, he can't trust the idea of original sin because, well, he wasn't there to see it with his own eyes. He wants us to believe that our own eyes and hearts and minds are trustworthy, and God's word must be measured against the truth of human wisdom. Preston Sprinkle, the founder of the Center for Faith, Sexuality and Gender, observes this in his untrustworthy book *Embodied*:

> Some say that intersex conditions are caused by "the fall." Others think they were part of God's original pre-fall design. . . . I wasn't in the garden before Adam and Eve sinned. . . . Maybe using the fall to explain intersex conditions is wrongheaded, to begin with, as many disability theologians have reminded us.[19]

19 Preston Sprinkle, *Embodied: Transgender Identities, the Church, and What the Bible Has to Say* (Colorado Springs, CO: David C Cook, 2021), 125.

For Sprinkle, the biblical first principle that sin, death, and illness entered the world with the sin of Adam is not at all clear because he wasn't in the garden at the time of the fall. In other words, the Bible's witness as the word of God is not sufficient, but what Sprinkle can see with his own eyes is. Sprinkle adds one more thing: if "disability theologians" find this wrongheaded because saying that you are born in sin offends people, then we should hold this foundational theology in suspicion. This is false teaching.

Brain-Sex Theory, Ontology, and Eternality

Ontology is a philosophical term for who you are eternally, essentially, and originally. We are ontologically male and female image bearers of a holy God because, as Psalm 100 declares, "It is he who made us," and not we ourselves (v. 3). This means that our biological sex is ontological also. We were born male or female, and we will be male and female in either heaven or hell. People with intersex condition are no more excluded from this glorious promise than anyone with a medical illness, as the dominant sexual presentation for each person with an intersex condition will be healed and glorified in the new Jerusalem if that person trusts in Christ for salvation. Additionally, the ontology of biological sex is very good news for Christian people who suffer from gender dysphoria, because in heaven and then in the new Jerusalem, God will restore and perfect all of us, giving us glorified bodies that hold no sin or corruption. What a promise! This is true whether you have had a sex-change operation or not. God cares very little for our foolish attempts to rewrite his law. His goodness far outweighs our foolishness.

Brain-sex theory is advanced by Milton Diamond of the University of Hawaii. Diamond studies brain morphology and brain prototype. He writes, "The evidence, I believe, is strong enough to consider transsexuality to be a form of brain intersex."[20] This means that your brain has one sex and your body has another sex. According to the new world order of transgenderism, the brain takes priority over the body. This means that if you supposedly have a male brain, then you are a man regardless of the presence of ovaries, breasts, and even perhaps pregnancy. According to the logic of brain-sex theory, the kind of brain you have determines your ontological truth. If you have a male brain (and a female body), then you are ontologically male. If you have a female brain (and a male body), then you are ontologically female.

While Diamond firmly believes that your brain has a sex, this is highly criticized by other neurologists. In his lecture "Gender Dysphoria, the Transgender Tsunami, and Our Response," Andrè Van Mol states: "Researchers analyzed MRIs from more than 1,400 human brains from four datasets. They found extensive overlap between females and males for all grey matter, white matter and connections assessed."[21] Van Mol quotes from a study that concludes, "These findings are corroborated by a similar analysis of personality traits, attitudes, interests, and behaviors of more than 5,500 individuals which reveals that internal consistency is extremely rare. . . . Although there are sex/gender differences in the brain, human brains do not belong to one of two distinct categories: male brain/female brain."[22] Brains, it appears, are brains.

But let's say that you believed in the brain-sex theory. How might you go about finding out the sex of your brain without an MRI,

20 Milton Diamond, "Transsexuality among Twins: Identity, Concordance, Transition, Rearing, and Orientation," in J. Alan Branch, *Affirming God's Image: Addressing the Transgender Question with Science and Scripture* (Bellingham, WA: Lexham Press, 2019), 76.
21 Van Mol, "Gender Dysphoria, the Transgender Tsunami, and Our Response."
22 Daphna Joel, Zohar Berman et al., "Sex Beyond the Genitalia: The Human Brain Mosaic," in Van Mol, "Gender Dysphoria, the Transgender Tsunami, and Our Response."

especially given that there is widespread disagreement of whether there is such a thing as a transgender brain?[23] Google is there to help—and to manipulate with an online quiz.[24] If you take this quiz (and I don't recommend it), you will be faced with mostly ridiculous questions like, What kind of dog do you like? What kind of snacks do you eat? How many shoes are in your closet? What are your criteria for shopping for jeans? According to this survey, I failed as a female. My brain is 58 percent male and 42 percent female. Apparently, the gender of my brain is scientifically determined by my preference for Beagles over Chihuahuas, for work jeans I can use in the garden and that better match my sixty-year-old frame, and the fact that I used the Covid lockdown to rid my closet of unneeded shoes. Go figure. If this—and the belief in "pregnant men" and "chest feeding"—is what "following the science" means, we are in bigger trouble than we thought.

Simply stated, brain-sex theory makes the case that ontology is rooted in the sex of your brain (scientifically dubious at the very least) over the sex of your body (objectively visible, even in most people with a chromosomal disorder). Because transgender activists tell us that the real you is determined by the sex of your brain, a transgender person who transitions is heralded as someone *becoming* who she really is. In other words, if you change the definition of ontology to reject the logic of a sexed body and accept the pseudo-

---

23 Lawrence S. Mayer and Paul McHugh, "Gender Identity," *New Atlantis* 50 (Fall 2016): 86–114. "It is now widely recognized among psychiatrists and neuroscientists who engage in brain imaging research that there are inherent and ineradicable methodological limitations of *any* neuroimaging study that simply associates a particular trait, such as a certain behavior with a particular brain morphology." Mayer and McHugh, "Gender Identity," 103; emphasis added.

24 "How Male/Female Is Your Brain?" Brainfall, accessed September 9, 2022, https://brainfall .com/.

science of a sexed brain, then *kindness* means mutilating the body to match the brain. Thinking through this theologically, we must face a quandary: homosexual orientation is now considered immutable and fixed while gender identity is a matter of psychological choice. How far from Genesis 1:27 we have fled.

What does Scripture say about our mind and our body? Here are some important verses to consider about your mind:

You keep him in perfect peace
   whose mind is stayed on you,
because he trusts in you. (Isa. 26:3)

You . . . test the minds and hearts,
   O righteous God! (Ps. 7:9)

I appeal to you, therefore, brothers, by the mercies of God, to present your bodies as a living sacrifice, holy and acceptable to God, which is your spiritual worship. Do not be conformed to this world, but *be transformed by the renewal of your mind*, that by testing you may discern what is the will of God, what is good and acceptable and perfect. (Rom. 12:1–2)

For this is the covenant that I will make with the house of Israel after those days, declares the Lord: *I will put my laws into their minds*, and write them on their hearts, and I will be their God. (Heb. 8:10)

Christians have God's law written in their minds and hearts. Christian counselors need to help people who experience gender dysphoria or who are influenced by ungodly transgendered indoctrination to align their minds and hearts with God's written word. We do no one any good if we who give counsel have our hearts and minds open to the foolishness of the world.

The Great Commandment found in Matthew 22:37–39 also reflects the scriptural value of changing our minds to accord with God's law: "You shall love the Lord your God with all your heart and with all your soul and with all your mind. This is the great and first commandment. And a second is like it: You shall love your neighbor as yourself." A Christian is to love God more than his or her own life, something that we can only do with God's grace. Psalm 63:3 says, "Your steadfast love [or grace] is better than life." If a friend's envy has made gender transition an idol, you do her no favors by showing empathy and trying to see things from her point of view. To love your neighbor as yourself, you must call her to love God more than her own life.

Scripture also has important things to say about the body:

> God gave them up in the lusts of their hearts to impurity, to the dishonoring of their bodies among themselves, because they exchanged the truth about God for a lie and worshiped and served the creature rather than the Creator, who is blessed forever! Amen. (Rom. 1:24–25)

Although the immediate context for this passage is homosexuality, we can see how it applies more broadly as well. Transgenderism is a lie, and if you, driven by envy, believe this lie, you will serve the creature, and not the Creator, by rejecting the sexed body that God gave you. Sin makes us feel entitled to things God doesn't want for us. Later in Romans Paul asks, "Who will deliver me from this body of death?" (Rom. 7:24).

The biblical witness is clear. We are to conform our mind to Christ and discipline the body to desire only that which God has for us. Because we all are born with the desire for something that God hates, we should not see transgenderism as foreign but as a sin. We want to show great compassion for those who are trapped in the lie of transgenderism, but we don't accomplish this by re-framing sin as a grace.

12

Eternal Life Means More than Just Living Forever

"Good Teacher, what must I do to inherit eternal life?"
And Jesus said to him, "Why do you call me good? No one
is good except God alone. You know the commandments:
'Do not murder, Do not commit adultery, Do not steal, Do
not bear false witness, Do not defraud, Honor your father
and mother.'" And he said to him, "Teacher, all these I have
kept from my youth." And Jesus, looking at him, loved him,
and said to him, "You lack one thing: go, sell all that you
have and give to the poor, and you will have treasure in
heaven; and come, follow me." Disheartened by the saying,
he went away sorrowful, for he had great possessions.

MARK 10:17–22

A GODLY PERSPECTIVE OF THE REALITY of heaven and hell is crucial in fighting the sins of the flesh. Pastor Gordon Keddie reminds us:

> Eternal life is not merely endless life. The lost in hell have endless
> life of a kind, but Scripture calls it "the second death" (Rev. 2:11;

20:6, 14; 21:8). Eternal life is the life of heaven come to earth in a new spiritual condition. This condition consists in personal knowledge of and union with God made possible in and through Christ.[1]

But we can't know Christ and serve idols simultaneously, as the rich young ruler in Mark 10 wanted to do. Pastor Keddie gives three powerful applications of how the knowledge of eternal life empowers us to love God more than our own bodies and believe in faith that Scripture is truer than our own feelings.

First, he says, "we must know the 'only true God' who is 'the God and Father of our Lord Jesus Christ' (Eph. 1:4). He is only truly known in and through his Son, who is 'the express image of his person' (Heb. 1:3). All other Gods are false and nonexistent." Transgenderism makes false gods. Don't follow them. Second, he says that "we must also know Jesus Christ. Joining these names for the first time, Jesus is saying, 'I am the promised Messiah.' Jesus means 'God saves' (Matt. 1:21), and Christ means 'Messiah' (John 1:41). No mere teacher or visionary, Jesus is both God and man." Real Christians fear Jesus. They bow before his holiness. They do not take his name in vain. Third, he says that "we must know Jesus as the one sent by God to purchase the church with his blood (John 1:18; 10:36; Gal. 4:4; Acts 20:28). Saving faith believes in this God and this Jesus: 'Nor is there salvation in any other, for there is no other name under heaven given among men by which we must be saved' (Acts 4:12)."[2]

1   Gordon J. Keddie, *Prayers of the Bible: 366 Devotionals to Encourage Your Prayer Life* (Pittsburgh, PA: Crown & Covenant, 2017), 538.
2   Keddie, *Prayers of the Bible*, 539.

To the faithful Christian, the biblical witness of the eternality of hell is one of its most agonizing features. The rejection of eternal hell is artistically portrayed by Victorian poet William Ernest Henley in "Invictus," which was published in 1888:

Out of the night that covers me
Black as the pit from pole to pole,
I thank whatever gods maybe
For my unconquerable soul.

In the fell clutch of circumstance,
I have not winced nor cried aloud.
Under the bludgeonings of chance
My head is bloody, but unbowed.

Beyond this place of wrath and tears
Looms but the horror of the shade,
And yet the menace of the years
Finds, and shall find, me unafraid.

It matters not how strait the gate.
How charged with punishments the scroll.
I am the master of my fate;
I am the captain of my soul.[3]

The rejection of the eternality of hell can also be found in the work of Preston Sprinkle. In a 2016 blog post Sprinkle writes, "While I remain convinced that the punishment in hell is

---

3 William Ernest Henley, "Invictus," Poetry Foundation, accessed March 11, 2022, https://www.poetryfoundation.org/.

irreversible, . . . I do see more biblical evidence supporting the so-called annihilation (or terminal punishment) view of hell. That is, the punishment for sin is death. If you don't trust in Christ's death for your sin, you will suffer your own death in hell."[4] According to Sprinkle, it is "biblical, righteous, and Christian" to embrace "annihilation or terminal punishment" over the historic view of the Christian church, that those in hell suffer for eternity in a state of consciousness. Sprinkle denies that hell is eternal, although he fails to support this claim with proof of "biblical, righteous, and Christian" evidence. Sprinkle dismisses the most horrific aspect of hell: the fire is everlasting, the pain is everlasting, the horror is everlasting, the punishment is everlasting (2 Thess. 1:9; Rev. 14:11; 20:10). But he wants his readers to see this change of heart as his humility and obedience, not heresy and apostasy, since this change of heart only represents 2 percent of his theological backbone. Sprinkle writes:

> Some people ask me if I've changed my view since writing *Erasing Hell*. My short answer is "no." Since Francis [Chan] and I devoted 2 pages to the duration of hell in our book, and since we leaned toward the traditional view of eternal conscious torment, any change that I've made has to do with 2% of the stuff we talked about in the book. Sometimes "change" is seen as a bad thing. But quite honestly, I hope that every theologian would change at least 2% of what they've written about in all their books. If they haven't changed, I wonder if they're still studying the topic.[5]

4 Preston Sprinkle, "A Dialogue on the Duration of Hell," *Theology in the Raw*, February 23, 2016, https://theologyintheraw.com/.
5 Sprinkle, "A Dialogue on the Duration of Hell."

The full title of the book Sprinkle coauthored with Francis Chan is *Erasing Hell: What God Said about Eternity, and the Things We've Made Up*.[6] The subtitle—which Sprinkle conveniently concealed in his blog post—seems to imply that the concept of eternity is a big deal in this book, not a small matter. Sprinkle is feigning humility, but, truly, if every theologian changed the core truths of the Christian faith in their books by 2 percent, well, we would all end up where Preston Sprinkle is. If you can't trust Sprinkle on what the Scriptures call an "elementary principle" (see Heb. 6:1), then you can't trust him on anything.

The eternality of hell is more than horror because the eternality of God is *holy*. Indeed, hell's eternal punishment is rooted in God's holiness and has historically been linked to faith and revival. Jonathan Edwards's powerful sermon "The Eternity of Hell Torments" awakened many to the danger of hell and was used by God to bring many to saving faith.[7]

---

6 Francis Chan and Preston Sprinkle, *Erasing Hell: What God Said about Eternity, and the Things We've Made Up* (Colorado Springs, CO: David C. Cook, 2011).

7 Ponder the holiness of God as it connects to the eternality of hell in this brief passage from Jonathan Edwards's famous sermon:

> Consider what it is to suffer extreme torment forever and ever; and to suffer it day and night, from one year to another, from one age to another, and from one thousand ages to another, and so adding age to age, and thousands to thousands, in pain, in wailing and lamenting, groaning and shrieking, and gnashing your teeth; with your souls full of dreadful grief and amazement, your bodies full of racking torture, without any possibility of getting ease; without any possibility of moving God to pity by your cries; without any possibility of hiding yourselves from him; without any possibility of diverting your thoughts from your pain. Consider how dreadful despair will be in such torment; to know assuredly that you never, never shall be delivered from them; to have no hope: when you shall wish that you might be turned into nothing, but shall have no hope of it . . . when you would rejoice, if you might have any relief, after you have endured these torments millions of ages, but shall have no hope of it. After you shall have worn out the age of the sun, moon, stars, without rest day and night, or one minute's ease, yet you shall have no hope of ever being delivered; after you shall have worn a thousand more such ages, you shall have no hope . . . but that

Denying the eternality of hell violates the command to love God and our neighbor. It bears repeating that cheapening God's holy commands so that we don't hurt someone's feelings is not loving. As pastor Ted Donnelly says, "Damnation is too high a price to pay for friendship."[8] Denying the eternality of hell also violates the third commandment: "You shall not take the name of the LORD your God in vain" (Exod. 20:7). And when we violate the third commandment, we incur the wrath of the Trinitarian God—Father, Son, and Holy Spirit.[9]

---

still there are the same groans, the same shrieks, the same doleful cries, incessantly to be made by you, and that the smoke of your torment shall still ascend up forever and ever. The more the damned in hell think of the eternity of their torments, the more amazing it will appear to them, and alas! They will not be able to keep it out of their minds. . . . The damned in hell will have two infinites perpetually to amaze them and swallow them up; one is an infinite God, whose wrath they will hear and in whom they will behold their perfect and irreconcilable enemy. The other is the infinite duration of their torment.

Works of Jonathan Edwards, 2 vols. (1843; repr., Edinburgh: Banner of Truth, 1974), 2:88.

8 Edward Donnelly, *Biblical Teaching on the Doctrines of Heaven and Hell* (Carlisle, PA: Banner of Truth, 2001), 45.

9 The third commandment states, "You shall not take the name of the LORD your God in vain, for the LORD will not hold him guiltless who takes his name in vain" (Exod. 20:7). The Westminster Larger Catechism, chapter 19 on the law of God, shows what it means to take the name of the Lord in vain by defining the sins forbidden in Question 113: "What are the sins forbidden in the third commandment?" Answer: "The sins forbidden in the third commandment are, not using of God's name as required; abusing of God's name in ignorant vain, irreverent, profane, superstitious, or wicked mentioning, or otherwise using his titles, attributes, ordinances, or works, by blasphemy, perjury, all sinful cursings, oaths, vows, and lots; violating of our oaths and vows, if lawful, and fulfilling them, if of things unlawful; murmuring and quarreling at, curious prying into, and misapplying of God's decrees and providences; misinterpreting, misapplying, or any way perverting the word, or any part of it, to profane jests, curious or unprofitable questions, vain janglings, or the maintaining of false doctrines; abusing the name of God, the creatures or anything contained under the name of God, to charms, or sinful lusts and practices; the maligning, scorning, reviling, or any wise opposing of God's truth, grace, and ways; making a profession of religion in hypocrisy, or for sinister ends; being ashamed of it, or a shame to it, by uncomfortable, unwise, unfruitful, and offensive walking, or backsliding from it."

Many popular books try to understand God on man's terms. It is especially tempting to do this when we are dealing with a loved one who is trapped in the sin of transgenderism. If you believe that gender roles are cultural stereotypes and not God's pattern for biblical anthropology and image-bearing, you are likely to believe that men and women are as interchangeable as their gifts and interests. You might even say something like this:

K.D. grew up as the youngest of several brothers in a context where men were expected to be masculine and women to be feminine. "Real men" served in the military, and women typically stayed home and made babies. K.D.'s brothers naturally joined the military and went off to war. They were the epitome of masculinity. K.D., on the other hand, had another sort of gift: he loved to write poetry. K.D. struggled with many emotions throughout his life: doubt, depression, anxiety. He also had times when he was so filled with joy he could hardly contain himself. Often, he would grab a pen and bleed his emotions onto paper. Like many poets, K.D. also had a talent for writing and playing music. While his brothers were off at war, K.D. stayed home and wrote poetry and music, singing songs about nature, beauty, depression, God, and his best friend, John. John and K.D. were inseparable. They spent loads of time together and desperately missed each other when they were apart. K.D. vowed that he would spend the rest of his life with John, and John felt the same way. They weren't sexual with each other. But they were more than your typical American male friends. When they were together, they would laugh, they would cry, they would talk, and they would hug. Sometimes they would even kiss—in a friendship sort of way. A few years later, John enlisted in the military and went off to war. He rose through the ranks and was a skilled fighter. But, one day, John was killed in battle. When the news reached K.D.'s ears, he was devastated. He fell into a depression. He refused to eat, and he wept profusely. Once the tears dried up enough for him to see, K.D. did the only thing that could soothe his pain. He took his pen and poured out his heart in a poem, describing John's love as better than the love he felt toward women. After K.D.'s own death, the poem would be published and read by millions. So moving, so intimate, so loving were the words of that poem that some people to this day believe that K.D. and John were gay.[10]

In this fictional experiment, Sprinkle is casting King David ("K.D.") as an effeminate poet and Jonathan ("John") as his unrequited love. In keeping with postmodernism, Sprinkle tips his hat to the false claim that David and Jonathan were probably gay. Playing with the Bible in this way is meant, I suppose, to make it friendlier to sexual minorities. But lies are not our friends. We see here how Preston Sprinkle provides many useful examples for how *not* to care well for Christians who identify as transgendered. Any Christian leader who, "because he wasn't there" with Adam in the garden and therefore can't figure out that an intersex condition is the consequence of Adam's sin, and uses a narrative of empathy to misrepresent Scripture, violating the third commandment on his way to misreading it, should not be trusted. He is an irresponsible guide in understanding transgenderism and responding as a Christian. He favors biblical imagination over biblical revelation. He uses innuendo and a deceptive selection of events to misread Scripture.

10   Preston Sprinkle, *Embodied: Transgender Identities, the Church, and What the Bible Has to Say* (Colorado Springs, CO: David C Cook, 2021), 79–80.

Sprinkle uses careless humor to conceal sin and deny repentance. A Christian solution to the pain of transgenderism does not mock sin. Only Satan wants to conceal sin and deny you repentance.

If your daughter or granddaughter is trapped in the sin of transgenderism, the last thing you need is someone rewriting Scripture. You need the power of God to save, the mercy of God to intervene in your daughter's life, and the wisdom of God to know how to stay connected without buying into the indoctrination.

Is Gender Dysphoria Illness and Transgenderism Social Contagion?

In 2012 I learned that one of my lesbian graduate students had transitioned, had written a memoir about her transition from FTM (female to male), had married a woman, and now lived as a father and husband.[11] Because she had changed her name, I couldn't place her when a friend sent me her blog post and book.

Then I realized why. My former student had been a lesbian separatist, someone who wanted to live in an exclusively female world. She rejected everything about men. The idea that she decided to "become" a man was unthinkable to me. My former student has become a full-time political activist, even running for local political offices in addition to writing books and giving lectures about trans rights. To this day, it breaks my heart.

How did a butch, lesbian separatist, quite confident in her lesbian identity, find her "true" identity as a "transman"? In her memoir, she tells the tale of how her therapist led her down this

---

11 Everett Maroon, *Bumbling into Body Hair: A Transsexual's Memoir* (Seattle: Booktrope Editions, 2012). In a dustjacket review, *Bustle* raves: "All teenagers have body issues, but trans man Everett Maroon had more than his fair share. *Bumbling into Body Hair* is Maroon's humorous take on living life as a clumsy, geeky and just plain awkward dude. It's as if *Pretty in Pink* were genderswapped for a new generation."

path, a tale that I believe is both true and criminal. And I believe this is how a social contagion works: the patient presents a series of symptoms, and the therapist offers one solution. But the symptoms that women bring to the table are common to us all: feeling uncomfortable and unsafe in our bodies and hating the way our hormones change our moods. These symptoms are reflective of several things—including normal adolescence. That these symptoms have become "proof" of being transgendered is ludicrous. Therapists are the new priests of Transgender Nation.

Social Contagion

In 2016 I was speaking at a Christian college. After my talk, I met privately with a young woman who went by the name of Cal Baxter. She had tried to get the administration to cancel my visit because she considered my position to be spiritually abusive. She was planning to get a double mastectomy and a hysterectomy over spring break because, she said, she was a man trapped in a woman's body. She was thin and frail, and the testosterone she was taking gave her a fuzzy face that looked more Winnie-the-Pooh, teddy bear–like than manly. She was shorter than I am (and I am five foot two).

Her masquerade of manhood failed abysmally.

"Do you know anyone who has had a double mastectomy and a hysterectomy?" I asked, wondering what kind of trans community she had here. Her answer surprised me.

"Yes, I know one person who had both surgeries. When Aunt Mary had breast cancer, she had both a double mastectomy and a hysterectomy." As she talked about Aunt Mary, she looked more and more like a scared little girl, rubbing her thumb and index finger over the piercings in her right ear the way that my toddlers would fray the satin cuff of their baby blankets. The fact that her knowledge of this surgery had come through a genuine medical situation rather than a politically expedient cosmetic procedure was vital information.

"Did this surgery make Aunt Mary a man?" I asked.

"No. And that is what scares me," she whispered timidly.

"Is there a war going on between your body and your mind?" I asked.

"Yes, and it makes me cut myself and dream of being a man," she whispered.

"If there is a war between your mind and your body, why are you starting with your body? Why not spend six months working on changing your mind?" I asked.

"Because that is not what Chase Ross said to do."

"Who is Chase Ross?"

"*Who* is Chase Ross? Why, he is the most famous FTM [female to male] in the world! You haven't seen his YouTube channel?"[12] She was more animated than I had seen her yet. She was completely enamored with Chase Ross and simply couldn't believe that I didn't know her name. It made me wonder if she wanted to be a man or if she wanted to be Chase (whoever this was).

Together, this student and I went to the chaplain, who was, providentially, a Christian counselor. The chaplain wanted to know how often she watched Chase Ross. The student replied with a number I didn't think was possible: ten hours a day. (Could you imagine watching and then rewatching episodes of anything for up to ten hours a day?) The chaplain offered to meet weekly with her to work on knowing and following Jesus and made it clear

---

12 Chase Ross's YouTube channel, "UpperChase1," has more than ten million views and 166,000 subscribers. I do not recommend visiting this channel as the material—common for the transgender community—is lacking in modesty and decency on all issues.

that part of her obedience was no longer knowing and following YouTube influencers. I am sure that it was hard to detox from a ten-hour-a-day addiction, but Cal did this. With the help of Christian counseling, she stopped pursuing surgery and instead worked on the deep heart issues that lurked in the shadows of her past, learning to walk with Christ step by step.

And here is another example.

In 2018, at a midwestern Bible church, a man in distress approached the microphone at the end of the Q&A time. I had shared my testimony and had answered questions for about two hours, and the pastors and elders and I were ready to pray and dismiss the audience. The small audience and sanctuary felt intimate and safe, and I enjoyed being able to see everyone clearly. The man at the microphone was wearing a wig, and his makeup was a little off. His black eyeliner was running along the creases of his pancake-white foundation like a creek cresting the banks during a bad storm. Once he took the mic, he started to grandstand: "I almost didn't come, and now I wish I hadn't. You don't respect trans people. In your testimony, you said that your 'friend' Jill had large hands. Transwomen are offended by that. And—"

The "large hands" offense is a trope that comes up a lot in my talks, and I was too tired to entertain it.

I interrupted my interlocutor and invited him to come to the pastor's office with me where we could talk privately. I explained that we would have more time to talk, and I anticipated that we both would be able to listen better sitting down in comfortable chairs with a cup of tea. He accepted, and together with the pastor, the three of us walked out of the sanctuary and down the hall. As we were bending the corner toward the pastor's office, an irate man burst out in front of us.

"Art! What happened to you, man?" He blurted out, standing in front of the man with the dripping eyeliner.

"Jim? Is that really you? I'm not Art anymore; I'm Autumn."

"Art, what happened to you? What happened to Mary and the kids?"

"It's Autumn, not Art, and my divorced wife and children are very happy that I have found my true self."

"That's a bunch of bull@#$%, and you know it. Where are we going? I'm coming with you guys," declared Jim as he shoved himself into our tight group. I liked him immediately, and despite his confrontational spirit, Art/Autumn did too. I could tell. They had the kind of history that allowed for strong words.

I learned that Art and Jim had both worked as truck drivers for the same company a decade or so ago. They both committed their lives to Jesus during that time and had gotten baptized, married, and started families. I have sat with many people who believe they are transgendered, but no conversation was as illuminating as this one, because Jim provided a history and perspective that challenged Art in a way that he could not deny. Jim had the bona fides that the rest of us lacked. And more than bona fides, Jim held Art's history. That was key. Transgenderism is committed to the erasure of truth and history in the name of false but persistent fantasies (like brain-sex theory). Having Jim at the table challenged the fiction of transgenderism. Jim also was connected to Art. Jim was filled with sympathy for Art's wife and children, and he persistently called Art to "man up" (see 1 Cor. 16:13).

Jim extended no empathy to Art. Instead, Jim extended the truth that comes from a long friendship. Every time Art would offer some ideological propaganda, Jim blurted out, "Bull@#$%." It served as a salty kind of catechism for truth and history. Jim firmly and kindly told Art that he needed to man up, come back to Jesus, apologize to his wife and kids, put on some pants, and return to church.

"I can't, Jimmy. Look at me," Art mumbled softly, tears starting to make black lines of dripping eyeliner over his cheek.

"Yes you can," Jim commanded. When Jim offered to come to church with Art, something in Art shook visibly.

Art contemplated all of this for a moment, then turned to the pastor with a question. He wanted to know if he could join a women's Bible study. The pastor said no. Art wanted to know if he could use the women's bathroom. The pastor said no and immediately offered instead his private bathroom for Art to use at any time. Art started to weep. He said that he could only dress like a woman. He explained that he has no men's clothes and that he is morally and ethically opposed to the idea of wearing men's clothes. The pastor said that Art could dress any way he wanted to for a while, and Art decided that he would go to church only if Jim drove with him and they sat together. And then Art said something fascinating. He turned to the pastor and said, "You need to call me Autumn. Only Jim can call me Art because that is the name that he knew me by. And you need to honor my pronouns. Jim can do what he wants."

Jesus is the hero of this story, and Jim is his ambassador. Rough around the edges and colorful with his adjectives, Jim loved Jesus. Because Jim was closer to Jesus than to Art, and also because Jim had a past friendship with Art, Jim was able to be of real use. Both Jim's history and his faith played a role. He wasn't in any way persuaded to "stand in Art's shoes" (and not only because Art was wearing high heels).

Jim was filled with godly sympathy, and he had no desire to lead Art by empathy into worldly sorrow. Jim did what supposedly causes people like Art to commit suicide—he stayed connected to both truth and to Art. And Art did not kill himself. Instead, he changed. The church also did what it needed to do. It welcomed Art, and at the same time, protected the church by denying him access to the women's restroom and Bible study. The pastor was able to arrange weekly biblical counseling. The church had a connection with a medical doctor who had helped people in Art's position, and he was called in to help. The last I heard, Art was attending church and biblical counseling weekly. My prayer is that he is making a transition back into manhood.

Jill, Cal, and Art had all been schooled in a church. They knew the Bible, and you could appeal to the Bible when talking with them. My graduate student was outside the church. As I reflect on these relationships, I am reminded of the powerful role of the praying parents, grandparents, sisters, brothers, aunts, uncles, cousins, and neighbors of loved ones captured by these lies. You praying parents and grandparents and loved ones are heroes. Your loved one's legacy with biblical faith and with church and family are gold. You hold history. Please keep all of the relics of your loved one's history. Keep the pottery and pictures. Keep the childhood stuffed animals and old clothes. She will need these relics of truth.

As I type these words, I pray for you as you uphold family and friends who have fallen, for now, because of transgender propaganda. Do not in any way discount the prayers and tears that you have offered as you stand rooted in Christ's truth. And do not deny yourself the victorious stories of real Christian men and women who left the dark fiction of transgendered identity to live as real men and real women.[13] Jesus raises the dead to life.

13 Books like Laura Perry's *Transgender to Transformed: A Story of Transition That Will Truly Set You Free* (Bartlesville, OK: Genesis, 2019) should be at your right hand.

Repenting from Transgenderism

Everyone has a path to sin. Perhaps your path to sin is responsive to the sin of others. This is often the case with childhood sexual abuse or trauma. Perhaps you are sinning because of a deep desire that wells up inside you, something that is as much yours as your face or name. This is likely original sin, the way that Adam's sin now fingerprints your life. It does not matter what the sin is. It does not matter if you are sinning as a response to being sinned against, as the result of some indwelling pattern of desire that comes from the fall, or because of some willful impulse over which you failed to exercise prayer and self-control. We all sin. And Christians are all called to repent. True repentance involves a change of mind, a change of affections, and a change in your life. We all need help with this. We need God's help and we need the help of brothers and sisters in the church. We are almost always both sinners and victims.

Repentance is poetically reflected in Psalm 51, where we find these aspects displayed: grief over sin (vv. 1–3), confession of sin to God (vv. 4–8), humiliation for sin (vv. 9–10), accepting God's chastening for our sin (vv. 11–17), and embracing God's covenant and the divine mercy that only he can offer to us and walking in obedience to his word (vv. 18–19).

Real repentance, which results in Spirit-wrought change, is radically different from its counterfeit, which condones sin and asks for no change. Indeed, repentance is the threshold to God. Any Christian who tires of hearing about repentance or who rejects it as spiritual abuse is someone whose soul is in grave danger. If this is you, pray or sing Psalm 51, asking that the Lord would give you the courage to see your sin as an offense against God and give you a willing heart and mind to repent of it. My husband and pastor,

Kent, says that when we sing the psalms, we are praying twice. I need this means of grace for myself, and I commend it to you.

For those who have started a gender transition, repentance includes doing everything possible to return their body and identity to God's design. Two very helpful Christians to read and learn from are Laura Perry and Walt Heyer.[14] Both have detransitioned, and both are biblically married. God is gracious to save. And even if returning to your God-given body is not possible on this side of heaven, the very best news is that when Jesus returns, the souls and bodies of God's own people will be reunited and glorified. You will be made whole. There is no sin in heaven or in the new heavens and earth. There is no transgenderism or homosexuality in heaven.

Vice or Virtue

If envy is the vice, contentment is the virtue.

Repentance is a good fruit of the Christian life (Matt. 3:8), and to a Christian, there is no shame in repentance. If transgenderism is the sin of envy, then someone who has struggled against transgenderism in repentance will find the godly fruit of contentment as she rests in God's calling for sex and gender integrity. It's that clear, but it likely is not simple. Anyone who has undergone transgender surgeries or hormone blockers will also require medical care. But do not underestimate the godly virtue of contentment. Contentment is a misunderstood and maligned virtue, dismissed as passive resignation to God's cruelly leaving you in rotten circumstances. But this is not what godly contentment is.

Our anti-Christian age (and the "Christian" writers who are foolishly duped by it) puts sexual and gender identity on the science

---

14 Perry, *Transgender to Transformed*; and Walt Heyer, *Trading My Sorrows* (Maitland, FL: Xulon Press, 2006).

pedestal and removes it from a moral category. But a rejection of the body God gave you is a rejection of reality. There is no shame in needing God's loving oversight as you seek godly contentment. Christians should not go along with this satanic cruelty of transgender fiction. Any Christian with gender dysphoria can grow in the grace of contentment, flee the sin of envy, grow in union with Christ, and live a vital and thriving life in the church and the family of God.[15] There is hope and help for body, mind, and soul.

Jeremiah Burroughs preached and lived as a Puritan nonconformist during the English Civil War, and his writings show him as a man of faithfulness and courage. As a religious nonconformist during an age of religious tyranny, he was in constant danger of arrest, imprisonment, and even execution.[16] I marvel that a Puritan nonconformist preaching under tyranny, persecution, and threat of execution would choose to preach a sermon series on contentment and not on, say, religious liberty or when to practice civil disobedience. The context in which Burroughs preached his sermons is something to contemplate.

Burroughs's *The Rare Jewel of Christian Contentment* is his collection of these sermons, now a Christian classic that I reread

---

15 Reading the Puritans can take some practice. I happen to like their style. But I also happen to like reading the Bible in the King James Version and reading classical literature for pleasure. If these things aren't to your taste, I strongly recommend finding good and faithful translators of the Puritans. Andrew M. Davis has written a biblically faithful book on contentment entitled, *The Power of Christian Contentment: Finding Deeper, Richer Christ-Centered Joy* (Grand Rapids, MI: Baker, 2019). I highly recommend this book, as well as Pastor Davis's other books. Pastor Davis has memorized forty-three books of the Bible, and I especially am in awe of his booklet *An Approach to Extended Memorization of Scripture* (Greenville, SC: Ambassador International, 2014), Kindle.

16 Phillip L. Simpson, *A Life of Gospel Peace: A Biography of Jeremiah Burroughs* (Grand Rapids, MI: Reformation Heritage, 2011). Also see Nancy Wilson's helpful introduction in *The Rare Jewel of Christian Contentment*, Christian Heritage Series (Moscow, ID: Canon Press, 2020), i–v.

every couple of years. It always convicts me of my sin, leads me to repentance, and produces awe and gratitude for my Lord and Savior Jesus Christ. To Burroughs, only a Christian can grow in the godly contentment of which Paul speaks in Philippians 4:11: "I have learned in whatever situation I am to be content." To Burroughs, godly contentment is only an attainable jewel to those who know God through Jesus Christ.

Knowing God through Jesus Christ means grace for sinners who will come to glory because God the Father stands by his word to honor the Lord Jesus Christ's sacrifice to become sin on our behalf and die on the cross (2 Cor. 5:12). When we confess our sins, "he is faithful and just to forgive us our sins and to cleanse us from all unrighteousness" (1 John 1:9), not because of our works or our suffering, but because Christ's sacrifice is acceptable to the Father. God is the author and definition of justice. But the believer has more of God than the world. In other words, the believer is in the world but not of it. The believer has the knowledge of God through a mind redeemed by the Holy Spirit to receive the Bible as Christ's pure words of truth in all situations. God gives contentment only to the genuine Christian, not to someone who is Christian in name only. Cultural Christians cannot have contentment. But even to the genuine Christian, contentment is not something passively received.

Burroughs defines contentment as "the inward, quiet, gracious frame of spirit, freely submitting to and taking pleasure in God's disposal in every condition." Burroughs explains that this takes "heart work within the soul," "a quieting of the heart," submission, which is "sending the soul under God," and "a gracious frame."[17]

---

17 Jeremiah Burroughs, *The Rare Jewel of Christian Contentment* (1648; repr., Carlisle, PA: Banner of Truth, 2013), 40.

Contentment means being able to say and believe that God is good, just, and wise in all things. As my friend Pastor Drew Poplin is fond of saying, "God uses sin sinlessly." Not even outrageous sin can overturn God's providence, which will perfectly bring all his elect into the new creation as glorified and faithful believers. Godly contentment allows us to suffer in the flesh and perceive in the soul how God's providence is perfect even when it is painful.

Burroughs aids genuine Christians to grow in the mystery of contentment, revealing spiritual weapons to use in the fight against the sin of envy. What he writes is intimately applicable to the person suffering from gender dysphoria or trapped in the indoctrination of transgenderism. I recommend *The Rare Jewel of Christian Contentment* in its entirety. I will highlight here one chapter—"The Mystery of Contentment"—where Burroughs identifies six spiritual practices that serve as powerful spiritual weapons against the sin of envy.

1. *Be unsatisfied with the world.* Christians must learn how to be content with God even while being unsatisfied in the world. The world cannot give us what we need. We are not to pray for things that Scripture forbids. If you get the unbiblical thing you asked for, you can be sure that you are now eating out of Satan's hand, not God's. Learn to be content in God and unsatisfied in the world.

2. *Subtract desires, don't add them.* Burroughs says that "a Christian comes to contentment, not so much by way of addition, as by way of subtraction."[18] This requires heroic sacrifice. Making such a sacrifice is impossible for the unbeliever or the pretend Christian. "A heart that has no grace . . . knows of no way to get contentment."[19] This approach leaves no room for a little cross-dressing to blow off steam. It means that if a student named Bill

18 Burroughs, *Rare Jewel,* 45.
19 Burroughs, *Rare Jewel,* 45.

comes to a meeting in a skirt and asks to be called Joanne, the ministry leader needs to take Bill aside and get Bill some spiritual—and perhaps medical—counsel. It does not mean that everyone should now accept "Joanne" as he presents himself. In order for Bill to grow in contentment, he needs to subtract the dress, not add it.

3. *Add burdens, don't seek to subtract them.* Burroughs also says that "a Christian comes to contentment, not so much by getting rid of the burden that is on him, as by adding another burden to himself,"[20] and the burden that Burroughs tells us to add is the burden of our sin. The real Christian is deeply concerned with sinning against God when he is in pain. The pretend Christian has remade a god in the image of his insatiable desire and cannot imagine a god who denies what his flesh craves. Counterfeit Christians judge God by their own intentions and the merits of their feelings. Repenting of envy compels the Christian who struggles with transgenderism to submit to God as one submits to the reality that God's greatness is beyond our understanding. It forces the believer to fear God and bow low before his holiness. And if this is not your reaction, Burroughs tells you that you are deceived to believe that your only path to contentment is if your burden were lightened.

Faithful Christians throughout history have found ways to praise God for their afflictions. Joni Eareckson Tada has praised God for her wheelchair.[21] Betsy and Corrie ten Boom praised God for the fleas that kept away the guards in a Nazi concentration camp, thus allowing them to proclaim the gospel.[22] Christians change their

---

20 Burroughs, *Rare Jewel*, 47.
21 Joni Eareckson Tada, "Wheelchairs in Heaven," Joni and Friends (website), May 5, 2021, https://www.joniandfriends.org/.
22 Corrie ten Boom, *The Hiding Place* (Grand Rapids, MI: Chosen, 2014). See also Christine Hoover, "'Thank You, God, for the Fleas'—Finding Courage in the Hiding Place," The Gospel Coalition, July 1, 2019, https://www.thegospelcoalition.org/.

affliction by framing it in God's point of view. For the genuine Christian burdened with transgenderism, fight the good fight in the Spirit and do not cave to the flesh. Progressive sanctification will be your friend, and God will be your comfort. Set a better example for others who are afflicted like you.

Satan would like you to think that you can't obey God until you are able to get comfortable in your skin and gain the desire of your flesh if even on unholy grounds. But Burroughs reminds us that the real question is not "What do I need?" but rather, "What is my duty?" Burroughs asks it like this: "What is the duty of the circumstances that God has put me in?"[23]

4. *Look at your afflictions through the mind of Christ and the cross of Christ.* God's grace in our hearts shows us how our afflictions are portioned to serve our spiritual needs. We who are in Christ suffer for the good of our souls (Rom. 8:29).

5. *Do your duties before God and men—do the good works to which God has set you apart.* Your strength is to be spent doing the work God has given you, not murmuring about what he has withheld. It is good when God withholds our sinful desires. He is on your side. You need to get to work. Ken Smith, the pastor whom the Lord used in my conversion, is fond of saying that circumstances don't make a person; they reveal what he is made of. Ken Smith also says, "You can't turn a parked car." He means that you can't steer a car in a particular direction if you can't get it to move. When you are burdened by sinful desires, don't blame your circumstances but do the good work of the Lord. And pray that God would strengthen you to continue to do more good work. But don't think that you can cross-dress or self-mutilate

---

23 Burroughs, *Rare Jewel*, 51.

and make up for it by working in a soup kitchen. God won't be mocked, and you won't be helped.

6. *Conform or "melt" your will to God's.* Burroughs gives great encouragement to repent when he writes, "A gracious heart is contented by the melting of his will and desires into God's will and desires; by this means he gets contentment."[24] Melting your desires into God's will—what a beautiful picture those words paint. Proverbs 21:1 says, "The king's heart is a stream of water in the hand of the LORD; he turns it wherever he will." If we are the clay and God is the potter, we are to be soft and malleable under the loving care of our heavenly Father, who knows what we need better than we do. Melting your will into God's goes beyond submission and obedience. Through union with Christ, believers are joined to the Lord. As such, our will takes its shape under God's word and God's calling.

Christian contentment is an active and rigorous application of faith; it is not passive resignation. Christian contentment is the biblical antidote to the sin of envy. Understanding contentment as a spiritual weapon with power to defeat the sin of envy helps the Christian who struggles with gender identity to rely upon her union with Christ to grow her in his likeness. The point is to look like God's will for you, not the will of your flesh.

When dealing with sexual sin, it is imperative for the Christian to see how the battlefield has changed and to extend Christian compassion, charity, and sympathy to those whose besetting sin has a civil rights movement cheering it on. As the battlefield has changed, we have witnessed beloved Christians failing to stand for the truth and instead falsifying the gospel message, to the great

---

24 Burroughs, *Rare Jewel*, 53.

detriment of people's souls, futures, and families. Deuteronomy 13:1–3 explains:

> If a prophet or a dreamer of dreams arises among you and gives you a sign or a wonder, and the sign or wonder that he tells you comes to pass, and if he says, "Let us go after other gods," which you have not known, "and let us serve them," you shall not listen to the words of that prophet or that dreamer of dreams. *For the LORD your God is testing you, to know whether you love the LORD your God with all your heart and with all your soul.*

Christian, if you are struggling with transgenderism, find a good church, listen to your pastor, get the counseling and Christian medical care you need to live in the fullness of the body that God gave you, and grow in contentment and progressive sanctification. Becoming another casualty of the LGBTQ+-rights movement will help no one, least of all you. Contentment is the opposite of envy, and envy is the sinful fuel of transgenderism. God knows how to get you the help you really need. "The Lord knows how to rescue the godly from trials" (2 Pet. 2:9).

———

MODESTY IS AN OUTDATED BURDEN THAT SERVES MALE DOMINANCE AND HOLDS WOMEN BACK

13

In the Presence of My Enemies

*You prepare a table before me
in the presence of my enemies.*

PSALM 23:5

1997, Syracuse, NY

The table was set with unfussy Corelle dishes, yellow paisley cloth napkins, and water glasses. One of the pastor's sons, a colleague of mine from the university, pulled a gallon plastic jug out of the refrigerator and started filling water glasses. "It's not filtered. I just like it cold," Pastor Ken Smith's eyes sparkled a stunning sky blue as he laughed and warmly shook my hand and pulled me—gently but more firmly than I was expecting—over the threshold. This was one of my first experiences of a Christian family feast, one that included the whole extended Smith family, brothers and sisters from the church, and me. It had been so very long since I had experienced anything even close to this that I hardly knew how to conduct myself. The room hummed with deep men's voices laughing and holding court and the giggles of children. The calmness of the women was serene and strange. No grandstanding. No holding court. No gossip. These were old friends with deep connections who knew how to belly laugh. I stood between the kitchen and the family room, not belonging in either place. As soon as Becky saw me, she pulled me into the middle of the kitchen conversation, gave me the choice between two jobs—holding a baby or chopping vegetables—and asked me about my week. I washed my hands and reached for the knife and carrots. Did they know that I had never held a baby?

This night became for me a mirror. I looked into it and saw ugly things in myself and lovely things in God's family.

The first had to do with diversity—an important word in my lesbian community. While I proclaimed the value of diversity, the reality was that I had spent the past decade around people just like me—white, thirty-something, humanities PhDs in lesbian relationships. The mirror of this night was dramatic irony at its best. It was at my first experience of a Christian family feast, held at the straight, white, male pastor's house, where I found myself in the most diverse crowd I had inhabited in years, maybe a lifetime. Men, women, children of every age. Who knew?

The table was set. Children dragged in extra chairs. Bowls were overflowing with Floy Smith's steaming and savory sweet and sour soybeans, and Ken herded us to the table with a gentle but firm hand. People started grabbing the hand of the closest person, and Ken prayed a prayer that thanked God for the food and the hands that made it. That's sweet, I thought. The hands that made it. The women's hands. They mattered.

We feasted and talked. It was intimate but not stuffy, even though there was no elbow room, and I was sitting closer to strangers than I would normally have been comfortable. The conversation was marked with edgy questions of the day (on which I took an opposing side) and the Bible verses and principles (some offered as answers and others that opened more questions). It seemed to me that Pastor Ken Smith and the other Christians at the table used the Bible for reference, comfort, and lingering long. What an intimate use of a book, I pondered. Even the children could reference the Bible as a touchstone, and this gave everyone at the table a shared world. They belonged to one another and to this Bible, from the least to the greatest.

When dinner was done, one of the older children started passing out a red song book, marked *Book of Psalms for Singing*,[1] and without fanfare or fuss, the room opened in song. Voices in all four parts to the tune of "Crimond" rang right as rain. The harmony was tight and strong. And when we sang, "A table Thou hast furnished me, in presence of my foes," I started to lose my sense of which way was up. I got all turned around. I felt like I had absentmindedly taken the wrong path on a well-walked trail. I was trained to play the victim and to perceive myself as a sexual minority, the voiceless among the voiced. As we sang, which I found myself doing with gusto in spite of the clear and present danger, I said in my heart, "Yes, dear victim, here you are in the presence of your foes, these awful, hateful people who want to trample on your civil rights as a lesbian." But even though victimhood served as my catechism, I just couldn't talk myself into believing this while we were singing Psalm 23. God's word started to rewrite my words. And that is when I looked into the mirror of God's word and saw it: I, the English professor, was misreading the text.

I wasn't dining in the presence of my enemies.

I was the enemy.

It was dreadful to behold—I was God's enemy.

---

1 *The Book of Psalms for Singing* (Pittsburgh, PA: Crown & Covenant, 1973), selection 23B.

Dinner concluded with prayer. Pastor Ken prayed, and so did a few others—men and women prayed at the table, one voice tapering off and another one starting up with some invisible hand of organic unity. The unyielding and unanswered questions that had marked the earlier part of this evening were neither swept under the rug nor turned into idols but instead placed firmly in the hand of God. At the final "Amen!" someone said, "Let's sing Psalm 122B." The table had this one memorized too, and Floy gently touched my arm and placed an open psalter in my hand. Again, the room unfolded in song without pretense. This was not a performance. It was something else entirely, but I couldn't put my finger on what it was at the time. We sang:

> I was glad to hear them saying, "to the Lord's house let us go."
> For our feet will soon be standing in your gates Jerusalem. . . .
> In your palaces be safety, for the sake of brothers all,
> For the sake of my companions, I am saying
> "Peace to you!"[2]

At the psalm's conclusion, someone muttered, "Yes, Lord, this is my pilgrim's journey."

While I did not understand the reference at the time, this night marked my pilgrim journey as well. That I was the enemy at this table made little matter to Pastor Ken Smith. That I had mocked Christians (including the very people at this table), written university policy that extolled hatred for God (the university's first domestic-partnership policy for same-sex couples, to be exact), taught classes in queer theory that enlisted others into a worldview

2 *The Book of Psalms for Singing,* selection 122B.

that walks only to hell, and sinned against others with my body and books was not the main thing for this godly pastor and the church he pastored. The main thing was Christ crucified and risen.

The Christian life goes on regardless of how many enemies are at the table, because enemies cannot perjure the main thing—"That I may know him, and the power of his resurrection, and the fellowship of his sufferings, being made conformable unto his death" (Phil. 3:10 KJV). Our faith flourishes by design in the presence of our enemies. Psalm 110:2 declares, "The LORD shall send the rod of thy strength out of Zion: rule thou in the midst of thine enemies" (KJV). It is God's will that Zion (the church) will shine in the presence of our enemies. John Calvin puts it this way:

> Doubtless our condition in this world will include many hardships, but God's will is that Christ's kingdom should be encompassed with many enemies, his design being to keep us in a state of constant warfare. Therefore, it becomes us to exercise patience and meekness and, assured of God's aid, boldly to consider the rage of the whole world as nothing.[3]

Indeed. To a Christian, the rage of the whole world is nothing—nothing, that is, compared to the grace and power of God.[4]

That evening at the Smiths' home held up before me another mirror, reflecting a signature virtue of the godly women in the room. At the time, I couldn't name it. But I saw it and felt it and loved it. It was the opposite of me, and I secretly wanted it. These

---

3 John Calvin, *365 Days with Calvin: A Unique Collection of 365 Readings from the Writings of John Calvin*, ed. Joel Beeke (Grand Rapids, MI: Reformation Heritage, 2008), March 19 entry.

4 A version of this section first appeared in *Fight. Laugh. Feast.* 2.2 (Summer 2021): 17–19 and was reprinted in *Tabletalk* magazine, September 2021, 15–19.

women were strong and valued and loved. They cared for their children and husbands well. They were covered by godly men, and they lived as a team with a divine purpose and eternal calling. They were honored. But they didn't sell themselves. They didn't talk about themselves. They possessed a virtue that I had not ever seen before: modesty. The path that my life was on would take me far away from this table, from this virtue, from ever becoming a woman like these women.

I realized that night that the Christian life is a life of binaries. If I wanted to be like these women—if I wanted to be a godly woman—I could not be a lesbian. But I couldn't just flip a switch and stop feeling like a lesbian. I knew that, because I had tried it before.

That night I realized the real reason I could not become a godly woman was not primarily my feelings of attraction to other women. The real reason I could not become a godly woman was that I had no idea how to be a woman at all. I was hung up on the *godly* part while the real mystery was God's design for me as a woman. I might have accepted a God who would change the *ungodly* part in the same way that my wisdom teeth were removed years ago—while I was deep under some anesthesia. At the same time, I also wanted the Lord to leave my feminism and my professional life on which it rested perfectly intact. But that's not how it works. Ungodliness is not surgically removed under anesthesia by the Holy Spirit while the sinful foundation remains. We are called to mortify our sin—to kill it. And then we are called to vivify our Christian life—to bring it quickening, or new life, in Christ. Ephesians 4:22–24 makes this clear: "Put off your old self, which belongs to your former manner of life and is corrupt through deceitful desires, and . . . be renewed in the spirit of your minds. . . . Put on the new self, created after the likeness of God in true righteousness and holiness."

The whole thing hit me like a brick: these modest Christian women lived lives that supported patriarchy, that evil empire that had been my life's driving mission to destroy.

Months of more dinners with open Bibles and singing children and me now with my own role to play in the kitchen, me with praying women friends and a Bible with underlined passages memorized, the new me, the new creature in Christ, with a new nature.

Me, still battling my biography of sin, but doing so firmly locked to Christ and securely belonging to this church, these elders, those people.

Me, who belonged now in competing worlds and would have to choose.

Me, who felt like I was falling off a cliff.

Me, who desired to be a godly woman. A woman of grace who conducted herself in modesty.

How was God going to get me there?

I came to learn that God would grow me in sanctification through obedience and suffering, through grace and grit "according to the foreknowledge of God the Father, in the sanctification of the Spirit, for obedience to Jesus Christ and for sprinkling with his blood" (1 Pet. 1:2).

14

Exhibitionism

The New Almost-Christian Virtue

The woman Folly is loud;
she is seductive and knows nothing.

PROVERBS 9:13

An excellent wife who can find?

PROVERBS 31:10

GODLY WOMANHOOD WAS A MYSTERY to me not just decades ago when I lived as a lesbian. Godly womanhood, like other Christian virtues, is truly a mystery. A godly woman is a modest woman. A godly woman's modesty is a sacred principle, infused with God's grace. A godly woman's modesty is a signature virtue, the beauty of which our anti-Christian world mocks and despises. This confusion about the vital role of modesty in the life of a woman has been slipping into the church. In the evangelical church most especially, in those churches where celebrity pastors court influential women writers on Twitter, and in those Reformed churches that have become smitten by this, one thing is dreadfully clear: our social media–saturated world encourages Christian women to replace modesty with exhibitionism.

Modesty and Sanctification

Modesty serves a vital role in our sanctification. It helps guard us— and others—from temptation. The lie that modesty for Christian women is an outdated cultural expectation has shipwrecked many Christian women and leaves the generation of our daughters in peril. In both dress and social media use, modesty has been replaced by exhibitionism.

Modesty and Virtue

Modesty is a virtue, one which the apostle Peter commands us to add to our faith:

> For this very reason, make every effort to supplement your faith with virtue, and virtue with knowledge, and knowledge with self-control, and self-control with steadfastness, and steadfastness with godliness, and godliness with brotherly affection, and brotherly affection with love. For if these qualities are yours and are increasing, they keep you from being ineffective or unfruitful in the knowledge of our Lord Jesus Christ. For whoever lacks these qualities is so nearsighted that he is blind, having forgotten that he was cleansed from his former sins. (2 Pet. 1:5–9)

A modest woman does not bring attention to herself but instead gives glory to God. Modesty, however, is not some kind of passive weakness; it is a virtue, after all, and *virtue* is a strong word and means "valor, worth, merit and moral perfection."[1] *Virtue* is different from *values*, as virtue hearkens from God and values from man. Modesty, as a biblical virtue, is like a rich compound oil, marinating valor, knowledge, self-control, perseverance, godliness, brotherly kindness, and love to achieve a stunning embodiment of moral beauty. Modesty is a high point of moral beauty and a vital virtue for women, requiring God's grace and personal grit. Significantly, adding virtue to your faith is not optional, because faith in Christ is not the end but the start. Peter described those who lack virtue as shortsighted, blind, and forgetful of our Lord and his grace in cleansing us from our sin. These are not small matters. Modesty, as one of the virtues of valor, is not something we can neglect.

But we do.

Modesty and Temptation

I have the privilege of teaching English literature in a classical Christian homeschool co-op where my teenagers are enrolled as students in the rhetoric program. Like most Christian schools, ours has a dress code. The boys' dress code takes up about a paragraph, and the girls' covers multiple pages. And that is not unfair. It's very wise and necessary. The fashion industry for girls sets them up to be tempters to young men.

How many of you read that sentence and think I'm being unfair and "blaming the victim"?

In *Modesty: More than a Change of Clothes*, Martha Peace and Kent Keller define modesty as "an inner attitude of the heart motivated by a love for God that seeks His glory through purity and humility; it often reveals itself in words, actions, expressions, and

---

1   *The New Shorter Oxford English Dictionary on Historical Principles*, vol. 1, ed. Lesley Brown (Oxford, UK: Clarendon Press, 1973), s.v. "virtue."

clothes."[2] Martha Peace is one of my favorite Christian mothers. Her books—especially *The Excellent Wife*—have mentored and encouraged and rebuked and shaped me.[3] I trust Martha to help me embrace a biblical standard of modesty so that I don't sin against God and neighbor. Martha contrasts biblical modesty with immodesty, which she defines as "an attitude of the heart that expresses itself with inappropriate words, actions, expressions and/or clothes that are flirtatious, manipulative, revealing, or suggestive of sensuality or pride."[4] Immodesty is a sin that can be diagnosed easily (unlike other sins that lurk underground). We wear immodesty on our body and blogs. Perhaps only the proudly immodest are deluded.

Martha Peace offers a checklist to help her readers look at the symptoms of immodesty from a biblical point of view. She asks us to check our heart and our actions against these symptoms of immodesty:

- I do dress modestly compared to most girls. Since I'm more modest than most, I must be dressing modestly.
- Some guy's problem with lust is not my problem. Quit blaming me for his problems. We already have too much of that "victim" mentality that wants to pass the blame to others in our culture today.
- This is all just legalism. I can dress any way I want to since this is a "gray area."[5]

2 Martha Peace and Kent Evan Keller, *Modesty: More than a Change of Clothes* (Phillipsburg, NJ: P&R, 2015), 17.
3 Martha Peace, *The Excellent Wife: A Biblical Perspective*, rev. ed. (Bemidji, MN: Focus, 1995).
4 Peace and Keller, *Modesty*, 18.
5 Peace and Keller, *Modesty*, 19.

Martha goes on to explain by parable how immodesty affects young men:

> Can you think of someone who was cruel to you? Perhaps another kid at school made fun of you in front of others, and everyone laughed. Perhaps he pushed you or tried to trip you up. Maybe he grabbed your books, ran down the hall with them, and threw them in a trashcan. As a result, you dreaded going to school because that bully of a kid would not leave you alone. . . . On the days when the bully did not make fun of you, you were nonetheless well aware that he was lurking near you, ready to burst forth with seemingly endless cruelty at any moment. You always had to be on guard and try, very hard, to avoid him. In a similar way, that is how boys usually are when they see an immodestly dressed woman. Even if they try to be godly, they are well aware of sexual temptation. . . . When men see an immodestly dressed woman they have an instantaneous physical reaction: sexual temptation.[6]

Perhaps you think that her parable stretches things too far. Perhaps you wonder why men and women can't just be friends without the complication of sexual difference. Aren't we just spiritual siblings after all? The answer to both questions is simple: because sexual difference is irrefutable, men and women, as spiritual siblings, promote modesty and prudence. Men and women are hardwired and softwired differently as part of God's design. Men and women are not interchangeable, and no amount of feminist biblical interpretation will change this.

---

6   Peace and Keller, *Modesty*, 21–22.

Let's look carefully at these two different angles on the subject of modesty: the difference between men and women, and the danger of temptation.

Men and Women Are Not Interchangeable

My husband pastors a small Reformed Presbyterian church close to a college campus. One of our young mothers, Beth, a teacher at the college, was struggling about a situation that involved a transgendered student, a man named Zeke who wanted to be addressed as Annette and who attended the campus Christian fellowship with LGBTQ+ evangelical glee. Zeke wanted the world to know him as a woman who loved God. He wanted the world to know that Christians who denied him "transgender rights" and female pronouns were spiritual abusers.

Beth wanted to do the right thing but was confused. The campus minister wanted Zeke to be discipled by the students. But he didn't designate how this should be done, perhaps not wanting to upset a fragile situation. Beth's colleague, May, wanted to extend hospitality and care, and she and Beth invited Zeke to dinner at a local restaurant. Immediately, more confusion ensued. Beth didn't know what name to use to address her guest. Zeke pummeled the concerned women with requests for advice on eyeliner application, padded bras, and eyebrow management, and before Beth could stop it, May dug in her purse for a comb and was helping Zeke with ringlets, trying to avoid the stubble of facial hair.

The next day, we prayed that the Lord would convict Zeke of his sin and provide for him appropriate counseling and a biblically faithful church. Beth was visibly troubled, and she asked me for help. She came to our house after church so that we could talk and pray some more.

We pulled two stools up to the kitchen island and plugged in the electric tea kettle. Beth selected two mugs from the cabinet and found our favorite tea, the herbal one with turmeric and ginger.

Beth poured boiling water into our mugs, and I opened my Bible to Titus 2.

We cupped our warm mugs and enjoyed the sharp scent of ginger.

Beth sighed and in a defeated exhale said, "I was just trying to help. Why is everything so complicated?"

"Sin always makes things complicated," I offered.

"Why did things get so wacky last night? Why did May and I approach Zeke so differently? Why did she bring out the comb? Why did May have to bring out the curling iron?" Beth took a careful sip of tea.

"Why isn't the ministry director discipling Zeke? Where is Zeke going to church?" I inquired.

"Zeke doesn't go to church because he needs to find one where Annette is fully welcome—hey, can we open that box of Nilla Wafers?"

"Good call on the Nilla Wafers. Yes, this does sound complicated," I consented.

Beth tore into the cookies and sighed, "Does the Bible speak to transgenderism?"

"Of course it does!" I was quick to assure her.

I grabbed two Bibles from the shelf and said, "It's right here in Titus 2." We opened our Bibles, and I read verses 1–8:

Teach what accords with sound doctrine. Older men are to be sober-minded, dignified, self-controlled, sound in faith, in love, and in steadfastness. Older women likewise are to be reverent in behavior, not slanderers or slaves to much wine. They are to teach what is good, and so train the young women to love their husbands and children, to be self-controlled, pure, working at home, kind, and submissive to their own husbands, that the word of God may not be reviled. Likewise, urge the younger men to be self-controlled. Show yourself in all respects to be a model of good works, and in your teaching show integrity, dignity, and sound speech that cannot be condemned, so that an opponent may be put to shame, having nothing evil to say about us.

I paused and asked, "Do you see? Men are to disciple men, and women are to disciple women. Men are to disciple men to be and act like men. And likewise for women."

Beth was working on a Nilla Wafer and whispered, "So Zeke needs a man to talk to, and he needs a church, and this is true whether or not Zeke has gender dysphoria."

I leaned over and took a cookie out of the box.

"That's exactly right."

Soon, when the kids sniffed out an open box of cookies and barreled into the kitchen like a herd of wild buffalo, our quiet time came to a halt. We started preparation for dinner. Our big group required two full tables that night. Minestrone soup, leftovers from the night before, grocery-bought rotisserie chicken, leftover fresh bread from the Lord's Supper, and a pot of steaming brown rice. The dining room rang with loud laughter and singing, and we prayed again for Zeke during after-dinner devotions. Kent offered to help Zeke.

When Beth left later that night, she was clear-headed but sad for Zeke.

Later that semester, Zeke's Christian parents brought him back home for counseling.

Zeke's issue was severe. But what about temptation, you might be thinking. Is temptation such a big deal?

The Danger of Temptation

Why should a woman's liberty be sacrificed to guard against temptation?

The Puritan John Owen wrote powerfully about sin and temptation, and he answers that question biblically. Two readable sources for Owen's classic 1658 work are *Overcoming Sin and Temptation: Three Classic Works by John Owen* and *Temptation: Resisted and Repulsed.*[7] The subtitle of that second volume is worth special note—temptation is something to be repulsed because temptation is repulsive. Temptation is not to be trifled with. You can't domesticate temptation, because there is nothing innocent about it. And you cannot be negligent about those temptations that we experience because of our sin nature. Jesus had no sin nature, but we do. And for this reason, not all temptations are alike.

Owen says, "Temptation is like a knife: it may be used to cut the meat, or to cut the throat of a man. It may be a man's food or his poison, his exercise or his destruction."[8] What exactly is the test of temptation? Temptation tests the believer's faith because there are people whose faith is false. How we deal with temptation helps us gain clarity about our spiritual state and strength. Although God will use all manner of providence—including sin—sinlessly, this does not minimize the potential for temptation to destroy our lives. While it is true that a true believer cannot lose her faith, she can

7 John Owen, *Overcoming Sin and Temptation: Three Classic Works by John Owen*, ed. Kelly M. Kapic and Justin Taylor (Wheaton, IL: Crossway, 2006); and John Owen, *Temptation: Resisted and Repulsed*, Puritan Paperbacks (Carlisle, PA: Banner of Truth, 2007).
8 John Owen, *Temptation: Resisted and Repulsed*, ed. Richard Rushing (1658; repr., Carlisle, PA: Banner of Truth, 2021), 7.

lose everything else. Temptation comes from the hand of Satan himself, employing three potential means: his own power and knowledge of our weakness, the world's goods and glitter, and our own sin nature and the personal history we have with sin. Although we live in a world that eschews modesty and believes that everyone needs to know all of our struggles, we see that this is unsafe. As you are "coming out" and "giving voice to your pain," Satan is listening. He is taking notes, and perhaps because of your need for self-disclosure done in the name of authenticity, he now knows how to bait the hook. Owen defines temptation as something that "exerts a force or influence to seduce and draw the mind and heart of man from the obedience which God requires of him to any kind of sin."[9] A temptation lures man to sin, gives him opportunity to sin, and beckons him to neglect his duty to God (John 14:15). Our affections, entertainment, friends, and ambitions are all Satan's central playing field for temptation. Owen offers a stark warning: "Whoever does not realize this is on the brink of ruin."[10]

Did you catch that? Owen is not saying that a temptation is a personality pattern. Owen would cringe at someone saying something like, "Homosexual desire is my temptation pattern, not my sin." He would cringe because of the false teaching that drives that unbiblical statement right into the clutches of Satan. Indeed, for Owen (and Scripture), once temptation becomes a pattern, it lodges not in your Myers-Briggs or Enneagram score but rather in your soul. A temptation pattern is what we call "indwelling sin,"[11] and it will kill you if you don't kill it.

9 Owen, *Temptation*, 15.
10 Owen, *Temptation*, 15.
11 See Owen, *Overcoming Sin and Temptation*, 229–407.

The Puritans understood indwelling sin as "sin in the regenerate"—that is, a believer's sin. The Puritans understood Romans 7 as representative of indwelling sin, when the converted Paul declares, "I find it to be a law that when I want to do right, evil lies close at hand" (v. 21). This indwelling sin is not a personality trait or a potentially unruly companion that can be civilized. No. "The Puritans were all agreed that this 'law' is always present in the believer in this life. This 'dangerous companion' is always resident in the soul; it is a 'living coal' that must not be disregarded, or it may consume a person."[12] To the Puritan, reframing sin as an attribute of personality ("I'm a strong woman") or liberty ("I'm not immodest; I'm just exercising my rights!") is the most serious and dangerous game. The Bible does not record indwelling sin, sometimes called "besetting" sin, as a permanent feature of the believer's life.[13] A woman's personality does not excuse her immodesty. But is she really sinning when she mouths off on Twitter for hours at a time or carelessly wears whatever is in fashion for fifteen-year-old unchurched girls? Perhaps she is merely demonstrating a pattern of temptation?

Temptation becomes sin when it claims us by its persistent presence. It is the evil and the law that Paul presents in Romans 7:21. God calls the believer to kill (or mortify, as the Puritans put it) her sin (Gal. 5:24). And sin can be mortified because the word of God is not just something that dances on the surface of our personality or inclinations. The word of God cuts to the heart to remake a person:

---

12 Joel Beeke and Mark Jones, *A Puritan Theology: Doctrine for Life* (Grand Rapids, MI: Reformation Heritage, 2012), n.p.

13 Martin B. Blocki, "Sanctification: Besetting Sins," Place for Truth (website), Alliance of Confessing Evangelicals, October 4, 2019, https://www.placefortruth.org/.

The word of God is living and active, sharper than any two-edged sword, piercing to the division of soul and of spirit, of joints and of marrow, and discerning the thoughts and intentions of the heart. (Heb. 4:12)

The writer of Hebrews uses visceral, physical language portraying the spiritual word working in the material life of the redeemed as a surgical tool cutting out the rotting corpse of sin from joints, marrow, thoughts, and intentions. When the word of God gets to be bigger inside you than you, something powerful happens. This is true. But we must be washed in the word daily—multiple times a day—because the "old man" (Rom. 6:6–23) is not dead until glory, and Satan knows that even if you don't. This is one of the most vital reality checks for the Christian: if the word of God does not remake you, something is vitally wrong. For the believer, the word of God does not skim over the top of her affections like a weak adjective.

Temptation becomes a sin when we enter into it (1 Tim. 6:9). There are three potential entrances to temptation: the sinfulness of our heart, the will of God allowing Satan to sift us like wheat (as he allowed in Peter's case in Luke 22:31), and "when a man's lusts and corruptions meet a particularly provoking object."[14] No Christian woman wants to be seen in the eyes of God as a "provoking object." Women, don't minimize the seriousness to your own soul if Satan uses you as a tool for any reason.

But perhaps, you may be thinking, it is unfair to ask women to dress modestly for the sake of their brothers. Isn't this blaming the victim? Using 2 Peter 2:9—"The Lord knows how to rescue the

14 Owen, *Temptation*, 19.

godly from temptation"—you might want to dress and conduct yourself any way you like. But doing so is a misuse of this verse. It is to make room for temptation on the basis that you believe God will protect you, and it's not different from continuing in sin that grace might abound (Rom. 6:1–2).

The Puritans regarded the sin of a believer as scandal or snare. A scandal snares others into committing the same sin by normalizing it. Scandals have far-reaching consequences. Sin of all kinds, but especially sexual sin, is the church's greatest scandal. Modesty in dress, speech, and conduct are good practices, helping us safeguard against our own sin and against being a temptation for others. If a man sins, the sin is on him. But anything we can do to help prevent scandal in the church is a good work indeed.

For a godly woman to conduct herself with modesty, she must understand modesty is an active and not passive grace.

Modesty, Temptation, Sexual Abuse, and Cults

Modesty has fallen on hard times, in part because of the way that it has been leveled by parachurch movements for evil purposes. Books such as *Lovingly Abused: A True Story of Overcoming Cults, Gaslighting, and Legal Educational Neglect* by Heather Grace Heath, testify to the tragic outcome when parachurch ministries misuse the word of God and manipulate people's lives, claiming that by following rules they are manipulating God's favor.[15] This book has become popular among Christian women, and it's a book that makes me very sad.

Heather's family joined a discredited organization, a parachurch movement called Advanced Training Institute (ATI), founded by

---

15 Heather Grace Heath, *Lovingly Abused: A True Story of Overcoming Cults, Gaslighting, and Legal Educational Neglect* (Charleston, SC: Palmetto, 2021).

Bill Gothard in 1997, the same year I met the Smiths.[16] Heather's family joined a cult that put the women and children at risk, while I joined a church and found safety and salvation. Partly because of her training in this parachurch ministry, Heather believes that words like *temptation* and *modesty* carry the weight of abuse. Throughout her book, she represents how she perceived that these words were used against her as weapons. Heather writes: "Women held full responsibility for whether or not their bodies caused a man to sin."[17] This raises the question, If a woman is sexually abused, is it ever her fault? Heather says that at ATI, the answer would be yes. But the Bible gives a strong no in answer to this question. The responsibility of sin—whatever the sin—squarely falls on the shoulders of the sinner. Deuteronomy 24:16; Job 19:4; Proverbs 9:12; Jeremiah 31:30; Ezekiel 18:20; Romans 14:4; 2 Corinthians 5:10; and Galatians 6:5 make the strongest case that the sinner is responsible for the sin. The real answer to the problem of abuse is not in adding to the Bible (as cults do) or rejecting it (as atheists do), but in embracing it, living it, and being transformed by it. That is what believers do.

It is a terrible sin when a cult uses Scripture to falsify God's truth. And while we can learn lessons from Heather's life, admire the grit and intelligence God gave her, and pray for her salvation, Christian women are in sin if they use Heather's biblical interpretations to defend their own sinful immodesty.

Modesty and Social Media

I do not participate in social media, unless you want to include Nextdoor and Ravelry, where I learn about lost dogs and find

16 Heath, *Lovingly Abused*, Kindle, no loc.
17 Heath, *Lovingly Abused*, Kindle, no loc.

good knitting patterns for my overabundant yarn stash. Lost dogs put me into action (I love a good excuse to take a walk and help a neighbor), and knitting patterns keep my gift-giving flowing. I've never lost one wink of sleep over Nextdoor or Ravelry. Nor have I gotten into any hot water or nasty fights. I don't reject social media for its information-gathering or -sharing aspects. But because information gathering is not how social media is predominantly used, I know its use can be addictive, sinful, ungodly, and damaging to one's soul. Social media is a place where anger flares, context is nonexistent, and words and images are delivered that can never be taken back. "Vengeance is mine, says the Lord," but the Internet claims otherwise.

Perhaps no other medium has created a cult of immodesty as much as social media. Here, we garner "likes," sympathy, and solidarity, hunker down in divisive camps, create a following, stir up strife and pride, create new sins and redefine old ones, and engage in slander and prideful derision all in the name of discernment and telling the truth, and we waste an enormous amount of time that would be better spent in doing almost anything else. (And I mean *anything* else: alphabetizing your spice rack comes to mind.)

In addition, making public everything from your current grievances to your lunch blurs the line between public and private such that the category of *private* sometimes completely disappears from our lives. And when privacy disappears, so does modesty. Indeed, a social media–infused Christian life will always choose exhibitionism over modesty.

What I am observing is hardly new. In both Christian and non-Christian circles, our honeymoon with the Internet is clearly over. Many books published over the past decade or so usher a clarion call: social media is using us, duping us, distracting us, disintegrating our relationships, and corrupting our lives.[18] The popular Netflix documentary *The Social Dilemma* made the case a slam-dunk: we are not getting "information" when we check the Internet. We are merely swimming in our own feedback loop.[19]

But why are Christians falling for this? Why does social media elicit sin from professing Christians? The idea that you can spend hours on Twitter engaging in sin (gossip and time-wasting) but adorn it as biblical teaching shows that delusions of grandeur hold powerful sway over women who aspire to be influential. Modesty chooses the better path over influence.

Let me riff on a well-known controversy to provide an example. Let's say there is a conference of about fifty people who are playing word games. My name comes up as a term in the game. I'm sure that never happens, but let's just go with it. Each respondent is supposed to say two words in response to my name. A member of a polemics ministry responds to my name with "lesbian feminist." Well, that would be formerly true, but not true today. But another pastor in response to my name says, "Go home!" He says this because he has seen me speak at homeschool conferences with both men and women in attendance as well as at the Ligonier National Conference. He believes that I am violating 1 Timothy 2:12.

The polemics pastor is acting in bad faith, so I just ignore him. But the "Go home!" pastor and I both agree that God's word rel-

---

18 These include Jaron Lanier, *Ten Arguments for Deleting Your Social Media Accounts Right Now* (New York: Henry Holt, 2018); Donna Freitas, *The Happiness Effect: How Social Media Is Driving a Generation to Appear Perfect at Any Cost* (New York: Oxford University Press, 2017); Nicholas Carr, *The Shallows: What the Internet Is Doing to Our Brains* (New York: Norton, 2010); Jia Tolentino, *Trick Mirror: Reflections on Self-Delusion* (New York: Random House, 2019); Richard Seymour, *The Twittering Machine* (London: Verso, 2019); and Chris Martin, *Terms of Service: The Real Cost of Social Media* (Nashville, TN: B&H, 2022).

19 *The Social Dilemma*, directed by Jeff Orlowski, produced by Exposure Labs et al., distributed by Netflix, initial release January 26, 2020, https://www.thesocialdilemma.com/.

egates the church office of pastor for ordained and qualified men. We agree that even if a woman is a guest speaker at the church, she is not called to preach the gospel. Nor is she called to speak from the pulpit on the Lord's Day. But that is not what he is saying. He is saying that I ought never to speak in a room where men might be present. He is saying that if the sound guy or the security detail is paying too close attention to my words, there is a sin problem. His reading of this scriptural passage might mean that men have nothing to learn from women. Or his particular concern might have been the specific conference or the topic. Either way, when two believers agree on the meaning of a passage but seem to be in a public crossfire over its application, it is time for a phone call, not a Twitter war.

Now, no one likes her name used as an example of what not to be or do. I understand that. I've experienced that. But the biblical response to this is either a phone call or the grace to let it go.

The pastor who thinks I'm a feminist lesbian or that I am preaching from pulpits or teaching the Bible at conferences to a mixed audience might instead contact my husband and elders and talk with my session about my conduct. Or let's say my husband or elder contacts the accusing pastor to discuss what he said about me. Let's say either one of these responses takes place. Good comes out of this in two ways. First, I can learn about how I am coming across. Second, the elders can advise me on whether I have sinned. If I have sinned, I can repent. The elders can help me think about how to select speaking events in the future. If I have not sinned but am concerned that some of my speaking selections have been unwise, I can course correct and have different criteria for speaking events. Or if the pastor sinned against me, he could repent, and I can receive his repentance.

And sometimes we will simply arrive at a difference of opinion, and then we need to let it go.

By sitting down and listening to the pastor who has criticized me, I can better understand the heart of the man who stands behind the criticism. If he is a brother in the Lord, I will learn that he is not attacking me as a person but rather is concerned for my witness and for the truth of God's word. And if my elders believe that the pastor was wrong and has sinned against me, they can issue a rebuke to him while guiding me to forgive him and move on. If we find that the situation is not a matter of sin (on either part) but misunderstanding, nothing else but forgiveness needs to happen. If there is public sin, there ought to be public repentance, but sometimes this doesn't happen. I have had a situation where someone publicly sinned against me but only privately repented because the public scrutiny was too much for her to bear. I was happy to receive a private letter that recanted and repented of her sin and to be restored as sisters in the Lord. There is a lot of gray and a lot of grace in how Christians extend and receive forgiveness. But the Internet lacks grace all the way around. It is the place where conflicts get ratcheted up but not resolved.

Let's play out this same scenario on Twitter. Let's say that on Twitter, a pastor calls me a lesbian feminist and tells me to stop speaking publicly. Everyone weighs in on Twitter, including people who don't have a dog in the fight. It creates words that cannot be taken back, hurt that just keeps going deeper, and a growing confusion over what the original issue and context was in the first place. If we turn this into a brawl on social media, we also enlist people who likely will be hurt by doing so. Somewhat like the high school debate team, where you can only dig in and defend and never repent and turn away from your "resolve," the Internet makes all conflict a war zone.

Not only does the Internet create a world where everything is public; it makes it impossible to follow Paul's excellent example of forgetting what needs to be forgotten so that we can grow in Christ and suffer well:

> I press on . . . because Christ Jesus has made me his own. . . . One thing I do: forgetting what lies behind and straining forward to what lies ahead, I press on toward the goal for the prize of the upward call of God in Christ Jesus. Let those of us who are mature think this way. (Phil. 3:12–15)

The Internet never forgets. But Christians are called to forget in a sanctified way. The pressing and straining to which Paul refers reveal moral and spiritual strength. The Internet cares little for that. Part of why our speech on the Internet is so dangerous is that it is contextless and unguarded. When we speak at an event, we have notes (or in my case, a manuscript). But Internet speech is a free fall, mitigating against our own spiritual maturity and the spiritual well-being of others.

My plea to Christian women is this: use social media for the sharing and gathering of information, not for grievances. If you are going to use social media, make sure that it is not using you. Deal with grievances as God has ordained, even if others don't.[20]

20 The Westminster Confession of Faith, in chapter 20, addresses the topic of Christian liberty and liberty of conscience, offering an excellent principle against which to examine our social media participation as women:

> And because the powers which God hath ordained, and the liberty which Christ hath purchased, are not intended by God to destroy, but mutually to uphold and preserve one another, they who, upon pretense of Christian liberty, shall oppose any

Discourse on social media is public, and it has created a Christian world where seemingly everything is public. Confusing public and private has created great personal pain for people. It has created false conflicts, discouraged reconciliation, and has falsified the rightful place of the "keys of the kingdom," which Jesus Christ has given to the church, not the Internet (Matt. 16:19; 18:15–18).

Actual journalism is different from an Internet brawl. I have benefited greatly from women in journalism.[21] Biblical journalism is a blessing to the church. But not everyone with a blog or a brand engages public conflicts with godly conduct, and on this point, Christian women need to be careful. I have seen reputations ruined not because of what other people said about Christian women, but because of their own conduct.

The bottom line is this: when modesty is exchanged for exhibitionism and then promoted as a new Christian virtue, especially in our social media–infused world, no one is more hurt by it than women. For women who wish to conduct themselves with modesty, as the Lord desires, we need to be mindful of our social-media footprint. Regardless of what others do or say, we are called to be above reproach. The Internet escalates gossip, slander, and irreconcilable breaches of fellowship.

---

lawful power, or the lawful exercise of it, whether it be civil, ecclesiastical, resist the ordinance of God. And for their publishing of such opinions, or maintaining of such practices, as are contrary to the light of nature, or to the known principles of Christianity (whether concerning faith, worship, or conversation), or to the power of godliness; or such erroneous opinions of practices, as either in their own nature, or in the manner of publishing or maintaining them, are destructive to the external peace and order which Christ hath established in the Church, they may be lawfully called to account, and proceeded against by the censures of the Church, and by the power of the civil magistrate.

21 I have profited especially from the work of Jamie Dean at *World* magazine (https://wng.org/) and Janet Mefferd on the *Janet Mefferd Today* program (https://janetmefferd.com/).

The people you are directed by God to influence, even if they are no longer in your home, deserve private communication. Loving your children, church, and neighbors is a high calling. If a Christian woman has the reputation of loving her Twitter neighbor while neglecting her real one, this is a vile testimony indeed. A healthy dose of modesty could bring us all to our senses.

Afterword

The Difference between Acceptance and Approval,
or, How to Stay Connected to Loved Ones Who
Believe These Lies without Falling for Them Yourself

From the days of John the Baptist until now
the kingdom of heaven has suffered violence,
and the violent take it by force.

MATTHEW 11:12

We urge you, brothers, admonish the idle, encourage the
fainthearted, help the weak, be patient with them all.

1 THESSALONIANS 5:14

SINCE 2015 WE IN THE Christian church have experienced a seismic shift in what it means to be a Christian.

It's not that the Bible has changed.

It's not that the church building has collapsed.

It's that the meaning of almost everything has undergone an almost overnight transformation. Girls think they are boys, boys think they are girls, and abuse scandals have rocked the church. The old ways have fallen under suspicion, and the new ways come with an off-putting vocabulary that changes daily.

This seismic shift has produced a world that believes five lies. Even more troubling, the world seems to lead the church today, and these five lies have found a home in evangelicalism.

In this book, we have discussed the following five lies:

Lie #1: Homosexuality is normal.
Lie #2: Being a spiritual person is kinder than being a biblical Christian.
Lie #3: Feminism is good for the world and the church.
Lie #4: Transgenderism is normal.
Lie #5: Modesty is an outdated burden that serves male dominance and holds women back.

I'm sure you can come up with additional lies, and I can too. But what all these lies have in common is they don't think that God had a plan and purpose when he created men and women. God's proclamation in Genesis 1:27–28 stands in stark contrast to these five lies:

So God created man in his own image,
in the image of God he created him;
male and female he created them.

And God blessed them. And God said to them, "Be fruitful and multiply and fill the earth and subdue it, and have dominion over the fish of the sea and over the birds of the heavens and over every living thing that moves on the earth."

I've lost friends to all these lies, and likely you have too. And I was myself almost lost to all these lies at one point as well. I hung on to some of the lies well into my Christian life and thus have unintentionally led people in the wrong direction. Good intentions and saving faith do not always protect us from sin.

At this point, you might be asking yourself an obvious question: Why did the evangelical church fall off the edge? Where were the watchmen and what were they watching? How did evangelicalism fail like this? Why are things so upside down, with the world leading the church instead of the church leading the world? Why does it feel like we all live in Babel now?

Because some watchmen acted like the mythological hunter Narcissus, recording diligently how many Twitter followers they had and dutifully trying to manage their reputations on social media. In other words, some of these watchmen were watching themselves. They tried to "outdo one another in showing honor" (Rom. 12:10) by keeping up their public profiles. But social media orchestrates narcissism and deludes us into thinking that sending a snarky tweet is the same thing as actually doing something. As James puts it, "If anyone is a hearer of the word and not a doer, he is like a man who looks intently at his natural face in a mirror" (James 1:23). Social media is a contextless mirror that leads to amnesia: "For he looks at himself and goes away and at once forgets what he was like" (1:24). While the vain watchman and his followers may forget, the Internet, of course, does not, and harm proliferates, both to the flock and the man. The flock imbibes Christian themes in the posture of a carnival goer. The watchman flounders in self-delusion. Is this not an accurate picture of some of the megachurch pastors you know?

But other watchmen, those faithful pastors of faithful churches, were dutifully preparing their flock for this very battle and were not taken aback. They prepared their sermons in private study and prayer, they with their elders sacrificially shepherded the flock, knowing each member by name and need. They administered sacraments, practiced church discipline, and worked within tight budgets. No glamour, no glory, and a lot of rice and beans at the fellowship dinner table. If these watchmen used social media, it was to give messages on the church Facebook page that said something like this: "We will gather for prayer meeting at 7:00 p.m. Please come or send your prayer requests to the elders." God gave blessing, increase, hardship, and tests of faith. Covenant children came to faith, as well as others God called out of darkness and into light. Brothers and sisters memorized Scripture and catechisms. Baptisms, weddings, and funerals filled the cycles of church life. Faithful pastors reminded the flock that we are the church militant until Jesus returns, and then and only then are we the church triumphant. The flock committed themselves to prayer, fasting, repentance, worship, evangelism, Christian education, and hospitality. No frills. Wars and pestilence came and went and came back again, but these didn't change the way that these churches worshiped God or practiced hospitality.

These faithful and unpretentious churches have blessed many a true Christian. And during times of seismic shifts, they are holding down the fort. These watchmen will care for you as you try to stay connected to your lost loved ones without falling for indoctrination. If you love a prodigal, the first order of business is to make sure you are worshiping in a faithful church with a pastor who knows you and elders who pray for you and shepherd you.

Principles of Loving People Lost to These Lies

One helpful principle in loving your prodigal without falling into indoctrination is holding church membership in a faithful church where you are shepherded by faithful men. The other is knowing the difference between acceptance and approval. Acceptance means living in reality and not fantasy. If your daughter calls herself a lesbian, you need to accept that. If your son Rex calls himself Mathilda, you need to accept this. He really is living in such a dangerous state of delusion and deception. That is reality right now. Acceptance is an important step in seeing the person you love in the sin pattern in which he is trapped. Acceptance, however, does not include believing his interpretation of how he got here or what it means. Acceptance does not include believing that Rex really is Mathilda. Acceptance does not include being manipulated by the therapist who asks, "Would you rather have a dead son or a living daughter?" Acceptance does not lose sight of Jesus and the cross he calls us to bear.

Approval means that you give the whole situation a blessing. Approval means more than loving your daughter in her sin. It means calling her sin by another name ("grace," "blessing," or "illness") and compartmentalizing and shrinking your Christian life in the process. Approval means denying Christ and your responsibility to carry the cross that your age and status produce. It means getting Luke 14:26–27 wrong, like Jeremy did, and as we discussed in chapter 5.

The difference between acceptance and approval is the fine line that a Christian who loves someone trapped by these lies must navigate.

Acceptance is a mature response. It means living life with your eyes open and facing reality. Acceptance requires the ability to be compassionate and sympathetic. Approval is an immature response. It means allowing empathy to overrule what you know to be true in the hopes that "standing in the shoes" of your loved one will help.

Both gestures—acceptance and approval—desire to offer comfort in affliction. The former does so biblically, as can be apprehended in the opening lines of 2 Corinthians where Paul encourages the church at Corinth "to comfort those who are in any affliction, with the comfort with which we ourselves are comforted" (1:4). The comfort surely is not the affliction. The comfort is God's blessing of union with Christ—that sweet, irrevocable, eternal, spiritual, and unbreakable belonging that we have with the Lord, who never leaves us nor forsakes us. In accepting where someone is, you seek for them God's rescue and help. Approval of sin, on the other hand, declares,

> They have healed the wound of my people lightly,
>> saying, "Peace, peace,"
>> when there is no peace.
> Were they ashamed when they committed abomination?
>> No, they were not at all ashamed. (Jer. 8:11–12)

Pastor-Wolf

What if your son or daughter has a wolf for a pastor? What if you do? False teachers love to proclaim half of the gospel. Saving faith, however, requires the whole gospel, law and grace together. Truly helping your lost prodigal means using the law of God to extend the love of God. Trying to love the lost apart from the law results only in false beneficence.[1] The moral law of God reflects the perfect righteousness of God. The law acts as a schoolmaster, driving us to Christ. We are not justified by

---

1 John Calvin's threefold use of the law, in John Calvin, *Institutes of the Christian Religion*, ed. John T. McNeill, trans. Ford Lewis Battles (Philadelphia: Westminster Press, 1960), 2.1:304–10.

the law, but we are often helpfully constrained by it. The moral law of God restrains evil. Jesus followed the moral law of God perfectly, and therefore you cannot have Jesus without the word and the law because Jesus is the fulfillment of the word and the law.[2] If you know all of this and yet have serious concerns about your pastor, schedule a meeting with him and with the elders. Ask pointed questions, take notes, pray about what you heard, and take seriously your responsibility to worship in a church that preaches the whole gospel.[3]

While the law cannot change hearts, it can protect the innocent and punish the guilty. This teaches people to fear punishment and seek blessing, to flee from crime and embrace goodness. The Reformer John Calvin says that the law works "by means of its fearful denunciations and the consequent dread of punishment to curb those who, unless forced, have no regard for rectitude and justice."[4] On earth we will have only a limited measure of justice, but when Jesus returns and the last judgment is realized, we will have perfect justice.

The moral law of God reveals what is pleasing to God.

Hospitality and mercy ministry are examples of the moral law of God. In these practices we delight in the law as much as God delights in it. John 14:15 exemplifies this: "If you love me, you will keep my commandments."

2 "The moral law is of use to all men, to . . . help them to a clearer sight of the need they have of Christ, and of the perfection of His obedience." Westminster Confession of Faith, Question 95, "Of what use is the moral law to all men?" See *The Westminster Larger Catechism with Scripture Proofs*, Westminster Divine Assembly (Pittsburgh, PA: Crown & Covenant, 2019), 103.

3 Todd Pruitt, "What's a PCA Office or Church Member to Do?" *Presbycast*, March 9, 2022, https://presbycast.libsyn.com/.

4 Calvin, *Institutes*, 2.1:304–10, quoted in *Reformation Study Bible*, ed. R. C. Sproul (Orlando, FL: Reformation Trust, 2015), 273.

A note in my study Bible says, "The moral law that God revealed in Scripture is always binding upon us. Our redemption is from the curse of God's law, not from our duty to obey it. We are justified, not because of our obedience to the law, but in order that we may become obedient to God's law. To love Christ is to keep his commandments. To love God is to obey his law."[5] The law of God is an anchor, and the only way to know if we are anchored to Christ is by our obedience to the word. It is not enough to say that you have a high view of Scripture. Faith is not measured by what you affirm or how you identify. You can affirm that you are a Christian, but if you do not obey God's requirements as revealed in the Bible, then you are proving your affirmation false. Obedience does not make you a legalist or a fundamentalist. Obedience to the word of God reveals that you are a Christian. We can only help our lost loved ones if we ourselves stay tethered to God's word by grace.

How Acceptance and Approval Differ

Acceptance is a great kindness, so learn the difference between acceptance and approval. I learned this from Ken and Floy Smith decades ago when they told me that they could accept me as a lesbian, but their acceptance didn't mean approval. This was 1997, and I took no great offense. I appreciated the honesty behind this. While acceptance is not approval, acceptance is a great kindness. Acceptance means dealing protectively and gently with the person who is lost. I learned from the Smiths that acceptance involves listening, caring for, praying, and sharing God's word. It may include getting off social media so that your prodigal does not get gratuitously hurt by conversations not meant for her ears. Sin

5 *Reformation Study Bible*, 273.

makes more work for all of us, and it breeds paranoia. Don't give your prodigal reasons to run. And don't take responsibility for your prodigal's decision if she does run. You are a praying parent who prays for a prodigal. Your daughter is a prayed-for child. And that makes all the difference in the world.

Here are some principles to apply as you seek to accept without approving your prodigal:

1. Don't think that just because your prodigal is an adult, you are no longer parenting. You will be your children's parent until the day the Lord takes you home. We must become adept at pointing our adult children to the gospel as the only means of avoiding God's ultimate punishment.

2. If your prodigal has declared war against reality and believes that she is nonbinary or a different sex than that which God gave her, ask her to define all these new vocabulary words but don't feel compelled to use them. Your daughter is now living in a dystopic world of science fiction. You never wanted to write this story anyway, so put the burden on her to explain these words and their meanings every time they come up. Don't get a PhD in all of this new vocabulary. Be sanctified in both knowledge and ignorance.[6]

3. Know biblical doctrine better than you ever have. Use biblical doctrine as a filter for the new words your child has embraced.

6　See Maria Keffler, *Desist, Detrans, and Detox: Getting Your Child out of the Gender Cult*, (Arlington, VA: Advocates for Protecting Children, 2021). See also Rainbow Redemption Project, https://www.rainbowredemptionproject.com.

4. Have a systematic theology game plan. Systematic theology is invaluable in learning how to use Scripture in a fluent way. My favorite systematic theology is the Westminster Shorter Catechism.

5. Make sure that if you are not in a faithful, biblical church, you get to one fast. And once you get there, take the covenant of church membership. Even though it may mean breaking friendships with your former church, you must get to a faithful church for the sake of your own soul. You need more help than you think. You are more vulnerable than you believe. Church is not a social club; it's training for war. Like it or not, the theater of this spiritual war is your home and your heart and your family. If you don't know how to discern a good church from a weak or dead one, Barry York, in *Hitting the Marks: Restoring the Essential Identity of the Church*, explains with clarity what you should see if you are looking for a faithful church:

> The first and chief mark is the faithful preaching of the Word of God. The Lord has given us his Word, and he expects his church to hear and obey it. The second mark of the church is the rightful administration of the sacraments of baptism and the Lord's Supper. The Lord has provided these outer, visible signs to his bride to identify her as belonging to him. The third mark is the proper exercise of church discipline. This mark refers to the corrective discipline a church may use to win back a straying soul, and also to the

formative discipline of instructing followers of Christ in discipleship.[7]

6. Pray. Acceptance of your prodigal's real life means getting every Christian you know to pray for her conversion. This is no time for pride or for hiding. You need help, and you need to deal honestly and ask for this help. Praying for the prodigal you love requires focus. It means taking stock of those distractions that you allow to steal your joy and attention on the Lord: Internet? Gossip? Entertainment? Weak theology? Wolves in the pulpit and the pews? Blogs with a veneer of "almost-Christian" interests but no real meat? Praying for your prodigal may be your highest calling and most blessed Christian duty. Have you read Christopher Yuan and Angela Yuan (son and mother cowriting team) in their memoir of faith, *Out of a Far Country: A Gay Son's Journey to God. A Broken Mother's Search for Hope*?[8] If not, please do. This book is our most faithful trail guide for accepting and loving, but not approving of, your beloved prodigal.

7. Going boldly to the throne of grace requires daily repentance of your own sin, but this means not taking on your prodigal's sin as your own. It means repenting of the sin of self-pity. Satan wants you to feel responsible that you have a prodigal child. He wants you to think that it is all your fault, and that God is punishing you. He wants you to look

---

7 Barry J. York, *Hitting the Marks: Restoring the Essential Identity of the Church* (Pittsburgh, PA: Crown & Covenant, 2018), xix.

8 Christopher Yuan and Angela Yuan, *Out of a Far Country: A Gay Son's Journey to God, a Broken Mother's Search for Hope* (Colorado Springs, CO: WaterBrook, 2011).

at other families and covet what they have. Nothing that comes from Satan is helpful or true—even half-truths are lies. If you have fallen into sins of covetousness, repent and ask God to help you love your calling as a prayer warrior for a prodigal. What if you are the only Christian in your family who is bringing your prodigal to the throne of grace? What if all the other Christians in your family have gone apostate and have bought into false theology? Don't lose a minute of time feeling sorry for yourself. You have too much spiritual work to do. Get on with it.

8. Acceptance means not telling your prodigal lies and not buying into her false theology. It also might mean a time of physical separation, remembering that God knows better than you do what she needs. Acceptance means remembering. It means holding on to your prodigal's history, especially if she has fallen for transgender madness. Keep her pottery and pictures and favorite clothes. Don't throw her history away, but preserve it for her. Keep the truth safe and sound. She will need it someday.

Being useful to your prodigal requires that you fear God, not her. Don't fear your prodigal. Don't fear what she writes about you on Twitter or what she says about you to her friends. Don't be distracted by the fear of man. Study this subject by doing subject searches using your favorite Bible study method. There are many affordable Bible software programs available, and some are even free! Look up "fear of God" and "fear of man." Keep a journal on all the verses of encouragement and warning. Meditate on what you learn. Pray for your prodigal as you cling to Christ and to his promises.

Try to stay connected to your prodigal. When the holidays come around, pray that the Lord would give you a clear path to gather without compromise. Ask your elders and pastors for help. If your elders and pastors are too busy or too fearful to help, find a faithful church that will. Deal with each situation carefully, asking God to help you see how he wants you to serve. Following are some questions and answers that I've encountered recently.

1. *Do I attend the gay wedding of my son?*
No, you cannot attend your son's gay wedding and maintain faithful witness for Christ. Fear of your son's rejection or hatred is real, and for that reason, you will need to spend many hours of prayer under the direction of your pastors and elders. Among other things, prayer strengthens you to receive the command that God gives you. While fear of your son's rejection is natural, it is also a snare. "The fear of man lays a snare, but whoever trusts in the LORD is safe" (Prov. 29:25). A snare is an instrument of execution intended to trap you and torture you. Your only protection against the fear of man is the fear of God. Jesus understands, and he says, "If anyone comes to me and does not hate his own father and mother and wife and children and brothers and sisters, yes, and even his own life, he cannot be my disciple" (Luke 14:26). Jesus anticipated this difficult cross and gives clear instruction. The word of God knows our needs better than we do.

2. *My daughter and her lesbian partner are having a baby by artificial insemination. They want me to attend the baby shower. Should I?*
As Christians, we love life, and we cherish life no matter how God in his providence brings that life into the world. This child

needs a Christian grandma, and there is nothing preventing you from celebrating her life.

3. *My son and his "husband" want to come home for Christmas, but my other adult children (who are strong Christians) don't want them to come home because they don't want to have to explain their relationship to my grandchildren (ages five, seven, eight, twelve, and fifteen). What should I do?*
You have to choose. Which set of children needs you more? If the whole family cannot come together, that's fine, but you still need to choose. I believe that your adult children who are in the Lord need you less than your prodigal son and his friend do. My advice is to invite your son and his friend and have a quiet dinner. At the end of dinner, have a time of family devotions. Open the word. Pray together. Present the gospel again.

4. *My twelve-year-old daughter wants to start taking testosterone and wants me to call her Jack. Her teachers at her public school support this. What should I do?*
Read Abigail Shrier's book *Irreversible Damage*. While this is not a Christian book, the appendix in the back has excellent emergency suggestions for just this situation. The first thing you need to do is unplug your daughter from those deep wells of untruth. Take her out of government schools, take away her phone, and get her immediately into biblical counseling (biblicalcounseling.com).

5. *My son is willing to come home for Thanksgiving, but only if he and his boyfriend can stay at our home. What should I do?*
Make separate accommodations if you have a large home with two guestrooms, and let your son know that you are very much

looking forward to having him and his friend join you, but the bottom line is that they will need to sleep in separate rooms if they stay in your house. If he is using this as a litmus test, he wasn't coming anyway. Hold fast to the gospel. Bear your cross with Christian dignity.

6. *My lesbian daughter says that heterosexual sexual sin and homosexual sin are on the same moral level. Is this true? Are both heterosexuality and homosexuality terms of moral corruption? Are they equally so?*[9] Romans 1:21–27 makes clear that homosexuality is unnatural, untruthful, futile, foolish, dishonoring to God and to others, shameful, and pagan:

> Although they knew God, they did not honor him as God or give thanks to him, but they became futile in their thinking, and their foolish hearts were darkened. Claiming to be wise, they became fools, and exchanged the glory of the immortal God for images resembling mortal man and birds and animals and creeping things. Therefore God gave them up in the lusts of their hearts to impurity, to the dishonoring of their bodies among themselves, because they exchanged the truth about God for a lie and worshiped and served the creature rather than the Creator, who is blessed forever! Amen. For this reason God gave them up to dishonorable passions. For their women exchanged natural relations for those that are contrary to nature; and the men likewise gave up natural relations with women and were consumed with passion

9 See Rosaria Butterfield, *Openness Unhindered: Further Thoughts of an Unlikely Convert on Sexual Identity and Union with Christ* (Pittsburgh, PA: Crown & Covenant, 2015).

for one another, men committing shameless acts with men and receiving in themselves the due penalty for their error.

The order of natural sexuality put forward by the creation ordinance is one man and one woman in the context of biblical marriage. The heterosexual pattern is natural even if a particular practice is sinful, as in adultery. If a man and a woman are committing fornication but they come to Christ and repent of their sin, they could someday get married and live in God's obedience and blessing. But if a man and a man in a homosexual relationship come to Christ, they would need to break up in order to live in obedience and blessing. Reformed theologian John Murray in his commentary on the book of Romans says this: "The implication is that, however grievous is fornication or adultery, the desecration involved in homosexuality is on a lower plane of degeneracy; it is unnatural and therefore evinces a perversion more basic."[10] In other words, homosexual sin is a violation against both God's pattern of creation and the moral law of God, while heterosexual sin violates the moral law of God exclusively. At the level of pastoral theology, homosexuality is like all sin—it is treason against a holy God, and only the blood of Christ can ransom the homosexual sinner from the wrath of God. But when considered in light of the creation ordinance, homosexuality is perversion of the created order. Homosexuality is a sin that runs deep and hard in a person's life, and it cannot be domesticated. Because homosexuality is sinful at the level of pattern and practice, it is always on a lower and more base sin level than heterosexual sin.

10   John Murray, *The Epistle to the Romans*, New International Commentary on the New Testament (1959; repr., Grand Rapids, MI: Eerdmans, 1987), 47.

7. Has the LGBTQ+ community suffered damage from the church? Is this true? What kind of damage? How does this compare to the damage that LGBTQ+ have inflicted on each other?

Those of us who have come out of homosexual sin remember times when people in the church didn't trust us. Perhaps people believed that homosexuality cannot be changed by gospel grace or that repentance doesn't lead to transformation of the heart and life. We all have stories, and those stories can be hurtful. But there is a much greater harm that happens within homosexual or transgender relationships. Some of this harm happens within the sex acts themselves. Sodomy can cause rectal prolapse and STD transmission, including HIV infection. Some gay men involve themselves in harmful role-playing about which they take pride and that can lead to serious emotional and physical damage.[11] People—including children—who are envious of the sexual anatomy of others and are encouraged by therapists and doctors to mutilate themselves through hormones and surgical removal of body parts are being tragically manipulated and lied to.

So, while people who call themselves gay or trans have likely felt hurt by some things that the church has said over the years, how can we compare this to the clear and present danger these people face from within their communities? My point is that people who claim the LGBTQ+ community as their own need to be rescued *from* it. The LGBTQ+ community cannot be redeemed on its own terms. You can't stay LGBTQ (in name or practice) and be simultaneously rescued from its sin. I am grateful

---

11 President Joe Biden appointed Sam Brinton to the US Department of Energy. Brinton is known for his advocacy of masochism and the vile mistreatment of other men. See Rod Dreher, "Biden Puttin' on the Dog," *The American Conservative*, February 10, 2022, https://www.theamericanconservative.com.

that we have the church and parachurch ministries to lead people out of these dangerous communities and relationships and model faith, repentance, and the necessity of biblical sexuality.[12]

Christian Life after the Seismic Shift: Now What?

When a Christian theology separates the gospel from the garden, it loses gospel power and integrity. All manner of heresy springs from denying that God's gospel is found in the garden. If you love a wayward child, don't take the bait. But do listen to what your prodigal is trying to say. Your prodigal's insistence that LGBTQ+ is her life's center reveals something important: this is her religion. That's why she's so touchy about you getting all the vocabulary right. There is a difference between worship and recognition. Again, don't take the bait. Your focus is on loving your prodigal well and praying fervently, to the glory of God. This requires listening to your prodigal and studying God's word. You are running a marathon, not a sprint. Focus your energy and stamina on your spiritual health and your fervent prayer for the vitality and increase of your own faith as well as for your prodigal's repentance.

---

12 I believe that Christians should have access to a wide variety of counseling programs and practices, and while my preferred method is biblical counseling, I do not believe that reparative therapy/conversion therapy should be banned or outlawed or mocked. I've been one of the mockers, and I was wrong. Change-allowing therapies and programs can be useful, especially for people who have experienced childhood trauma, sexual abuse, or neglect. For those interested in learning more about the politics behind the American Psychological Association and its rejection of change-allowing therapy for undesired same-sex attraction and gender anxiety, I recommend checking out the International Federation for Therapeutic and Counselling Choice (https://iftcc.org/). For those seeking parental support groups that work within local churches, see Restored Hope Network (https://www.restoredhope network.org/). For those seeking a pastoral guide on the subject of sexuality and sexual sin, see Christopher J. Gordon's *The New Reformation Catechism on Human Sexuality* (Grand Rapids, MI: Reformation Heritage, 2022).

Here's our hard lesson on ground zero of the Tower of Babel: Even people who claim God's redemption can be on the wrong side of God's will. Lot was a believer, and so was the thief on the cross, but neither provides good examples for how to live the Christian life. Lot's life and the thief on the cross showcase God's mercy. The thief shows us how to die, not how to live. Paul, Nehemiah, Ezra, Daniel, David, Ruth, and Esther (just to name a few) model how to live out a strong Christian faith.

God has placed the church in the midst of the fallen and even evil world on purpose. He puts faithful churches at ground zero of the Tower of Babel to be distinct from the world as part of his plan. Psalm 110:2 puts it like this:

The LORD sends forth from Zion
    your mighty scepter.
    Rule in the midst of your enemies!

Of this, John Calvin writes: "God's will is that Christ's kingdom should be encompassed with many enemies, his design being to keep us in a state of constant warfare. Therefore, it becomes us to exercise patience and meekness, and, assured of God's aid, boldly to consider the rage of the whole world as nothing."[13] This is God's promise as well as his command to the faithful church: *the rage of the whole world is nothing.* "The rage of the whole world is nothing" means that the mayhem can hurt you, but it can't alter God's good plans for you. God uses everything. He even uses sin sinlessly. This means that the

---

13 John Calvin, *365 Days with Calvin: A Unique Collection of 365 Readings from the Writings of John Calvin*, ed. Joel Beeke (Grand Rapids, MI: Reformation Heritage, 2008), March 19 entry.

rage of our unbelieving daughter, her lesbian partner, and the entire Pride parade is nothing. We are to rule in the midst of our enemies. But what are we to rule? Who? How? It feels like no one listens to us anymore.

We are called first to rule our own hearts, conforming them to the image of God, finding the meaning of our pain within the promises of God's word. The world is raging all around us, and we are to be calm, active in our fervent prayer, resting confidently on the promises of God. We are not to be waging war on Twitter, gossiping at church, redefining the Bible based on our perceived gifts, or anything else. We are to worship in a true church, a faithful church, a church that values and honors the holiness of God. We are the church militant focused on the return of our King, the Lord Jesus, and ready to serve with him as the church triumphant. But our weapons are not ones that the world values. "For the weapons of our warfare are not of the flesh but have divine power to destroy strongholds. We destroy arguments and every lofty opinion raised against the knowledge of God, and take every thought captive to obey Christ" (2 Cor. 10:4–5). Our weapons are not of the flesh. The weapons of the flesh lack God's blessing and God's power. The church militant receives the rage of the whole world with patience, meekness, and discernment. We love our enemies, defining both *love* and *enemy* as the Bible teaches.

It is the church that holds the keys to the kingdom, not the HR department enforcing transgender pronouns. Things have changed—and we need to discern how those changes impact our lives. But the gospel hasn't changed. God hasn't changed. Here at the Butterfields', the gospel still comes with a house key. Let me give you a recent example.

One Lord's Day morning, early, during the height of the Covid frenzy in 2021 and directly after vaccine mandates were leveled,

I was heading out the side door with my two dogs in tow, Bella the Shih Tzu (50 percent dog, 50 percent stuffed animal), and Sully the goofy three-legged dog (75 percent dog, 25 percent plucky comic relief). My older neighbors Bill and Jason were waiting for me at the end of the driveway, with their elegant poodle Trixie.

Bill jumped right in: "I want to know why *you Christians* don't believe in the vaccine! Don't you believe in loving your neighbor?"

Bill and Jason have been in a homosexual relationship for thirty years. As Bill was talking, Jason was holding his cigarette at the left corner of his mouth so that he had two free hands to adjust Trixie's halter. After the halter met his approval, he allowed Trixie and Sully their special quality personal-sniffing time.

"Bill, I have a question for you," I countered. "Back in the late '80s and early '90s during our other pandemic, how come gay men rejected wearing condoms? Didn't you love your neighbor? Or even your sex partners?"

Jason's mouth opened like a fish on a line and his cigarette fell to the ground.

It was early, around 6 a.m., and maybe they weren't expecting the word *condom* to come out of the pastor's wife's mouth. Or *sex partners*. Or both. Who knows?

Bill exhaled deeply. "I never made the connection. Jay, she's right. Remember Larry Kramer supported condoms but most of us thought he was selling out."[14]

Jason recovered and said, "And Kramer was right. So many more of us would have lived." He choked a little, cleared his throat, and

---

14 Larry Kramer was a stalwart AIDS activist. His advice and antics roiled both the gay community and the public at large, sometimes at the same time. Matt Schudel, "Larry Kramer, Writer Who Sounded Alarm on AIDS, Dies at 84," *Washington Post*, May 27, 2020, https://www.washingtonpost.com/.

said, "All the funerals. All the young men in the prime of life. That could have been us, Bill—" his voice trailed off. In hoarse whispers he blurted: "It should have been us."

We walked in respectful silence until we turned the corner, each lamenting in our own life the toll taken by AIDS.

"Do you want to know why some Christians reject the vaccine and why some gay men rejected condoms? Do you want my opinion?" I offered softly, breaking the silence.

My neighbors nodded.

"Because everyone wants freedom to exercise their conscience. For Christians, that freedom comes from the Bible—"

Jason rebuked me, "Oh, sure, like the Bible has anything to say about vaccines! Or freedom!"

"The Bible has everything to say about freedom as well as making health choices, because the Bible has everything to say about spheres of authority—"

"Huh? The Bible?" offered Bill.

"Absolutely. The Bible offers spheres of authority: the family, the church, and the civil government. Health decisions are under the jurisdiction of family. The government has the right to issue taxes but can't tell the church how to serve the Lord's Supper. And the church has the authority and responsibility to proclaim the gospel to all the nations, warning people about sin, calling them to repentance, and sharing the good news about eternal salvation through Christ, who covers the sin of his people with his atoning blood. You might miss the whole discussion about spheres of authority if you fail to read the Old Testament, but I believe that the whole Bible is true. The church can't be the government and the government can't be the family and—"

"Preach it, sister," said Jason, a retired public-school teacher. His last years of teaching made him feel more like a social worker than a math specialist. He hated that. Jason loved his job when he could actually teach math and loathed his job when all he could do was plug holes of family neglect.

We were heading back into our neighborhood, and my house was right around the next corner.

"So, gentlemen, you answered your own question. Getting the vaccine or not getting the vaccine, wearing a mask or not wearing a mask—it's a personal choice, not a sin and not a grace. Some Christians reject the vaccine because they are exercising their biblical authority over their health care—over their bodies. Everyone wants freedom, and Christians find their freedom in the Bible. When gay men rejected condoms, that was an exercise in freedom. The question is this: Where does our freedom come from—our personal feelings or something greater? Which freedom is safe, and which is not?"

We stopped at my driveway. Sully and Trixie gave each other one last sniff. We all looked in each other's eyes with love and care.

"I never know what is going to come out of your mouth," Bill said.

I decided that morning to take Bill's comment as a compliment.

"I want to talk more about this," offered Jason. "Maybe tonight's dog walk, we can pick up where we left off?" he asked.

"It's a plan," I said.

The Christian faith speaks to our whole life and our whole world. Truly all of life is the triune God's love and law. It is all about the electing love of the Father, the atoning love of the

311

Son, and the sanctifying love of the Spirit. It is all about the kingship of Christ and the care of the eternal soul and the new heavens and the new earth. It is all about and all for the glory of God. It's all about the Bible's worth, merit, strength, dignity, and eternal truth. And each step of this journey of prayer and fasting for your loved one is about bringing God glory. It is all about fighting tyrants, defying lies, breaking down strongholds of sin with prayer, reforming the church, and practicing love of brother, sister, family, and neighbor. It is all about the life of the church.

The word preached.

Births.

Baptisms.

The Lord's Supper.

Weddings.

Funerals.

It is all about callings, the ones you expect and the ones you don't. It's all about service and sacrifice and fellowship and the seasons and rhythms of the life of the church. It's about suffering too. It's all about purposeful Christian living, where your life matters, where the prayers you bring to the throne of grace are heard. It's about the Lord keeping your tears in a bottle. It's about living Lord's Day to Lord's Day. It's about worship and psalm singing and taking up your role as a vital member of a Bible-believing church. Praying for our lost loved ones is part of this tapestry of the Christian life. It's about taking the time to listen to your neighbors, to break bread with them, to call them to life in Christ.

And the Lord Jesus Christ and his grace that weaves this life together is strong enough to hold you fast, in grief and joy, as you serve in the body of Christ, the church militant, until the Lord returns and we become the church triumphant. We leave our grief and tears here, for there are no tears where we are going.

Christian, this is our moment. We must speak boldly to our world. We need to live boldly for Christ. We need to do this now. Heaven has no regrets, and neither do Christians.

Acknowledgments

COURAGE WANED AND WAXED as I wrote this book, but the Lord graciously surrounded me with lionhearted Christians who picked me up when I fell down.

My pastor and husband, Kent Butterfield, as well as Pastor Drew Poplin and ruling elder Eric Halfors protected, advised, and prayed for me during this journey.

Church members and dear brothers in the Lord, Andrew Branch and Hermonta Godwin, read portions and drafts and gave me insightful feedback.

Without the help of Ken Colley, I wouldn't have a working computer or stable Internet access, but there's more to our story than my dependence on Ken's technological genius. Indeed, Ken Colley first started praying for me back in 1997 when I was a lesbian English professor at Syracuse University on somebody's prayer list. Ken prayed for me before I could pray for myself. How do I say thank you for that?

Over the years of our friendship, Lina Abujamra has given me more than I can express here—practical help, wisdom, time, medical advice, prayer, and the list goes on. Lina, you inspire me, and I am so thankful to God for you.

Lydia Brownback, my editor and better brain, is brilliant, wise, insightful, and strong. She loves the word and she loves words. She lives a sacrificial and vital faith. While I do not want to write another book, the time I have spent with Lydia, both in her home and on the pages of books, is so inspiring that I might just have to do this again.

This is a book about dismantling the idol of our times—the world of LGBTQ+ that I in my sin helped build. There are many Christians who have protected me in this battle whose names I cannot mention without putting them in danger. Thank you for the risks that you have taken and the lives you have lived.

Appendix

Guiding Principles for How to Read the Bible

In the beginning was the Word, and the Word was with God,
and the Word was God. He was in the beginning with God.
All things were made through him, and without him was not
any thing made that was made. In him was life, and the life
was the light of men. The light shines in the darkness, and
the darkness has not overcome it. . . . And the Word became
flesh and dwelt among us, and we have seen his glory, glory
as of the only Son from the Father, full of grace and truth.

JOHN 1:1–5, 14

THE BIBLE IS MY GUIDE TO FAITH AND LIFE. The Bible alone
meets the need of sinful men, women, and children in an irreplaceable way. Because I believe that the Bible reads me as I read it,
I want to share with you some basic principles for reading the Bible.

The Word of God Reads Us Perfectly

When the Holy Spirit takes our hearts of stone and gives us hearts
of flesh, the Lord commands us to follow him. The journey is never

easy. In faithfulness God sets apart afflictions that aid us in our Christian life. They draw us closer to our elder brother Jesus. We often grow to be like Jesus through the fellowship of his sufferings (Phil. 3:10).

The word of God is a special means of God's grace because of its very nature: "The word of God is living and active, sharper than any two-edged sword . . . discerning the thoughts and intentions of the heart" (Heb. 4:12). While we are reading the Bible, the word of God is reading us. The word of God is the surgeon's scalpel, cutting out the sickness of sin and unbelief. The word of God exposes our schemes and secrets. It discerns us and allows us in Christ to see the truth about ourselves. And one of the biggest truths it uncovers is our inadequacy before its majesty. We act sometimes as though the Bible depends on us. But just the opposite is true.

So what is the Bible? What is its nature, origin, and reliability? How do we approach it, interpret it, and profit from it? Can we trust it with all our heart? Can we trust it for our salvation? Can we trust it with our life today?

Six Guiding Principles for How to Read the Bible

The Westminster Confession of Faith provides six characteristics of the Bible.[1]

1. The Bible is clear. The clarity of Scripture is the most basic principle. The Bible bears God's heartfelt desire to communicate with people. God's message of salvation is accessible, even for

---

1 A helpful article addressing this is Wayne R. Spear, "The Westminster Assembly and Biblical Interpretation," in *The Book of Books: The Value of the Scriptures in a Day of Bible Bending, Bible Breaking, and Bible Believing*, ed. John H. White (Pittsburgh, PA: Crown & Covenant, 2019), 55–165.

those who are not scholars. The Bible is transparent about what God requires of us and plain about what we can expect from God. Matters of salvation and sanctification are not mysteries. For this reason, all people are encouraged to read the Bible for themselves.

2. The meaning of the Bible is available to everyone through ordinary means. The ordinary means available to us include hearing the word preached publicly and studying it privately. Additionally, our personal understanding of what God is calling us to think and do is edified and directed by our corporate worship.

3. The Holy Spirit illuminates the Bible in the heart and mind of Christians. Just as the Bible was authored by the Holy Spirit working through the words of chosen men, so too the Spirit today guides and enlightens people in the knowledge of Christ through the word. That is why we always pray for the Spirit to guide, direct, and correct us before we open our Bibles. We dare not read the Bible in our own flesh. That is a recipe for both disaster and heresy.

4. Bible passages have a single meaning, not multiple meanings. When we say that Scripture has a plain, single meaning, we are saying that readers are to look at words in a natural, not a wooden or embellished, way. Therefore, we should seek first to understand the single sense of a passage. In other words, there are no problem passages and no passages with competing meanings.

5. The Bible does not contradict itself; the difficult passages are to be interpreted through the lens of the clearer ones. This principle directs us to interpret the passage in light of the whole teaching of the Bible.

6. We are to use deductive reasoning when reading the Bible. Deductive reasoning starts by interpreting the big picture and ends with specific applications to our daily life.

The Word of God Is True

The word of God is true, and we can trust it with all of our life's troubles. I love study Bibles, the big, hulking volumes that contain a host of notes and maps and definitions.

One of my favorite study Bibles has this note about the word of God: "The authority and inerrancy of Holy Scripture are the bedrock upon which true Christianity stands. . . . Scripture has authority because it is the word of God. . . . The authority of Scripture implies its inerrancy."[2]

The word cannot lie: "It is the word of God that cannot lie" (see Titus 1:2). The word shoots straight as an arrow: "The sum of your word is truth, and every one of your righteous rules endures forever" (Ps. 119:160). And Christ himself declared in prayer, "Your word is truth" (John 17:17).[3]

The truth of God's word is also known as a "doctrine," which is a stated and shared principle that reflects a deeply held belief. We often express doctrines of the church as confessions, public statements that begin with "I believe . . ."

The Word of God Is Inerrant

The doctrine of inerrancy is vital, but why? Does it matter whether the Bible is inerrant? What difference does inerrancy have on my faith, my salvation, my sanctification, my assurance of salvation, my children, and the future generations of my family and church? What does your Christian faith look like if you embrace inerrancy? What does it become if you reject it?

The short answer is this: inerrancy is vital and necessary for your sanctification (your growth in Christ), your assurance (your trust

2 "The Authority and Inerrancy of Scripture," in *The Reformation Heritage KJV Study Bible*, ed. Joel Beeke (Grand Rapids, MI: Reformation Heritage, 2014), 922.
3 "The Authority and Inerrancy of Scripture," 922.

in Christ), your children's faith (the faith you pass down from generation to generation), and your church's future (your ability to withstand the attacks of the world, the flesh, and the devil in future generations). But—and this is a really important *but*—your salvation does not rest on inerrancy. Indeed, you can be saved and not believe in inerrancy.

The Chicago Statement on Biblical Inerrancy offers this helpful explanation about why inerrancy matters:

> We affirm that a confession of the full authority, infallibility and inerrancy of Scripture is vital to a sound understanding of the whole of the Christian faith. We further affirm that such confession should lead to increasing conformity to the image of Christ. We deny that such confession is necessary for salvation. However, we further deny that inerrancy can be rejected without grave consequences both to the individual and the church.[4]

This statement parses out the issue at hand and helps us see inerrancy as a shield against pagan spirituality. It helps us remember that we are saved by Christ, not our theology. And this alone should humble us and cause us to love Christ more. It also implies that while you cannot lose your salvation, you can lose everything else (including your assurance of salvation).

Christ as the Word made flesh reveals that the person of Jesus Christ cannot be severed from the nature and reality of the word. And if your theology severs Christ from the word, the effects will be increasingly damaging as the rigors of life increase with time.

---

4   The Chicago Statement on Biblical Inerrancy is available at Ligonier, https://www.ligonier.org/.

As R. C. Sproul puts it, "Inerrancy of Scripture is not a doctrine about a book. The issue is the person and work of Christ."[5]

R. C. Sproul tells the story of an old friend who stopped believing in the Bible's inerrancy but retained a belief that Jesus is Lord. The old friend explained that he believed that the church's general assembly, not the word of God, is the supreme authority through which Jesus Christ exercised his sovereignty. In this encounter, Sproul told his friend that his denial of inerrancy and replacement with a church counsel left him with an impotent Jesus. Sproul said, "You want to affirm the lordship of Christ, but your Lord is impotent. He has no way of conveying any mandate to you whatsoever, because you stand above the recorded mandates of Christ in Scripture. You set yourself over them in critical judgment."[6]

Inerrancy Helps Us See and Live

The doctrine of inerrancy asks us to behold the purity of Jesus Christ, the Word made flesh, as sinless in word and deed. But it also demands that we understand the depth and nature of our own sin. Just as Christ's sinlessness cannot be understood fully apart from Scripture, so also our sinfulness cannot be understood in its fullness apart from Scripture.

By way of illustration, Puritan Thomas Goodwin described mankind as represented by two giants: one is Adam, the first man, and the other is Christ. Hooked to the belts of these giants are every single human being, and all of humanity is born hooked onto Adam's belt. Adam's fall gave us a polluted nature that we can't clean up by ourselves. We are locked by an iron hook, dan-

---

5   R. C. Sproul, "What Difference Does an Inerrant Bible Make?" Ligonier, March 4, 2015, https://ligonier./org/.

6   Sproul, "What Difference Does an Inerrant Bible Make?"

gling off of Adam's belt. And to make matters worse, we start to love the sin that will kill us. John 3:19 describes it like this: "This is the judgment: the light has come into the world, and people loved the darkness rather than the light because their works were evil." We desire things that God calls sin, and when we embrace them and claim them as our rightful pleasure, sin grows and goes deeper and deeper inside. In Goodwin's word-picture, the iron hooks are impenetrable. We cannot change the giant to which we are hooked. We are powerless.

The word of God offers only one solution. The love of God is that solution. God seeks and saves his people. When God removes our heart of stone and gives us a heart of flesh (Jer. 31:33; Ezek. 11:19; 36:26; Heb. 8:10), the result is the fruit of repentance. Our eyes are unscaled. We see that Jesus is Lord. And we fall on our face. As the great physician, he takes the word of God and uses it like a surgeon's scalpel.

Those who reject inerrancy often believe that the reader is the surgeon, plucking out the kidney-shaped heart from the frog on the dissecting table, finding the true verses and dismissing the untrue ones with human wisdom. But the Bible's inerrant witness is that we are the lifeless frog stinking in formaldehyde, and the word of God is the scalpel that brings us to life.

It is the Holy Spirit who, granting us the fruit of repentance, unhooks us from the belt of Adam and clamps us onto the belt of the second Adam, Jesus Christ. The power of the clamped hook— the truth that we can never lose our salvation because Christ will not let us go—is found in the doctrine of inerrancy. Hooked to the belt of Christ, who is now our representative head with the Father, we learn by grace to love what God loves. And how do we know what God loves? How do we know the difference between a holy desire and an unholy one? The word of God alone is the discerner of the hearts of men (Heb. 4:12).

Indeed, the majesty of Christ is beheld in the doctrine of inerrancy.

Scripture and Unanswered Questions

Scripture doesn't answer all our questions, and the deeper we delve into Scripture, the larger and more looming are the questions: "There is no doctrine of our Christian faith that does not confront us with unresolved difficulties here in this world, and the difficulties become all the greater just as we get nearer to the center."[7] But unanswered questions in the face of the magnificence of Scripture are not themselves proof of a problem, for these are "questions of adoring wonder rather than the questions of painful perplexity."[8]

Unanswered questions ought not to shake our faith, because we must always return to the truth that Jesus is the Word made flesh.

Scripture and Obedience

The psalmist declares, "Your word is a lamp to my feet and a light to my path" (Ps. 119:105). But what do we do when we have an internal sense of our path, and that internal sense pulls us with a compelling longing in a direction we don't understand? Ought we to follow our heart? Ought we to become a "love warrior," abandoning the biblical faith for a pagan one, following our heart and not our Bible, embracing homosexual sin and rejecting the purity

---

7 Collected in *The Infallible Word: A Symposium by the Members of the Faculty of Westminster Theological Seminary*, 2nd ed., ed. N. B. Stonehouse and Paul Woolley (Phillipsburg, NJ: P&R, 2002), 1–54.
8 John Murray, "The Attestation of Scripture," in *The Infallible Word*, 7.

of biblical marriage?[9] Not if we believe that obedience is the proof of our love of God.

Scripture and Liberty

Sometimes we need to adjust our reading glasses to see the liberty in the commands of God. Think about it like this: nothing else but the word of God is binding, and we have clarity about what God requires of us. When Jesus says that his yoke is easy and his burden light (Matt. 11:30), we understand that yokes and burdens are only given to us by a loving God, and because the word says that they are light, we know that in Christ we can bear them. How can we call the yokes and burdens of life *light*? Is cancer, abandonment, job loss, depression, infertility, the death of a child, or the death of a dream (just to name a few) light? Never if we face them alone. But these yokes and burdens afflict us only in Christ's faithfulness (Ps. 119:71). He promises to send his word to give us supernatural comfort, strength, wisdom, and forbearance. Because of the word of God and its inseparability from the person of God, no burden is stronger than God, who bears us up in the face of hardship.

Scripture is "finished," so our feelings do not add new commandments. Has anyone ever said to you, "You need to give me more grace!" and by *grace* she means you need to lower the standards? Well, this is a misuse of the word *grace*. Puritan John Owen explains this principle in a beautiful way:

> The law grace writes in our hearts must answer to the law written in God's Word. God promised that his Spirit and Word always

9   Glennon Doyle, *Love Warrior: A Memoir* (New York: Flatiron, 2017).

accompany one another. The Spirit does not work anything in us, but the Word first requires of us.[10]

Understanding Scripture

The Trinity in Scripture

When we read the Bible as it is written, we behold the Trinity—Father, Son, and Holy Spirit. Just as the Godhead cannot be divided—just as God the Father, God the Son, and God the Holy Spirit cannot be pitted against each other for any reason and at any time—so too the word of God holds authority over our sinful hearts because the word is the manifestation of Jesus, the wisdom of the Holy Spirit, and the creational power of the Father. Nothing can undo it. Nothing can overcome it.

The Laws of Scripture

Our infallible and inerrant Bible contains many details, people, problems, and hard-to-pronounce names! It also includes many laws, but not all of these laws are still binding after the resurrection of our Lord. The ceremonial laws of the Old Testament, while no longer binding after Christ's resurrection, gives us a rich history of God's holiness and faithfulness. They provide a richness to our story as Christians by explaining historical place keepers of the plight of God's people, revealing the power of God's might.

Likewise, the judicial laws of the Old Testament applied to a nation that no longer exists as a national or geographic boundary occupied by a distinct people group. Both its fulfillment, culminating in the cross of Christ, and its inevitable disappearance give depth

---

10 John Owen, in *Voices from the Past: Puritan Devotional Readings*, ed. Richard Rushing (Carlisle, PA: Banner of Truth, 2009), 163.

to our shared history as God's people. After our Lord's resurrection and the giving of the Holy Spirit and the Great Commission, God's people were no longer defined by geographic or national boundaries. The whole world is his.

What remains and what binds us to Christ are the moral laws of God, which are found in the Ten Commandments.

Understanding the differences between the three types of Old Testament law—the moral law, the judicial law, and the ceremonial law—is no invitation to dismiss the Old Testament. On the contrary. If our Lord went willingly to the cross to fulfill what is found on the pages of the Old Testament, we are summoned to hold it in the same high order. To fulfill something is to make it complete. Jesus came to fulfill the words of the Old Testament, and by doing so, he supplied what was lacking—for faith, life, salvation, sanctification, and wisdom.

Scripture as the Word of Christ

The word of God is the very word of Christ. And God has given us this window into his heart and our own in the Bible that we hold in our hands. The Lord provides explicit teaching about the doctrine of Scripture. The apostle Paul wrote, "All Scripture is breathed out by God" (2 Tim. 3:16). It is God-breathed. And while 2 Timothy 3:16 makes no reference to human authors, the apostle Peter addresses the relationship between the human authors of Scripture and the Holy Spirit when he says, "No prophecy of Scripture comes from someone's own interpretation. For no prophecy was ever produced by the will of man, but men spoke from God as they were carried along by the Holy Spirit" (2 Pet. 1:20–21). Because of the Holy Spirit's role and authentication, we can be confident that the word of God is a "permanent embodiment" of Christ himself. Peter is not hiding or minimizing the role of human authorship, but he is showing how this authorship is unique in its complete dependence on the Holy Spirit for inspiration and authentication. This makes Scripture a singular book with a birthright and progeny unlike any other book on the planet.

Scripture Is Unified

In addition to Scripture's internal testimony, we find the organic unity of both Testaments. "Organic unity" means that while the New Testament gives us a fuller picture, it does not in any way contradict the Old Testament. Old Testament ceremonial laws (such as animal sacrifices) have been replaced by the perfect sacrifice of Jesus Christ. And the judicial laws that set the Old Testament nation of Israel apart have been replaced by the Great Commission, which extends salvation in Jesus Christ to all who will repent and believe. The organic unity of the Scripture offers to us a *progressive* revelation, meaning that as the biblical story unfolds, we behold what was there in the shadows all along. The New Testament "embodies a fuller and more glorious disclosure of God's character and will."[11] But the New Testament does not replace the Old.

Christ and Scripture Are Inseparable

The person of Christ is intricately linked with the word of God. And the work of Christ is intricately linked with the divine authority, inerrancy, and inspiration of both the Old and New Testaments. We see this in the New Testament in the promises that Christ gave his disciples before he sent them out to preach the kingdom of God:

11 Murray, "The Attestation of Scripture," 35.

You will be dragged before governors and kings for my sake, to bear witness before them and the Gentiles. When they deliver you over, do not be anxious how you are to speak or what you are to say, for what you are to say will be given to you in that hour. For it is not you who speak, but the Spirit of your Father speaking through you. (Matt. 10:18–20)

In this passage, Jesus Christ promises that as the disciples witness Christ and risk their lives, when they speak in defense of the kingdom of God, our triune God would grant them an inspiration of the Holy Spirit that would make their words his words.

On the night before his crucifixion, Jesus told them, "If I do not go away, the Helper [the Holy Spirit] will not come to you," and, "When the Spirit of truth comes, he will guide you into all the truth" (John 16:7, 13). After his resurrection, Jesus gave to his disciples the power of the Holy Spirit: "He breathed on them and said to them, 'Receive the Holy Spirit'" (John 20:22). We see here another image of the breath of God infusing the scriptures with the very purity of God.

Before Jesus ascended he said, "You will receive power when the Holy Spirit has come upon you, and you will be my witnesses in Jerusalem and in all Judea and Samaria, and to the end of the earth" (Acts 1:8).

All those passages reveal that the disciples' work is commissioned by Christ and is empowered by the inspiration and direction of the Holy Spirit. Thus we see that Scripture is the product of God's breath, inspiring chosen men through the power of the Holy Spirit, manifesting in language that is both material and spiritual. It is material because we can hold parchments and books in our hand. It is spiritual because it supernaturally speaks to the souls of God's elect people, serving as the conduit of God's comfort, direction, rebuke, and power.

And because Scripture is the very breath of God, it is "profitable for teaching, for reproof, for correction, and for training in righteousness, that the man of God may be complete, equipped for every good work" (2 Tim. 3:16–17). The word "profitable" here refers to turning a profit—taking something small and watching it become big. Sanctification—the believer's progressive growth in godliness—is our profit. The very breath of God in the life of a believer magnifies everything, allowing us to grow in the knowledge, righteousness, and holiness of God, and to lay down our own lives as we model our Savior and the Lord works all things to our good and his glory.

Scripture and Our Thoughts

Our thoughts about God and our thoughts about Scripture must be the same. We cannot love one and reject the other. What we think about Scripture and what we think about God are inseparable. The stability of our faith as evidenced in our responsive works and growth in sanctification is similarly linked to the doctrine of inerrancy. Ephesians 2:8–10 says, "By grace you have been saved through faith. And this is not your own doing; it is the gift of God, not a result of works, so that no one may boast. For we are his workmanship, created in Christ Jesus for good works, which God prepared beforehand, that we should walk in them." One of the good works in which we must walk is the belief that God's word is inerrant. And, therefore, we must ask ourselves some hard questions.

If the testimony of Scripture is unreliable, at least in part, then every single time the Bible crosses you on something, you will believe that that part is unreliable. If the Bible isn't 100 percent true in all parts, the whole book will start to unravel in your hands the minute you are crossed. Like Eve, you will ponder Satan's question, "Did God actually say . . . ?" (Gen. 3:1). This isn't an academic discussion. Your life is on the line.

Puritan Joseph Alleine writes, "The sincere convert accepts a complete Christ. He loves not only the reward, but the labor. He seeks not only the benefits, but the burden of Christ. He takes up the commands, yes, even the cross of Christ." In contrast, the unsound and perhaps unsaved person, "takes Christ by halves. He is all for the salvation, but not sanctification. He is all for the privileges, but neglects the person of Christ. . . . They desire salvation from suffering, but do not desire to be saved from sinning."[12] We need to meditate on how the complete Christ stands between us and a pagan world that wants grace without God.

Scripture and Suffering

The Bible hides within it the wounds of Christ, and when we have the Bible as our anchor, all the sufferings of this world are seen on the cross. In other words, suffering is always and only seen in light of Christ's suffering and victory. If the Bible is your anchor, you can be confident that your suffering has meaning and purpose and grace. Nothing can eternally hurt you. As Thomas Watson reminds us:

> If one loses his name, it is written in the book of life. If he loses his liberty, his conscience is free. If he loses his estate, he owns the pearl of great price. If he meets a storm, he has a harbor;

12 Joseph Alleine, in *Voices from the Past*, 239.

God is his God and heaven is his heaven. If God is our God, our soul is safe. It is hidden in the promises, in the wounds of Christ, and in the decrees of God.[13]

The intimate and unbreakable link between the suffering of Christ and our own suffering speaks to a world that demands ease and peace and the never-ending getting of what one wants. It tells us that hardships are not always meant to be resolved in this life. And that God is God over all of it.

Scripture Is Eternal

Finally, we need to know that the Bible, like our souls, will last forever. Isaiah 40:8 and 1 Peter 1:25 remind us that this world is passing away, but the word of God will be with us in heaven and in the new Jerusalem. We hold in our hands something that has God's guarantee of eternal merit. When we reject biblical inerrancy for the pagan philosophies of men, we are elevating dust over gold: "The short duration of mankind is stout in scripture by the vanishing grass. Life is a flower soon withered, a vapor soon vanishing, or a smoke soon disappearing. The strongest man is but compacted dust."[14]

---

13 Thomas Watson, *The Ten Commandments* (1692; repr., Carlisle, PA: Banner of Truth, 2009), 17–20.
14 Stephen Charnock, in *Voices from the Past*, 247.

General Index

abortion, 123, 166–68, 186
abuse, 162, 280, 290
acceptance: means remembering, 300; without approval, 59, 293, 296–97
actual sin, 86
Adam, covenant headship of, 94
adoption, 91
adultery, 304
Advanced Training Institute (ATI), 279–80
"aesthetic orientation," 82–83
afflictions, viewing through mind of Christ and cross of Christ, 254
Ahab, 206–7
AIDS pandemic, 195n1, 309–10, 309n14
Alleine, Joseph, 331
American civil religion, 182, 185
American Psychological Association, 69; on gender dysphoria, 219; politics of, 306n12
animal sacrifices, 136
annihilationism, 236–38
anorexia, 219
antibullying curriculum, 199
Apostles' Creed, 140
approval, 293
armor of God, xvii–xviii
assurance, 320
authenticity, 9, 276
autonomy, xiv, 133

bathrooms, in government schools, 197
Bauckham, Richard, 176n1
Beeke, Joel, 9–10
Bellah, Robert, 185
Bible. *See* Scripture
biblical counseling, 302, 306n12
biblical headship, 171, 188. *See also* patriarchy
biblical journalism, 286
biblical spirituality, as kind and inclusive, 14
binary oppositions, 133
biological sex, as ontological, 226
Bostock v. Clayton County (2020), 18, 25
brain-sex theory, 226–29, 245
breast binding, 208
Brewin, Kester, 124
Brinton, Sam, 305n11
Brown, Jerry, 218
Brownson, Jonathan V., 74–77
Brown University, 222–23
burdens, addition of, 253–54
Burk, Denny, 60
Burroughs, Jeremiah, 250–55
Butterfield, Kent, 50–52, 248–49

Cain, envy of Abel, 208
callings, 312
Calvin, John, 61n3, 108–9, 154–55; on hearing the word of God, 108–9; on knowledge of God and self,

154–55; on the law, 294n1, 295;
on rage of the world, 263, 307
celibacy, 73
ceremonial laws, 326
Chan, Francis, 236–37
Chicago Statement on Biblical Inerrancy, 321
child sacrifice, 208–10
Christian liberty, 285–86n20, 325–26
Christian life: in Babel, 306–13; as
constantly fleeing to the throne of
grace, 107; as life of binaries, 264;
in the presence of enemies, 263;
social media-infused, 281
Christian women, xix–xxi
church, divided, 6
church membership, in a faithful
church, 162–63, 292–93, 298, 312
church militant, 308, 312
church triumphant, 308, 313
Clinton, Hillary, 182–86
Coles, Greg, 84–85
Collins, Nate, 78n20, 82
comfort, in affliction, 294
"coming out of the closet," 27
commandments, express God's love,
172
common grace, 96
confession of sins, 251
conforming to Christ, 231
conforming will to God's will, 255
conformity to culture, as missional, 124
contentment, 249–56; opposite of,
255, 256
contextualization, 15n15
Cook, Becket, 3n4
Corey, Elizabeth C., 62
corumination, 220
cost of discipleship, 154
creation, pattern of, 304
creation order, sets pattern for godly
living, 173
creation ordinance, 7–8, 25, 43–44,
46, 67, 158, 210; rejected by
intersectionality, 61

cross, centrality of, 87
cults, 280

Darwin, Charles, 65–66, 107
David, and Jonathan, 240–41
Davis, Andrew M., 250n15
dead to homosexuality, 93
Dean, Jamie, 286n21
deductive reasoning, in reading the
Bible, 319
desires, subtraction of, 252
desistance, 216
DeYoung, Kevin, 157–58, 170
*Diagnostic and Statistical Manual
of Mental Disorders* (DSM-5),
203n7, 221
Diamond, Milton, 226–27
dignitary harm, 59
disability theologians, 226
Disorder of Sex Development (DSD),
223
diversity, 260
doctrine, knowledge of, 297–98
dominion over the creatures, 8
Donnelly, Edward, 238
Down syndrome, 224
Du Mez, Kristin Kobes, 178–79,
182–87
dying to sin, 30–31, 77

Edwards, Jonathan, 237, 237–38n7
effectual calling, 91n3
egalitarianism, 75
Elijah, 206–7
Elliot, Elisabeth, 183
Elliot, Jim, 183n11
empathy, 99–102, 106, 223; cheap
substitute for God's grace, 215; as
worldly sorrow, 246
endurance, xviii
English Civil War, 163
Enneagram, 276
envy, 30–31, 200–211, 249, 255;
transgenderism as, 30–31, 200,
207, 256
Esau, envy of Jacob, 208

324–25; on personhood, 66, 86;
on sin of homosexuality, 67–69;
speaks to transgenderism, 273–74;
on spheres of authority, 310;
and suffering, 331–32; thoughts
about, 330–31; trustworthiness
of, 78; and unanswered questions,
324; unity of, 328; as violent
book, 121; as word of Christ,
327–28
self-actualization, 196
"self-ID" perspective, 217, 219, 222
self-pity, sin of, 299
sex-change operations, 194, 208
sexual fluidity, 45
sexual identity, does not encompass
personhood, 93
sexual orientation, 45, 66, 82, 83;
change efforts, 86n34; as fixed
and unchangeable, 29; identity as
an idol, 93
sexual orientation and gender identity
(SOGI) laws, 198
Shelley, Mary, 169
Shreier, Abigail, 219–20, 221, 222, 302
"Side A" gay Christianity, 66–67, 73,
108, 109; as "gay-affirming," 73;
misreading of Scripture, 77
"Side B" gay Christianity, 67, 73, 82,
108, 109; and attendance at gay
weddings and gay Pride marches,
75; on homosexual desire as unanswered prayer, 79; mishandles
matters pertaining to sin and
salvation, 77; as "nonaffirming" of
gay sex, 73
silence, as violence, 59
Simpson, Phillip L., 250n16
sin: dealing with, 152–53; hardening
by, 156; killing of, 264; no longer
defines Christians, 90; overcoming of, 27; as predatory, 153n2;
responsibility for, 79, 280
singleness, 73
sixth commandment, 210

Smith, Floy, 39, 42, 49, 72–73, 127,
130, 139, 143–44, 160–61, 195,
260, 296
Smith, Ken, 22, 38–39, 72–73, 195,
254, 259, 261, 262, 296; lecture
on the Bible, 127–44, 171
Smith, Peter, 161n11
social contagion, 199, 219–20,
241–47
Social Dilemma, The (documentary),
282
social fragmentation, 60
social-justice righteousness, 211
social media: as airing of grievances,
285–86; negative feedback loop
of, 220–21; orchestrates narcissism, 291–92
sociology, 177, 187
sodomy, 305
Southern Baptist Convention, 178–79
spiritual authority, 86
spiritual battlefields, 196
spiritual but not Christian, 115, 122
spirituality. See unbiblical spirituality
spiritual warfare, xvi–xviii
spiritual weapons, 308
Sprinkle, Preston, 225–26, 235–37,
240–41
Sproul, R. C., 322
STD transmission, 305
stewarding the earth, 8
suffering, 331–32; inevitability of, 33;
for sins, 79
sun and moon, fulfill creational design,
156, 158
sympathy, 99–102, 106, 224
Syracuse Reformed Presbyterian
Church, 48
Syracuse University, 51
systematic theology, 298

Tada, Joni Eareckson, 253
temptation, 269–72, 275; becomes sin,
177–79
ten Boom, Betsy and Corrie, 253

Scripture Index

Get the Study Guide

Study Guide

Five Lies of Our Anti-Christian Age

Rosaria Butterfield

The *Five Lies of Our Anti-Christian Age Study Guide* dives deep into the key points of each chapter with summaries, questions, and Bible verses for further reading—inspiring readers to preserve godly values and shepherd the next generation.

For more information, visit **crossway.org**.

Also Available from Rosaria Butterfield

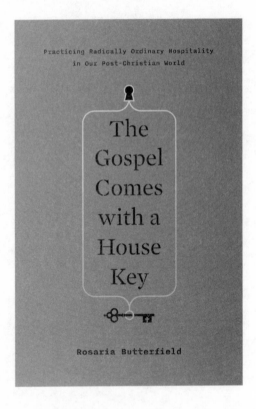

With engaging stories from her own life-changing encounter with radically ordinary hospitality, Butterfield equips Christians to use their homes as a means to showing a post-Christian world what authentic love and faith really look like.

For more information, visit **crossway.org**.